The Human Mother

Unraveling the Twisted Expectations of
Motherhood to Reclaim the Role and Become
Whole Again
Claudia Leona

SACRED
REBELLION
BOOKS

Sacred Rebellion Books

The Human Mother
© 2025 Claudia Leona

For permissions or inquiries,
contact:claudialeona.books@gmail.com

Published by Sacred Rebellion Press
Printed in the United States of America

Cover design and interior layout by Sacred Rebellion Books
First edition, 2025
ISBN: 979-8-9932180-0-7

This book contains personal reflections and stories drawn from lived experiences. Some narratives have been adapted or generalized to preserve privacy and honor the spirit of shared truth.

For more information, visit:www.claudialeona.com

Contents

Introduction

This isn't a parenting book. This is a deeply honest reminder of the infinite self that should outlive every title, including Mother.

If you're looking for tips on how to be a calmer mom, a more organized mom, a more grateful, regulated, ever-patient mom...

You can put this book down.
Because this *isn't* that book.

And if you're looking for a book that highlights only the beautiful, heartwarming parts of motherhood (the joy, the bonding, the magic worth celebrating - which do exist), this isn't that book either.

This book isn't about fixing or glorifying your mothering. It's about remembering the woman inside the role and reclaiming her humanity.

This is a soulfully bold book that confronts the reality of being a mother in a world that routinely asks you (and every woman who becomes a mother) to disappear.

A world that romanticizes your suffering. That praises you for smiling while you wither away. That tells you your rage is the problem, your selflessness must be unending, your exhaustion is normal, and your silence is sacred.

This book isn't sugar-coated. It isn't sanitized. It isn't domesticated. And it isn't "grateful for the journey."

It's raw.
Honest.
Even disruptive.
It's sacred.
Furious.
And free...

Free from the invisible shackles that have kept mothers small, silent, and split off from the depth and wholeness of their own sacred life force.

Whether she leads the PTA, runs a business, tends a garden barefoot, home-schools four kids, posts curated chaos, rides the bus with a stroller, or manages hidden symptoms from the couch - the shadows of old myths tug at her sleeves.

Sometimes she fits the mold.
Sometimes she defies it.
Some thrive in this role,
while far too many end up losing their soul-self in the midst of it.

No matter how different she looks, the demands are similar: stretch yourself endlessly, ask for crumbs, and give until there's little to nothing left *of you*.

She's exhausted, *but won't admit it.*
Rageful, *but only in secret.*
Disappearing, *but always with grace.*
Grieving, *but expected to be grateful instead.*

We've read the books that tell us to be mindful, be positive, be gentle, or to be present.

But what about being *human?*

What about being a woman who sometimes doesn't want to be touched? A woman who misses who she used to be? A woman who loves her children so deeply it aches yet also resents how invisible she's become?

A woman who feels, deep in her bones, that there *has* to be a better way - a better way to mother, to be mothered, and to be seen. A better way than the one we've been handed, the one society expects of us, or even the one we expect of ourselves.

This book, *The Human Mother*, is a reckoning. It's a confrontation with truth that demands awareness, accountability, and change.

It's a roar from the bones of every mother who's ever laid in bed at night, wondering:

"Why does it feel like everyone's thriving off my silence?"
"Why do I feel guilty for being tired?"
"Why do I have to earn rest?"
"Why do I feel like I'm not even real anymore?"

And perhaps most devastating of all:

"Why does it feel like motherhood swallowed me whole?"

This is for the mother who carries it all, wondering if she still exists under the weight.

This is for the woman who stopped writing, painting, dancing, or hiking. Who put her education on hold, gave up little adventures, and slowly pushed her own needs aside until she stopped dreaming.

Until she stopped *being*.

This is for the mother who wants to scream. Or run away. Who wants to *remember who the hell she was* before she became everyone else's lifeline.

For generations, mothers have been shaped into selfless providers of comfort and labor. Their dreams were erased so their sacrifices could fuel everyone else's neediness and survival. This lineage of quiet depletion is so old. It sits on top of hundreds of years where mothers were conditioned to disappear into duty and praised for it.

Capitalism, colonialism, generational patterns, and religion have all demanded mothers be the endless well, giving everything and asking for nothing. Your erasure didn't start with social media. That's just the newest face of an old story.

We deserve to have these truths laid bare - and to let them set us free.

This book is a weapon for waking up. A permission slip to take your life back. A map back to the woman beneath the mother, the girl before the expectations, the voice tired of being silenced - and the body and soul that are rejecting the continuation of self-denial.

This book pulls back the curtain and reminds us that a mother can be both the role she carries *and* the soul she came here to live as.

You don't need to heal yourself to earn this reclamation.
You don't need to be soft and submissive to be worthy.
You don't need to be constantly self-regulated to be a safe and reliable guide.
You don't need to be grateful for what broke you.
You don't need to pay the lessons you've learned forward.
And you don't need to keep it pretty ... or pink.

You just need to tell yourself the damn truth.
(Or at the very least, let the pages in this book help you remember it.)

This book is for you if you've ever:

- Wondered if "being a good mom" just means being quiet about what hurts.
- Been praised for your patience and endless endurance when what you needed was someone to rage with you.
- Secretly grieved the woman you used to be, even as you celebrated your children.
- Questioned if your love still counts when it has edges, limits, and anger inside it.
- Been told you were too intense, too sensitive, too everything, and started to believe it.
- Felt the crushing weight of being the center of your child's universe, with no one orbiting yours.
- Wished someone had mothered you the way you're expected to mother now.
- Been shamed for needing support, wanting space, or simply existing beyond your role.
- Craved real, unvarnished connection with women walking this same path.
- Felt, deep in your body, that something about all of this has been built to keep you small.

And this book is for you if something in you knows *we can't keep doing it like this.*

Something has to evolve.

Even though this isn't a book about how to love your kids better, it *is* a book about how to stop disappearing *in the name of loving them.*

It's about remembering that you aren't just a mother.
You are a woman.

And even more than that,
you are a full,
breathing,
flawed,
glorious *human*.

It's okay to come back to your whole, radiant self-
and to stay there,
even while being a mother.

About that one word.

Yes, I used *that* word. Not for shock value. And not to be edgy. But because it was the only word that carried the full weight of what I needed to say.

I spent the first 40 years of my life never swearing (not even the word *hell*) because of religious teachings and purity culture. I believed that silence, sweetness, and self-restraint made me holy. But once I realized I could say whatever the hell I wanted, something cracked open. Swearing, I realized, especially in moments of pain or truth, wasn't shameful.

It was *liberating.*
And it was *mine.*

You won't find many swear words in this book, but when they appear, it's because they came from a place of genuine rage: warranted rage I want you to feel with me. Rage that deserves to be heard.

This book is about *that* kind of liberation.
About seeing the unseen.
Naming the unspoken.
About breaking the spell of soft politeness and suppressing silence.

And about telling the raw and blunt truth about the disappearing act women have been forced into, shaped by myths, sustained by silence, and ignored by the very societies that depend on them.

We've been quiet long enough.
It's okay if the truth makes a bit of noise.
It's okay to not smile while saying it.
It's okay if your love has sharp edges.
It's okay if you miss the woman you were before-
and if you yearn for the woman taking shape.

What comes next isn't perfect, but it's real. The words I've written in this book were written to help set a mother free from the cage of silence and self-erasure. We've lost too many women to quiet suffering and suppression. Perhaps what the world needs is unhidden, unashamed, and unmuted women.

Perhaps it needs us to be loud in our truth while also being rooted in our wholeness.

May these pages help you come back home to your soul-self.

Before We Begin

Where Did I Go? (A note from the author.)

There comes a point where the silence becomes unbearable... the silence of a life where no one asks how you're doing.

Where your feelings echo back unanswered. Where your contributions are assumed and your exhaustion becomes normal.

Where you're so deeply woven into everyone else's survival that you become a ghost in your own story, or worse, a ghost to yourself.

And then, one day, something inside you snaps awake.

Maybe it's during a fight with your partner where you're, once again, the one translating everyone's emotions, fighting for the well-being of the family while trying to keep your sanity intact.

Maybe it's when your child (your beloved child) pulls away instead of leaning in when you finally try to share a sliver of your truth.

Or maybe it's just that dull ache you've been ignoring for years - the one that whispers, "No one really sees you. Not fully. Not truly. Not as a person with needs of her own."

I don't know about you, but I'm done being silent.

I'm done being the emotional sponge, the health coordinator, the peace negotiator, the background support system, the unpaid everything. I'm a mother, yes, but more than that, *I'm a human being.*

And I'm reclaiming my humanity.

This book is the dismantling of the sainted, self-sacrificing, silent archetype that has imprisoned mothers for generations. It's a call to remember that mothers aren't martyrs - we're souls.

We feel. We rage. We break. We heal. We need.
We doubt. We spiral. We numb. We ache. We long.
We expect. We reflect. We process. We disagree.
We witness. We wake. We try. We shift. And then we try again.

It's like learning to ride a bike again.
Wobbly at first. Unsteady. Unsure if we still remember how.
But we try.
And when we fall, we try again.
Because remembering who we are isn't a one-time thing.

It's a returning.
A relearning.
A sacred persistence.
It takes practice.
And it welcomes mistakes.

Every attempt becomes part of the becoming. And every time we get back up, we reclaim a little more of ourselves, piece by piece.

Because news to everyone on the planet:

Women who are mothers have thoughts that don't revolve around grocery lists or permission slips. We have dreams we buried. We have sacred anger that's starting to break through the cracks. We have pain that deserves to be held, not just managed quietly in the dark while the family sleeps or shared only in the secret corners of therapy sessions where no one else is listening.

We have been taught that "good mothers" don't complain. That "strong mothers" don't share too much. That "healthy families" mean mothers keep it all together, all the time, at all costs.

And it's slowly killing many of us.

Motherhood has become a performance of self-erasure, one that strips us of our sacred individuality. But I won't do it anymore. Not for appearances. Not for comfort. And certainly not for a culture that has *no idea* how to truly honor the feminine.

This book is a love letter to every mother who has felt like she had to be more than human in order to be good enough. It's for the mothers who are tired of being rocks and would rather be rivers - flowing, emotional, wild, and, above all things, *real.*

If our children are ever to grow into whole human beings,
they must witness *whole mothers.*

Not shells.
Not servants.
Not submissive housewives.
Not martyrs in leggings and mascara.
Not women who vanish behind clean counters and fake smiles.

Humans.
Soul-selves.

Our soul-self is sacred.
Even if it's been buried.
Even if the world bristles when we let it breathe.

We matter.

And we deserve to matter - as full, feeling, ever-evolving beings.
As a *Human Mother.*

Let this be the beginning of something brave and sacred.
Something that finally gives motherhood back what culture stole from it:

Its wholeness.
Its voice.
Its fire.
Its soul.

As you read this book, may you begin to remember what you were never meant
to forget.

May you remember yourself as you read these words, as being the full, radiant
being you were shaped over millions of years to become in this one unique,
unrepeatable lifetime.

From one soul to another,

Claudia

An Opening to the Woman You Still Are

She was never meant to disappear.

The woman who is a mother was never meant to disappear.

Not beneath the dishes.
Not beneath the praise for self-sacrifice.
Not beneath the aching back, the whispered resentment, or the guilt.

She was meant to *evolve.*
To *rise.*
To mother in a world that, dare we say, mothered her back.

But the system doesn't really mother mothers.
What it does do is:
It demands.
It depletes.
And it even shames.

It tells her she's noble when she erases herself.
It crowns her selfless, then walks away.
It doesn't ask her what she *really* needs.
And it doesn't wonder if she's *truly* okay.

Somewhere along the line, motherhood became synonymous with martyrdom.
Somewhere, the collective agreed that a mother's love meant giving to the point of disappearing.

That the smaller she became,
the better her children would thrive.
That there was only room for *their* growth,
not theirs *and* hers.
That love meant silence.
And that exhaustion was the defining proof that she was doing it right.

But what if the most noble thing she could do - was to remain whole?

What if her children didn't need a mother who gave everything,
but a mother who modeled boundaries, aliveness, and self-respect?
What if they needed to watch her say no sometimes,
needed to see her ask for help,
needed to witness her joy,
her ambition,
her fire?

What if they needed to see her *being* – not just endlessly *doing*?

And what about the little girl inside her?
The one who once twirled in the sun,
dreamed of big things,
loved with abandon,
and knew exactly what made her feel alive.

She wasn't meant to vanish either.
She was the north star,
the quiet compass pointing toward the life we were meant to live.
She held the blueprint for joy, for desire, for magic.

But somewhere along the way, we were taught to silence her.
To call her silly.
To grow up, give in, and forget.
Forget what we loved.
Forget what we actually wanted.
Forget who we were before we were needed.

But that little girl holds the keys.
She remembers the dreams we shelved.
And she remembers the version of us who was never afraid to shine.

What if mothering didn't mean losing her?
What if it meant bringing her with us -
letting her dance at the center of our lives,
keeping her dreams alive,
and reminding us what matters most.

What if we stopped calling it "love" when a woman disappears?

And what if we asked an even better question:

What do you need to stay alive in your own story?

Because mothers don't just give life.
They *are* life.
They are the pulse that holds the center.

But there are two pulses she can live by:
The hollow rhythm of the shell,
Or the deep, steady beat of wholeness.

And holding the center shouldn't mean becoming the shell -
a ghost of herself,
convenient and comforting for everyone but her.

Because when she disappears...
So does something incredibly vital in the world.

So let her stay.
Let her be seen.
And let her rewrite what it means to mother.

Let her stop apologizing for the space she takes up.
Let her children watch her evolve, not dissolve.
Let her rise.
And let the little girl rise with her.
Still twirling in the sun.
Still dreaming of big things.
Still the north star pointing toward what is true.
Dancing at the center of her own story.
Holding the keys to dreams reborn.
Reminding us what it would take to stay alive.

Let this become the new normal in family dynamics, where mothers don't disappear to meet impossible standards of motherhood.

And where growth is shared, *not sacrificed.*

— ·)◯(· —

Reflection Prompt

Consider taking a moment to ask yourself:

- What did I love as a little girl?
- What made me feel alive, curious, or full of wonder?
- What parts of her have I left behind in the name of being responsible, selfless, or "grown-up"?
- What would it look like to bring her with me now - not just as a memory, but as a guide?
- What do I need to stay alive in my own story?

Let these questions gently guide you back to your center. And let them help you remember who you are and help you become the person you long to be.

PART ONE

Unraveling the Myths
of Motherhood

Intro to Unraveling the Myths of Motherhood

The Shape of the Cage

Before we unpick the myths, we need to see the walls that hold them up and understand the shape of the prison that protects them.

Because these ideas (about what a mother should be, how she should give, what she should tolerate, how quietly she should disappear, etc.)...
They didn't rise out of *nature*.
They didn't come from *Spirit*.
And they *definitely* didn't come from *women*.

They were constructed.
Repeated.
Rewarded.
And handed down like heirlooms that bind women to the same worn-out roles, over and over again.

They were designed to feel like the rules of life - even as they siphoned the life right out of us.

This is the shape of the cage.
And before we can break free,
we have to see it.

The Function of Myths in Society

Myths aren't just children's stories. They're systems - a structure that shapes behavior and belief. They are the emotional code embedded into culture, teaching us what's good, what's worthy, what's expected, and what will be punished.

Throughout history, myths have shaped entire civilizations - guiding laws, customs, and identities. They were how humans made sense of the world, explained the unexplainable, and passed down lessons in a form that outlives generations. Stories have always had the power to bind people together, but unfortunately they also have the power to bind people in place.

They create truths without ever proving them.
They deceitfully whisper, "This is how it's *always* been."
And they become the rules we follow without knowing we've agreed to them.

In a world that demands invisible labor from women, myths have become an effective form of subtle control. Because if we believe that a good mother never complains, never rests, never needs, never breaks, then no one has to *change* the systems that are breaking her.

And if we believe she's naturally built for this kind of motherhood, then no one has to share the load she was never meant to bear alone. Then nothing has to shift, women carry the wounds, and everyone else gets to pretend that's just what "love" looks like - and that this is all normal.

That's how *mythology* becomes *machinery*.

Ghosts in the Hallway

Before something can change, it has to be seen. We can't free ourselves from what we haven't yet recognized. Awareness is the beginning of change.

But not everything that shapes us is obvious. Some lies are absorbed into our thoughts, expectations, and routines, so subtly, we don't even realize it's happened.

The most dangerous lies are often the invisible ones. I call them "the ghosts in the hallway," the ones we don't even realize we've let slip into our lives. They become the wallpaper of our days, the atmosphere of our homes, the low, familiar hum shaping our choices, our self-worth, and our place in the world.

I've felt this. In my home, in my role as a mother, and in the invisible beliefs I carried.

As a child, I experienced ghosts.

Literally.

From age six to nineteen, I lived in a haunted house. A literal one.

I didn't realize this was the case during my younger years. But it became clearer the longer I lived in those conditions. The heavy presence behind me every time I walked downstairs to my bedroom. A dark, invisible thing pressing in, never touching but never gone. Terror when I knew the sun was going down for the night. For years, it stayed that way.

Unseen.
Unnamed.
And always there.

And then more obvious things started happening. Lights began turning off when no one was in the room. Sounds came from places no one else was. And breathing was heard (outside of myself) when I was alone.

And that's when I *knew*.

So I spoke to it. I said, "I see you. You don't get to haunt me anymore. Leave now!"

And it changed.
The grip was broken.
And things began to shift.
Simply because I saw it, called it out, and said: *not anymore.*

That's what this is.
That's what we need to do with myths!

That's what so many women are living with right now - silent "ghosts" of expectation, obligation, guilt, shame, pressure, and performance, swirling around the shape of their lives.

These ghosts don't scream.
But their impact runs deep.
They cower in dark corners.
They slip into our speech,
our choices,
our words,
our inner talk.
They shape us until we think we're shaping ourselves.

But we aren't.

And the minute we name them, really *see* them, it's like flipping on the lights in a room where a ghost is hiding. A deer in the headlights. A child mid-hide-and-seek, frozen because they've finally been caught.

Everything changes once you see it.

This book won't be offering fixes before we flip the lights on the lies. Because nothing heals until the lies have been exposed. Growth can happen once the dark corners have been lit. And freedom will come after first seeing what (or who) has been stealing it.

This first section of the book, *Unraveling the Myths of Motherhood*, is the unveiling. This is where we name the "ghosts." This is where we say, "I see you. And no, you don't get to stay hidden anymore."

Once we name the shape of the cage, the door appears. And once we see the way out, that new level of awareness gives us the option *to walk out*.

The Cage is Made of Ideals

The bars of these cages aren't made of metal.
They're ideals.

Selflessness.
Strength.
Sacrifice.
Perfection.
Purity.

They *sound* noble.
But they function as shackles.

They turn a mother into a concept, not a full-spectrum human being.
And we measure ourselves against them daily, wondering why we always fall short.

What's wrong with me?
Why can't I be more patient?
Why does this feel so hard?
Why do I feel so hollowed out?

But the problem was never you.
It was the *invisible script* you were given.
And the roles you were taught to play.

The Convenience of Her Silence

There's something I've realized, something that settled in like a thunderclap once I truly saw it.

When a woman doesn't speak up in her home, when she swallows discomfort, shrinks her needs, and holds her tongue to keep the peace...

She becomes convenient.

Not cherished.
Or respected.
Convenient.

And the people around her, often without realizing it, begin to take advantage of her.

Because unspoken boundaries are more than likely to get crossed.
And unmet needs become the mother's quiet burden to carry.

At first, it might look like a few extra tasks here and there.
A lack of consideration.
A growing silence.
But over time, it becomes a pattern.
A normalization of her disappearing.
A home that runs on the fuel of her self-erasure.

If we look beyond this, we'll see that *it doesn't stop in the home.*

That same dynamic plays out in marriages, in families, in workplaces, in churches, in the very culture itself.

The woman who doesn't speak becomes the woman who gets used.
The mother who doesn't name her exhaustion becomes the mother expected to carry more.
The caregiver who never says "this isn't fair" becomes the one holding the world on her back.

Her silence becomes a systemic convenience - one that's gladly taken advantage of until she sees it.

That moment of seeing is what begins to shift everything.
It's when the silence, creeping through this particular haunting, finally reveals itself.

And the spell begins to dissolve.

And once you see it, you can then remember how to use your voice, and then begin to make necessary changes to reclaim your humanity.

Your Real Voice

Myths hum.
They sneakily hide inside compliments, parenting advice, commercials, family traditions, and even spiritual teachings.

They disguise themselves as encouragement:
"You're such a strong mama."
"God gives the hardest battles to His toughest soldiers."
"They'll thank you someday."

They become the voice in our heads saying:
"You should be grateful."
"You're just being dramatic."
"Other moms have it worse."

But there's another voice - perhaps a quieter voice.
The voice of wisdom.
The one that might be saying:
"This isn't love."
"This isn't me."
"I'm so tired."
"I want to stop making excuses for him, for them, for this."
"I don't want to be invisible anymore."
"I want to be known. And chosen by *me*."
"I want my life back."
"I miss myself."

That voice? That's her.
The real her.
Learn to recognize that voice.
Your own unique messages.

She's the one who can name the cage.
She's the one who can say,
"I see it. I see you. And I'm not playing along anymore."

That is the moment things can begin to shift.

Turning the Lights On

The following section of this book won't ask you to work harder on yourself but it *will* ask you to turn the lights on – to illuminate the unseen and unspoken myths of motherhood and to face the truths that will help set you free.

It will invite you to turn on the lights in the room you've been walking through in the dark and to name what was never yours to carry.

You might grieve what you were told to lose and you might rage at the myths you were taught to embrace that kept you small.

But, in the end, hopefully you'll remember the fullness of who you were *before* you were shaped to serve.

Because once you see the shape of the cage,
you can stop blaming yourself for not being free.
For not being *you*.

And once you recognize the myths,
you can finally begin to write your own truth -
and return to the human you may have lost somewhere along the way.

The human you were always meant to be.

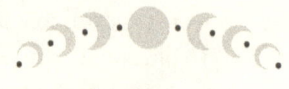

Chapter 1

The Saintly Mother

Myth: A good mother is selfless, saintly, and always serene.

She's praised in hushed tones.
Revered in scripture.
Romanticized in culture.
Marketed in magazines.
Memed on Instagram.

The Saintly Mother.

Religious or not, the ancient myths of the "saintly mother" still reach us – woven through politics, laws, media, and stories. Born from texts written thousands of years ago, they press into every corner of womanhood.

She's endlessly giving and endlessly forgiving. She rarely cracks, complains, or crumbles. She meets the daily needs before they're spoken. She has few boundaries, little need for rest, rarely any hunger for her own unfolding – and little left for herself, her *real* self.

She's the gold standard of womanhood!
And this version of a mother is everywhere.

We meet her in the pages of religious texts, in mid-century homemaker ads, and in the smiling influencer with a magazine-cover-worthy home. The details change, but the demand remains the same: a good mother gives everything and asks for little to nothing.

But beneath the saintly glow is a problem.
Because this isn't just a story.
It's a *blueprint*.

A blueprint that's been handed down through generations, shaping not only how mothers are seen and what's expected of them, but also how they see themselves and what they come to expect from their own lives.

This chapter is about that myth.
Where it came from.
How it evolved.
Who it serves.
And why it's *not divine.*

It isn't said outright. And it doesn't need to be.

It's in the sideways glances, the quiet judgments, the way the world gasps when a mother breaks away from religious norms. It's in the veiled undercurrents woven through films, therapy advice, religious teachings, and even well-meaning parenting books – all whispering the same thing, again and again:

Rest frequent enough to restore you isn't for you.
Help that doesn't vanish the second you're fine again.
Boundaries that protect your time, your body, your sanity, aren't for you.
Desire followed without shame or apology isn't for you.
Rage honored as truth without being branded as hysterical isn't for you.
Freedom that doesn't cost you everything else isn't for you.
(Not really anyway.)

Because *you* are the one here to soothe, to sacrifice, to disappear quietly (and beautifully, of course) while holding the center, tending to everyone else, and filling the cracks left by a society that doesn't offer (or refuses to offer) mothers.

The "sainted mother" is one of the first myths we're handed the moment we hold our first child or even the moment we dare to consider motherhood. She's gentle, smiling, and endlessly available. She has no shadows, no rightful outrage, and no personal ambition that isn't important enough to be postponed for *two decades.*

She's praised when she disappears in all the right ways, when she gives endlessly, performs without pause, and meets every need but her own. But the moment she shows up fully for herself, the boat rocks and those aboard panic. Suddenly, she's seen as selfish, unstable, or too much.

The drive to nurture, to protect, and to give with our whole hearts is real and meaningful. This kind of selflessness *can* be sacred.

But when did that sacred instinct turn into an expectation that you need to give *all* of you?

And when did love become measured by how much of yourself you *erase*?

We've turned this saintly mother into a cultural altar - no matter the version:

The church-going mother.
The influencer mother.
The grungy DIY homesteader.
The barefoot crunchy mom.
The spiritual energy-healing mom.
The CEO in heels.
The gentle parenting homeschooler.
The single mother holding it all together.
The activist mom marching with a baby on her hip.
The chronically ill mom doing her best from the couch.
The artistic mom turning chaos into creation.
The immigrant mother carrying the weight of two worlds.
The queer mother, unseen and unaccepted by the system.

She's expected to give her all, erasing herself along the way, and raise successful, well-adjusted children who fit neatly into society's expectations.

Saint Mom: always calm, always present, always giving.

She's glorified in commercials, canonized in religion, and polished in therapy language that encourages her to regulate herself for the benefit of everyone around her, even if no one's regulating for her.

What gets lost in all of this?
The fact that mothers are *people.*

We're taught to become a role.
A service.
A lifeline.
An unpaid worker.
A container for other people's feelings.
And a background character.

And if we dare to be something more than that, if we want to be seen as full humans, if we want to live life to the fullest, we're often dismissed, judged, or emotionally distanced. Support might be withdrawn. Approval fades. And suddenly, we're no longer the "good" mother but the difficult one, the extreme one, the out-of-touch one, etc.

No one might say the words out loud. But the warmth cools. The praise dries up. The silence grows heavy. And the message is clear: "You're not what we expected you to be. You've changed, *and not in a good way. This is concerning.*"

But how did we get here?

The Machinery Behind the Myth

This myth about the saintly mother doesn't seem accidental. Perhaps this subtle trap was carefully and deliberately built by systems and people that thrive on women's unpaid labor, emotional and physical availability, and constant self-monitoring. It keeps mothers endlessly giving, endlessly doubting, and disconnected from their own needs and from connecting with other women. (Because a woman too exhausted to ask for more is easier to control after all.)

From rigid systems like religion and capitalism to more subtle influences like family culture and internal pressure, each one has contributed to the beliefs we now confuse with "maternal instinct."

It's worth taking a closer look at the major forces that have shaped our story - religion, society, capitalism, family culture, and the pressure we place on ourselves.

▸ Religion: The Sacred Disappearance of the Mother

In many dominant religions, especially Christianity, mothers were lifted up in name but stripped of humanity in practice. Mary, the mother of Jesus, is painted as the perfect mother - silent, compliant, unbreakable. We know little about her fears, her mess, or her dark nights. She isn't allowed complexity. Only reverence.

And reverence without humanity is just another form of erasure.

In these traditions, a woman's highest calling is to serve. Her suffering is often portrayed as holy. The "Proverbs 31 Woman" in the Bible is praised for rising early, serving her household, never complaining, keeping quiet, doing everything, and needing nothing.

That's not a woman.
That's a machine.

Even spiritual phrases like "die to self" or "lay down your life for your children" have been weaponized against mothers. Tucked at the end of sermons, slipped into devotionals, or wrapped around biblical quotes.

These words quietly and continually reinforce the idea that dissolving ourselves is the most righteous thing we can do. It's the slow martyrdom, they framed as virtue. The more she suffers in silence, they teach, the holier she appears.

They don't just glorify mothers, they martyr them.

Christians praise Jesus for being crucified. They honor His pain, His sacrifice, His willingness to lay down His life for others. They build entire faiths around His suffering. They sing songs about His wounds and kneel before His statue.

But they ignore, expect, and continue to teach about the daily crucifixion of mothers.

She's crucified quietly.
Not with nails, but with endless expectations -
reinforced in every church sermon about women.
Not with thorns but with self-erasure dressed up as love.
Not with a cross on a hill but with a high chair, a time card,
and a house that never stops needing her.

She's told to "lay down her life" for her children.
And so she does.

She lays it down in dishes and doctor visits.
In midnight rocking and morning rush.
In checking bank accounts and checking temperatures.
In giving up her body, her mind, and her emotional well-being to bring even *more* babies into the world.
In giving up her dreams, future, and lifelong ambitions.
In saying "I'm fine" while something inside her quietly disappears.

They say, "die to yourself" and call it godly.
So she stops asking for more.
Stops claiming space.
Stops recognizing the voice inside that says,
I was meant for more than this disappearance.

Her body tightens, her dreams go quiet, and her voice becomes background noise. She, too, calls it love because she was told that love should cost her everything. She, too, calls it faith because the church praised her silence and her sacrifice.

But this isn't holiness.
This is slow erasure.
The slow annihilation of a soul.
This isn't sacrifice - it's slaughter.

We glorify Jesus for being crucified.
But mothers are crucified daily.
We say she's a saint.
We say she's strong.
And so we post memes that praise her ability to endure...once a year, on "Mother's Day."

We hand her the nails and say,
"Isn't this what a good mother does?"
We wrap the hammer in scripture.
We hide the violence in virtue.

And still, she shows up.
She gives.
She holds.
She bends.

If we're going to crucify her daily, then at the very least she deserves a snippet of what we give to Jesus - continual reverence, remembrance, and the unshakable support of a community that never lets her carry the "cross" of motherhood alone.

▸ Society: The Modern Saintly Mother

Fast forward to the 1950s and beyond: the "perfect housewife" is born. Smiling, lipstick on, dinner in the oven, waist cinched, problems invisible. She has few friends of her own, little to no aspirations that don't revolve around family. Her pain is unspoken. Her worth? It's measured in how tidy her home is and how quiet her discontent remains.

That image was shaped, sold, and endlessly reinforced by the media. Commercials, sitcoms, and magazine ads all polished the same message: the ideal mother is cheerful, composed, and content with her role. Even in modern media, that narrative persists, just with new packaging.

Today's "saintly" mother is the upgraded version. She's still selfless, still expected to hold the center, but now she's also energetic, fit, stylish, and thriving - *like she's immortal*. She's organized, but effortlessly so. Her house smells amazing, her sheets are crisp, the toilets are polished, and the pantry is stocked with labeled glass jars.

She plans thoughtful birthday parties, special gender reveals, balances a business, keeps her marriage alive, and still finds time for green smoothies, exercise at the gym, gratitude journaling, and holiday magic. *And* somehow does it all while smiling into a ring light.

Self-erasure has been rebranded as aspiration, packaged in pretty content, productivity hacks, and gratitude captions.

Children in movies are allowed full arcs of rebellion, growth, and emotion. Fathers often get to be aloof or even self-focused while still being framed as lovable. But mothers? They rarely allowed to falter. If they do, well, then they're the villain.

The packaging has changed over time, but the pressure hasn't.

The saint still smiles.

‣ Capitalism: The Saint Works for Free

Capitalism is the silent architect of maternal burnout.

It depends on mothers providing free labor - not just physically, but emotionally, spiritually, and logistically. It celebrates productivity and output but refuses to acknowledge the full-time, unpaid, unrelenting job that is motherhood.

When we do try to seek help or vocally express that perhaps such needs ought to be taken care of by the systems we are a part of (childcare, therapy, healthcare, rest) we're often met with judgment. We're seen as entitled, privileged, extreme, or even radical. We're told we're lucky, or made to feel that needing more is a personal failing. As if asking for support is a luxury and disappearing into the role is the price we're expected to pay.

The nuclear family model (that picture-perfect Christian ideal of the tidy home with a smiling mother, hardworking father, and well-behaved children) was never built to support human thriving. In practice, it cut mothers off from the webs of extended kin and communal care that once made parenting sustainable. It was designed for economic efficiency, not emotional well-being. The result? Mothers cracking under impossible pressure, while still smiling for school pickup.

Mothers have become the shock absorbers of a broken system. When healthcare fails, when schools are underfunded, when wages stagnate, mothers are expected to stretch. To fill the gaps. To make do.

The saintly mother doesn't protest the system's failures but absorbs them - quietly and gratefully.

And yet, despite this collapse, political leaders continue to urge women to have more babies. They cite falling birth rates as a crisis while ignoring the real crisis - that systems built to extract from mothers still refuse to invest in them.

Paid leave, affordable childcare, universal healthcare, community-based support - none of it exists at the level it's needed. The message is clear: reproduce, then fend for yourself.

And all of this is compounded for single mothers, poor mothers, BIPOC mothers, neurodivergent mothers, disabled mothers, and queer mothers. Those who fall outside the narrow mold of "acceptable" motherhood are punished even more harshly for daring to need or want anything.

She is the backbone of an economy that never intended to carry her, holding the cracks in the system with her bare hands and still wondering if she's doing enough.

▸ Family Culture: The Water She Swam In

Children or spouses often end up expecting everything from a mother. They learn it by watching her give everything away.

Over time, a quiet understanding forms within the home: *mom will take care of it.*

She'll remember.
She'll soothe.
She'll sacrifice.
She always does.

This isn't because children or partners are inherently selfish. It's because it's human nature to acclimate to what's consistently offered - especially when it's offered with a smile. When someone constantly centers others and neglects themselves, those around them begin to assume that's just who they are and that's how they should be.

And the quiet tragedy is that mothers often participate in it without even realizing they're doing so.

They want to give.
They want to love well.
They want to hold the center.

But in the absence of structural support, emotional validation, and shared responsibility, mothers begin to perform the impossible: they show up for everyone *at all times*, until their own needs feel disruptive. And eventually, aren't part of the equation at all.

This is how the saintly mother myth gets handed down: not through ideology, but through dinner routines, permission slips, and bedtime stories. It lives in who holds the clipboard, who wakes up early to make the lunch, who apologizes first after an argument, who keeps her breakdowns quiet so she doesn't "ruin the mood."

Spouses begin to depend on it.
Children grow up expecting it.
And no one stops to ask:

But who holds her?

I think back to my own mother.

We were never especially close growing up. She was the background of my childhood. The one who made meals, cleaned the house, reprimanded me, and drove me to where I needed to be. I didn't really know her though.

One day, after I was married, I ran into an older librarian who had known my mom for years. She looked at me and said, "Your mom is one of the neatest people I know. She has such a fun energy around her."

I was stunned. Wait, my mom? A fun energy? A whole personality that someone outside our family had not only noticed, but admired? It hit me like a wave - someone else had experienced something in my mother that I had never experienced. Because her personhood had been hidden behind duty. Behind service. Behind the role.

Why didn't *I* know her? Why had *I* never really seen her as more than a caretaker?

Although it may not happen in every mother-daughter relationship, it's common enough to ask: how do we stop this cycle from repeating itself across generations?

Family culture becomes the most intimate reflection of societal expectations. And like society, it rarely challenges the mother's role, because her selflessness keeps things running. Her exhaustion makes everyone else more comfortable. And as long as she doesn't name it, no one has to confront it.

But what mother would dare name it?

Religion tells her to be long-suffering.
Media tells her to be grateful and picture perfect.
Capitalism tells her to stop complaining and get back to focusing on her home.
Patriarchy asks her to carry the weight - quietly, and without recognition.

She knows not to speak too loudly, feel too strongly, or take up too much space. Quiet is how she stays admirable and lovable and respectable.

So she disappears quietly, efficiently, and invisibly, into the center she was told to hold.

▸ Self-Expectations: The Voice in Her Own Head

By the time the world has praised her selflessness, by the time her family has come to depend on it, and by the time the mirror no longer reflects who she once was, she believes this is just who she is. This is how the saintly mother myth finishes its work - with unseen external pressure and relentless internal expectation.

No one has to tell her to give more - she's already whispering it to herself:
I should be more grateful.
II should be able to handle this.
I should be doing better than I am.

I'm lucky to have this life.
What am I even complaining about?

She becomes both the performer and the enforcer, the caregiver and the critic.

She holds herself to impossible standards of calm, balance, and control because that's what the world rewards.

And the hardest part is that she often doesn't realize it. Because she's been trained, slowly and subtly, to believe that her worth is measured in output. That good mothers don't need frequent rest. That the best mothers don't want anything for themselves. That a worn out mother is a badge of honor and a resentful one gets quietly labeled as not quite mother material.

She scrolls social media and sees other moms smiling through the chaos, so she pushes herself harder. She compares. She shames herself. She stays quiet.

This is deeply embedded (and repeated) programming.

It's the final layer of the saintly mother myth, where the world no longer needs to erase her, because ... sadly, she's learned to erase herself.

One act of over-giving at a time.

A Word for Those Who Choose Traditional Motherhood

This chapter isn't about judging individual choices. If you find fulfillment in traditional motherhood, if staying home with your children brings you joy, if serving your family feels aligned with your values, that's beautiful and valid.

The problem isn't mothers who choose these paths. The problem is a system that demands this choice be made in isolation, without support, and with the expectation that choosing it means you forfeit your right to struggle, to need help, or to want anything else as well - a system built on the ancient myth of the saintly mother who suffers silently, asking for little, and giving everything.

You can choose to be a stay-at-home mom **and** expect your partner to share household responsibilities.
You can love serving your family **and** ask for help when you're overwhelmed.
You can find purpose in motherhood **and** maintain friendships, hobbies, and dreams that are just yours.

The saintly mother myth tells us these things are contradictory.

But they're not.
They're human.

The Saintly Trap We Walk Into

Whether we're religious or not, but especially in religious cultures, the trap begins long before we become mothers. As little girls, we're taught to be helpful, sweet, and selfless. We're fed stories (through books, media, and movies) that reward the girl who gives, the woman who sacrifices, the mother who smiles through everything. Then religion sanctifies it. Society reinforces it. Capitalism exploits it. And slowly, quietly, we begin to believe that this is what it means to be good.

The trap is subtle. We're praised for how much we do. We're complimented for how patient we are. For how quiet we stay. For how well we play the martyr without making anyone uncomfortable.

We're noticed only when we're not "doing well"... and then we're met with concern that treats us like a risk to be managed, not a mother to be cared for. We try to live up to this impossible ideal because we want to be good. We want to love our children deeply. And we do. But we're set up to fail.

I became a mother at just 20, not because I dreamed of it, but because I was taught it was my divine duty. That God wanted more children for His church and I was the vessel. I was a go-getter by nature, so I gave it my all, even though being a mom didn't come naturally to me.

I had once dreamed of becoming a veterinary assistant, a path rooted in a deep childhood love for animals. But that desire, like so many others, was quietly folded away.

I went on to have four children, and between being young, financially unstable, choosing to homeschool, and striving to do everything "right," I lived under the weight of constant pressure.

Every night for nearly *ten years*, I went to bed with the words *"I failed"* echoing through my mind. Because once again, somewhere in the day, something from the impossible list fell through, whether it was the house, the kids, the meals, the outings, or the needs of my spouse. No matter how much I gave, it felt like I had fallen short.

I think back on those years, alone, and feeling alone, within the walls of the home where I was raising my children. I was surrounded by the expectations of my religion, dictating what kind of mother I should be. With society offering its own version of that ideal. And by my own self-imposed standards, which sometimes gave me a glimpse that maybe I was doing okay but never enough to feel it in my bones.

If I could go back, I'd give that younger version of me the hug she never got. I'd tell her she was doing more than enough. I'd help her see the injustice of the broken systems that were failing her, not the other way around. I'd tell her perfection was never the point, and that everyone would turn out just fine, though in ways she never could have imagined. I'd remind her to make time for what she loves and to share that joy with her children and the world. And I'd point her toward spaces where she could finally feel supported - places that would hold her up when she couldn't hold herself.

And I'd tell her it isn't just okay to take breaks and be with herself but it's essential.

That's the final cruelty of the saintly mother myth: *it keeps us blaming ourselves for what the world refuses to carry with us.*

And once you begin to see that, once you stop mistaking exhaustion for failure and silence for grace, you begin to ask the question that's been buried for years:

Where did I go?

And slowly, quietly, or all at once - the halo begins to crack.

What Cracking the Halo Looks Like

Breaking free from the saintly mother myth doesn't mean becoming selfish or neglecting your children. It means recognizing that you can be a loving, devoted mother **and** a complete human being with needs, dreams, and boundaries.

Here's what it might look like in daily life:

- Asking for help without apologizing for needing it
- Taking breaks without guilt or justification
- Saying no to requests that drain you
- Expressing anger or frustration instead of swallowing it
- Pursuing interests that have nothing to do with your children
- Setting boundaries around your time and energy
- Speaking up when you feel unsupported
- Taking care of your own needs without calling it "selfish"
- Letting your children witness your full range of emotions
- Refusing to perform gratitude for circumstances that deplete you
- Choosing presence over perfection

The mother who lets her halo crack doesn't love her children less. She teaches them that women are full human beings deserving of care, respect, and space to exist as themselves.

The Breaking of the Halo

She was never golden. She was gilded.
Plated in expectation, wrapped in roles not of her choosing.

She smiled with cracked lips.
Held babies with sore arms.
And learned to cry without sound.

But halos were never meant for humans.
She was never perfectly divine.
Like a canonized saint or an angel.
She was blood and fire, bone and breath.

And one day, she stopped polishing the lie.
She let the halo slip.
She began to see herself.
And she let herself be seen.

She no longer wanted to be seen as a saint,
but as the un-anointed one who chose her own crown.

The one who shattered the mold.
The one who became something authentic, colorful, and real.

The whole mother.
The human.
The Soul-Self.

Encouragement for the Mother Who's Been Disappearing

If this chapter stirred something in you (grief, anger, disbelief, or recognition) you're not alone.

You were never meant to carry what the world placed on your back. You were never meant to disappear in the name of love. You were never meant to crucify your needs to prove your worth.

The myth of the saintly mother is not your truth.
Nor is it your blueprint.
Or your destiny.

You're allowed to be a mother and a full human being.
You're allowed to need help, rest, joy, passion, support, connection, relief, and recognition.
You're allowed to take up space in your own life.

You're allowed to *still be you.*

And the next time the religious rhetoric creeps in – the one that tells you to be quiet, to be good, to be grateful, to mold yourself into their version of "perfect" – pause and ask yourself:

Who benefits from me disappearing right now?
What would change if I chose to stay visible and in tune with my needs instead?

The impossible halo was never meant to be a cruel and punishing crown of thorns.

Let it crack.
Let it fall.

Stand in the power of who you authentically are...

And crown yourself on your own terms.

Chapter 2

The Natural Mother

*Myth: She was born for this. So being a
mother should come easily to her.*

From the very beginning, mothers are primed to meet certain expectations about
what motherhood should be.

Before the first contraction.
Before the first positive test.
Before any real choices of mothering are made - gathered like berries in a basket
from stories, advice, and expectations - we're taught to believe it will come naturally.

That we were *made for this.*
That our bodies *will know.*
That our hearts *will just open.*
That instinct *will kick in.*

And so when that doesn't happen, we tend to question ourselves.

The myth of the "natural mother" is a quiet, cruel lie.

It tells us that the love, ease, intuition, selflessness, and the satisfaction that comes
with motherhood will arrive with ease, as if stitched into our DNA. That there
isn't much of a need to *learn* how to be mothers; we should simply *be it.* It
presents motherhood as a state of being that should feel automatic, effortless, and
fulfilling.

This myth becomes the standard against which mothers silently measure themselves. (And often fail.)

The origins of this myth run deep in our culture.

For generations, we've romanticized motherhood as woman's "natural calling," ignoring the reality that parenting skills, like any others, must be learned, developed and practiced.

We've built an impossible standard that serves no one. Not the mothers living it, nor the generations of daughters who will one day carry its weight.

The Instantly Bonded Mother

One of the first points of presumed failure begins in the delivery room, or even before. The myth of the "instantly bonded mother" tells us we should feel a wave of love the moment we see our child. That our bond should be instant, overwhelming, and enough to unlock every instinct we'll ever need, turning us into natural caregivers without hesitation.

And sometimes, it is. Sometimes that love crashes in like a tidal wave. It can be euphoric and life-altering. Sometimes a mother will hold her baby and feel her heart expand in ways she never imagined.

This can and does occur. And when it does, it's beautiful. There's little that compares to it. Moments like these are deeply sacred.

But what if it doesn't happen like that?
What if the birth was traumatic?
What if depression rolls in like fog?
What if ambivalence (real, human ambivalence) colors those early days?
What if the only thing you feel is exhaustion, or fear, or nothing at all?
What if you grieve your old life or body, or both?

Research shows that up to 20% of mothers don't experience immediate bonding with their newborns. Studies also share that for many women, maternal attachment develops gradually over the first year, sometimes longer. ([1],[2],[3]) Yet we rarely speak of this reality. There has been little room for that in this myth.

No space to say,
"I feel numb."
Or: *"I don't recognize myself."*
Or: *"I'm not sure how I feel about this little stranger I just brought into the world."*
Or: *"I need a break - some time away from this."*

Becoming a Mother

I became a mother at just twenty years old. I was young, still growing into myself, but I had been taught through the lens of my religion that becoming a mother was the highest and holiest path a woman could walk. In my faith community, we were taught that women were divinely designed for motherhood, and that our spiritual worth was intimately tied to our ability to nurture and sacrifice.

The rhetoric felt beautiful but was binding: "No other success can compensate for failure in the home," they told us again and again. Every lesson, every talk, every example of womanhood held up the selfless, joyful mother as the pinnacle of righteousness. If you struggled with motherhood or didn't resonate with it, it felt like a spiritual deficiency.

I remember having several conversations with my friends while we were young, dreaming about what we'd be when we grew up. Most of them dreamed of being stay-at-home moms. But that never resonated with me. I loved animals and wanted to devote my life to helping them somehow - or doing something else big with my life that didn't involve having babies or raising children.

But, in the end, I did what I believed God wanted me to do. So I married young, and even though my husband and I were incompatible, immature, and far from stable, we followed "God's plan" and began having babies.

Our first daughter was born within a year of being married. Soon after, we moved out of our apartment and into my parents' home to save money and to help us eventually buy a house. Right before the move, continuing to follow "God's plan," I became pregnant with our second child. I believed God would be pleased with us and that He would bless our path.

But the pressure of that season was immense. Living with my parents brought stress and unspoken tension. Our attempt at starting a business was unsuccessful. Finances crumbled. Our car was stolen. The weight of our situation seemed to grow heavier by the month.

To their credit, my parents were generous in letting us live there. They never asked us to leave. But we could feel the quiet hope that we would soon be on our own. It was warranted.

And yet, even in all of that, I genuinely enjoyed being a mother to my daughter. I felt a strong bond with her. Watching her grow, witnessing her milestones brought joy and meaning amid the chaos.

But then my son was born. And things changed.

When I held him for the first time, I felt very little. No euphoric love. No magical bond. Just numbness. And beneath that numbness, a current of resentment grew.

I felt that he had taken something from me, having stolen the closeness I had with my daughter. He added to the noise, the pressure, the overwhelm. He was colicky and cried constantly, especially at night, and I was drowning in the demands of a life that felt too heavy, too fast, and too much.

Month after month, I carried those feelings. And I felt riddled with guilt. What kind of mother feels nothing for her newborn child? What kind of woman resents her baby? I believed something was wrong with me. There *had to be*. Flooded in shame and confusion, I told no one, so I carried these feelings alone.

But now, looking back, I wish I could go back and hold both myself and my son. I would whisper to us both that it wasn't our fault. It wasn't a lack of love. It was a lack of space. A lack of support. A lack of timing.

The reality was, my son was born just a year and a half after my daughter and that time frame was too soon. I wasn't ready. My *body* wasn't ready. My *heart* wasn't ready. Our *situation* wasn't ready.

It wasn't that I didn't love him. It's that I hadn't had time to return to myself before being asked to give myself away again.

I wish I could have told myself that it was okay not to bond instantly. That sometimes love grows slowly. That just because it doesn't feel natural right away doesn't mean it won't come.

Eventually it did come.

Around eight months in, something shifted. One morning, I looked over at him and felt something warm and new beginning to form. I remember thinking, "Huh. I really like you."

From there, the connection grew. And over the years, we've built a strong, healthy relationship, one grounded in presence, in growth, and in love that arrived in its own time and with continual effort to get it there.

I now know that there was never anything wrong with me. And there was never anything wrong with him. The unnatural part was the pressure to feel something I hadn't had the conditions to feel.

I learned that sometimes what's natural isn't an instant bond.

Sometimes what's most natural is *needing time*.

The Myth of the Forever Bonds

Mothers, especially new ones, often suffer in silence, believing something is deeply wrong with them for not feeling what they were promised or what they assumed they'd feel.

The myth leaves mothers feeling ashamed for needing to take time to bond. It obscures the truth that love can grow slowly, like moss. That not every bond begins as lightning.

Even more, the myth pretends that bonds *stay* consistent.
But they don't.

The attachment a mother feels to her children will ebb and flow over the years.

There are times of closeness and times when that closeness feels frayed or distant. There are moments when you care deeply and moments when you're simply surviving.
There are seasons when your children are your sun and seasons when you need to put yourself in the center again.

But this, too, tends to be hidden. Because the natural mother, we're told, *naturally* doesn't feel this level of contradictions.

Somewhere along the way, we came to believe that love would arrive on its own. That the bond between a mother and her child stays strong throughout a mother's life. That bonding would bloom instantly, without effort or complexity.

But real connection is rarely that simple.

And when it doesn't happen right away, it doesn't mean something is "unnatural." It's proof of your beautifully complex humanity.

But when the thread of bonding is broken or paused, another myth can quietly sneak in - the one that says real mothers should feel completely fulfilled by the role.

The Complete Mother

This myth builds on the last. If being a natural mother means love should come instantly and remain constant, then surely, if you were truly born for this, it should also fulfill you completely.

If you feel lonely,
if you miss your freedom,
if you still yearn for creativity,
connection, adventure, solitude, purpose,
then ... something must be wrong with you.

This myth tells you that your children should be your everything. That if you still long for more, then you're clearly not meant for motherhood. You must be selfish. You must not love them enough.

Although motherhood may awaken parts of you, it doesn't erase the rest.

You're still a whole person with a soul of your own.
Your dreams don't die at the feet of your children.
They may shift.
They may stretch.
But they are still yours.

It isn't selfish or betrayal to want to live beyond the title of "mom."
And it isn't wrong to miss the parts of yourself that feel buried under responsibility.

*You can be a loving mother **and** long for more.*
*You can be devoted to your children **and** still chase your own dreams.*
*You can be a good mother **and** a whole person at the same time.*

The myth of the complete mother asks women to shrink themselves down to a single role and to find their *entire* identity in their relationship to their children.

But no human being, regardless of how much they love their role, should be expected to find complete fulfillment in any single aspect of their life.

We don't expect this of any other role!

We don't tell teachers that loving education should be all they do or all they are, or ask doctors to find their entire identity in medicine. Yet we expect mothers to disappear completely into motherhood.

We don't expect this of fathers, of nanny's, of any other role that involves caring for others. And when we demand it of mothers, we don't create a better parent - we create women who slowly disappear, believing that's what love requires.

This expectation doesn't create better mothers, it creates exhausted, resentful, and hollow women who have nothing left to give because they've been asked to give *everything*.

When mothers dare to speak this truth aloud, when they admit to feeling restless or unfulfilled, another myth might rise to silence them.

The Unconditional Mother

If the last myth tells you your children should be your everything, this one tells you you must always be enough for them - endlessly, unquestioningly, and unconditionally.

Beneath all of this lies perhaps the most weaponized myth of all: *the Unconditionally Loving Mother.*

The belief that a mother's natural love for her child should be endless, and should never falter, and should ask for nothing in return.

We're told it is the one love that never runs out.
We're taught that this is what makes mothers holy.

But what this myth asks of mothers isn't unconditional love; *it's self-erasure.*

We're expected to love endlessly,
perfectly,
and without boundaries.
To give our bodies,
our energy,
our identities,
and our futures.

To love our children no matter how they treat us.
To keep showing up even when we are breaking.

And while the love between mother and child can be fierce and enduring, to expect that love to always be available, unshaken, and selfless at any cost is *inhuman*.

Even nature doesn't ask this of mothers!

Lessons from the Animal Kingdom

Consider the animal kingdom...

Elephant mothers are devoted and protective, yet they return to their own needs when nursing becomes unsustainable. When drought hits, they prioritize the herd's survival over individual calves.

Bird mothers feed their young tirelessly, but when winter comes, many species abandon their nests to migrate. Survival of the species depends on the mother living to breed again.

Even primate mothers, our closest relatives, will reject offspring when resources are scarce or when their own health is threatened.

Polar bear mothers will abandon cubs if food becomes too scarce, knowing that their survival ensures future offspring.

Wolf mothers will drive away adolescent pups when the pack's resources are stretched thin, teaching independence while preserving the group's stability.

Of course, I'm *not* suggesting human mothers should abandon their children or neglect their basic needs. But these examples reveal something profound: even in nature's most devoted mothers, self-preservation isn't selfish - *it's essential*.

The principle applies to human mothers too, just in different ways.

In the wild, mothers give a great deal to their young, *but they don't dismember themselves.* They *preserve themselves* because survival depends on it. And they definitely don't die slowly for the sake of upholding an ideal or meeting invisible expectations.

They feed their young, yes, but they also protect themselves. They retreat when needed. They abandon their young when conditions become unlivable. They preserve themselves because survival depends on it.

But human mothers are praised for the opposite. For giving everything. For never breaking. For smiling through the dismemberment of herself.

How is any of this "natural"?
How did we become so disconnected from what nature clearly shows us?

What's Actually Natural

It isn't natural to expect every mother's experience to be the same, or to ask her to dismember tooth and limb, heart and soul, ambition and curiosity, again and again, for the sake of a single role.

And it isn't natural to silence your desires, your rage, your need to run, your yearning to create or rest or be free, just to fit someone else's skewed definition of a good mother.

What we call "natural" is often just training - generation after generation of women molded into a shape that fits someone else's comfort. And when a mother doesn't fit that mold, she is called "unnatural."

But it isn't unnatural to need help.
To want more.
To bond slowly.
To feel distant sometimes.
To long for yourself.
To have love and connection ebb and flow.

It isn't *unnatural* to be human.

And the moment we stop measuring mothers by how "natural" they are is the moment we start returning to something far more powerful: the truth.

Reclaiming What's Actually Natural

What's *most* natural is a mother who's allowed to feel, struggle, question, and adapt.

Nature was never about perfection;
But it's about adaptation, instinct, and survival.

Real mothers need *support systems*.
They need *breaks*.
They need help naming the unspoken realities of birth and postpartum:
trauma, hormonal storms, depression, even psychosis.
They need time to recover between children.
They need space to maintain their identities beyond motherhood.
They need permission to struggle without shame.

Real mothers bond in their own time, in their own way. They love imperfectly, with boundaries, with needs of their own. They give generously but not at the cost of their own existence.

And so are you.

You aren't defective if motherhood doesn't come naturally.
Or selfish if you need more than your children's love to feel complete.
You aren't ungrateful if you struggle.
And you aren't unnatural if your love has limits.

You're human.

And that, more than any myth, is your greatest strength.

She Was Supposed to Be a Natural

She was supposed to melt into motherhood like butter in warm hands.
That's what they told her anyway.

Instead, she found herself staring at the ceiling at 3 a.m.,
empty, unsure, numb.
She worried something inside her had gone wrong -
because she didn't feel the rush of joy they said would come.

She fed the baby.
She held him.
She smiled at visitors.

But inside, she was screaming:
Where did I go?
Why don't I feel anything yet?
Why does everyone else seem to know how to do this?

Weeks turned into months.
Some days the love came like a warm tide.
Other days it was just muscle memory.

Still, she stayed.
She learned.
She grew.

And slowly, she began to understand:
Motherhood wasn't something she was born to do.
It was something she was becoming.
Her own being mattered -
and it mattered just as much as the life she brought into this world.

Encouragement for the Mother Who Thought It Would Come Naturally

If you didn't bond right away...
If you felt numb instead of euphoric...
If you questioned whether you were made for this...
You aren't a bad mom.
And you aren't the only one this has happened to.

Love doesn't always rush in.
Sometimes it arrives in small, quiet moments.
Sometimes it grows slowly - through presence, through learning, through time.
And that is just as sacred.

You're allowed to learn.
To adapt.
To need support, space, and time.
To become.

Motherhood isn't something you were born to master but it *is* something you're allowed to grow into.

And it's okay if it doesn't look or feel the way you were promised it would - or the way you thought it should.

You don't need to perform some ideal of "natural" to be worthy of love or respect. And you aren't less of a mother because you feel more like a work in progress than a glowing instinct machine.

You're a beautiful human being.
Still becoming.
Still worthy.

Still here.
And that's more than enough.

You weren't meant to become a mother in the birthing room, but in the thousand small moments that follow - in the choice to stay, to keep trying, and to let love arrive on its own terms.

And through it all, may you never forget that your life is just as precious as the life you brought into this world.

References:

[1] NHS, *Bonding with your baby.*https://www.nhs.uk/conditions/pregnancy-and-baby/bonding-with-your-baby/

[2] Taylor A, Atkins R, Kumar R, Adams D, Glover V. *A new Mother-to-Infant Bonding Scale: links with early maternal mood. Arch Women's Mental Health.* 2005;8(1):45–51. doi:10.1007/s00737-005-0074-z

[3] APA, *Postpartum depression and the baby blues.*https://www.apa.org/topics/depression/postpartum

Chapter 3

The Unbreakable Mother

Myth: A strong mother never falters.

She carries it all.

The schedules. The emotional tone of the household. The daily chores and tasks. The weight of her children's hearts and the health of her partner's mind or the fulfillment of their needs.

She's the regulator, the healer, the safe place, the unshakable one.
The one who never lets the thread slip.
She's celebrated for the strength that holds everything together -
and expected to use that same strength to keep herself from coming undone.

But underneath that image, something is likely breaking, and it's rare for those around her to see it.

The myth of the unbreakable mother has been etched into our culture as the gold standard. She's strong, grounded, emotionally regulated, and endlessly available.

She doesn't cry too much. She doesn't lose her temper. She doesn't ask for too much. She doesn't mind doing endless tasks. She doesn't break. And she *certainly* doesn't *need* a break (or need one regularly) and without apology.

This myth doesn't just deny mothers the right to express their needs; it denies them the right to be human. Because being human means faltering sometimes. It means breaking down.

And it means *needing*.

In a culture that glorifies resilience and mistakes suppression for strength, mothers are left with three choices: stay silent, speak and be dismissed, or quietly collapse under the weight of it all.

But what happens when the performance becomes impossible to maintain?

Learning From Luisa

We see an example of this in Disney's *Encanto*, through Luisa, the strong sister. Praised endlessly for her strength, she's the one everyone depends on. She carries donkeys, lifts buildings, and meets expectations - at every turn. Her entire identity revolves around how much she can carry (and do) for everyone else.

But beneath her strong exterior, she's falling apart.

In the song "Surface Pressure," she confesses:
"I'm the strong one, I'm not nervous / I'm as tough as the crust of the Earth is..."
"Under the surface, I feel berserk as a tightrope walker in a three-ring circus..."
"I'm pretty sure I'm worthless if I can't be of service."

Does that sound familiar?

They are similar to the underlying fears and pressures mothers carry: How can I keep everything around me functioning? If I stop holding everything, who will? If I fall apart, does that make me weak, unlovable, or a failure?

But Luisa's strength is quietly suffocating her. She's being slowly crushed beneath the weight of a thousand expectations, carefully balanced on trembling shoulders. It's the performance of being okay while silently unraveling.

And we see so many mothers just like her. Carrying the world. Praised for their strength. Terrified of what might happen if they ever set the weight down.

But real strength isn't measured by how much you can hold for everyone else. Real strength is knowing when to say, "This is too heavy," and putting it down anyway - even if no one else picks it up.

Even if some things around us crumble because we chose to set it down.

What Breaking Really Looks Like

To falter, in the eyes of the myth, is to lose emotional control and fail to keep up with the daily demands. It's to stop holding it all together.

But in real life, "faltering" can look like a thousand ordinary things:

• Crying in front of your kids
• Losing your temper
• Asking for help
• Saying "I can't do this right now"

• Lying on the floor and not getting up
• Dropping the ball on something important
• Not having the answers
• Wanting to be left alone
• Saying "no" to someone you love
• Letting dinner be cereal and dishes pile in the sink
• Being emotionally unavailable for a while
• Going quiet because you can't hold one more conversation

These types of "faltering's" aren't signs that you're falling apart.
They are *thresholds* more than anything.

They're signs that your humanity is speaking louder than the role you've been
taught to perform.

This kind of "breaking" isn't random weakness. There's a deeper explanation for
why mothers reach these breaking points, and it starts with understanding what's
really happening in our bodies and minds.

What the Body Knows

Most of us "falter" because we've had enough: mentally, emotionally and physically. This and we falter because our nervous systems are overloaded. We've been
living in survival mode for too long, but we're expected to perform like we're
thriving.

Fight. Flight. Freeze. Fawn.

These are protective responses. And they are the body's way of saying: *this is too
much.*

When a mother has been carrying stress, pressure, noise, and responsibility without pause, her body keeps score. Her brain rewires for vigilance. Her nervous
system doesn't know how to relax. Her adrenals burn out. Her muscles tighten
into tension that have forgotten how to release and relax.

And then, one day, she cries in the closet.
Or she screams into a pillow.
Or she stares blankly at the wall.
Or her nerves are shot.
Or her immune system falters.

Or her libido wanes.

Or her eyes lose their sparkle.

This happens because she's been carrying too much, for too long, without enough support.

This is why breakdowns matter. Breakdowns are a sacred message from within that says: *Something needs to change.*

But this nervous system overload didn't start with us. What we're carrying is also the unspoken, inherited pain from those who came before us.

The Weight of Generations

For generations, women were told to endure. To survive. To push forward without processing. To swallow the pain, trauma, abuse, and bone-deep exhaustion. And now, *only now,* are we beginning to name this for what it is: *generational trauma.*

Thanks to voices like Gabor Maté and others, healing is slowly becoming normalized. But we're still in the early stages.

So maybe now isn't the time to hit the gas pedal on having more children, no matter what religions or political leaders are urging. Maybe now is the time to pause and acknowledge what we're carrying – to admit that many of us are holding not only the stress of daily life, but the inherited wounding of entire family lines, and the pressure of pretending we're fine through it all.

At the very least, we should point it out for what it is. (Because you can't regulate what hasn't been recognized. And you can't heal what you've been taught to hide.)

Not only are we carrying the pressure of modern motherhood - we're also carrying generations of distorted beliefs, silenced pain, and what was never healed before us.

This layered burden helps explain why motherhood can feel so overwhelming. But for many women, it goes beyond overwhelming into territory we need to name more honestly.

When Motherhood Becomes Trauma

Motherhood can be beautiful. It can crack your heart wide open in the best way. It can stir a love so deep it feels like the very pulse of your being. It can bring meaning, magic, and a fierce sense of purpose. It can shape you into someone stronger, more alive, more grounded than you ever imagined.

But in truth-telling, when we dare to name what's often left unspoken, we should also admit that for many women, motherhood is also stretching and exhausting and overwhelming.

And for many - it's traumatic.

Not in the metaphorical sense. Not in the "oh this is hard" kind of way. In the body keeps the score, nervous system on fire, soul in survival mode kind of way.

When you live in a constant state of stress...

When you wake up each morning bracing for meltdowns, overstimulation, and emotional management before your eyes have fully opened...

When you spend all day multitasking, soothing, planning, reacting, adjusting, and just need one minute of silence (a minute you can't seem to find)...

When you go to bed every night feeling like you're failing, no matter how hard you tried to keep it together...

That's not just "mom life."
That's trauma.
Deeply ingrained,
subtle trauma.

Is it any wonder so many mothers are sick, exhausted, or silently unraveling when motherhood today means chronic sleep deprivation, nonstop emotional labor, financial strain, and the expectation to do it all without help, rest, or recognition?

The data doesn't lie. Women who mother in unsupported environments face higher rates of anxiety, depression, autoimmune disease, and burnout. This occurs because they're carrying too much, for too long, with too little support.

This isn't just "hard."
It's biologically unsustainable!

It's layered. subtle. unacknowledged. *trauma.*

Year after year. Day after day. Hour after hour.

This kind of chronic stress changes you:

• The way you breathe.
• The way you think.
• The way you respond to everything around you.
• The way you take in life.
• The way you see yourself.

And the most painful part is you often don't even realize it's happening.

Like a frog in water as the temperature gradually rises to a boil, you don't jump out - you gradually adapt. You keep adapting. You become accustomed to the emotional intensity, the deprivation, the demands.

Until one day, you realize you don't want to anymore. You can't! And the realization that's been quietly surfacing is: *This is damaging me.*

You've been carrying more than any one person should. You've been bending so long, you didn't notice you were breaking. You've been holding everything for everyone, running on fumes, offering a calm face to the world while your insides unravel, and suddenly, there's nothing left to hold it all together.

You feel like a shell of who you used to be. Because you've been overextended beyond what is humanly sustainable.

And still, you kept going. Mostly because you weren't allowed to fall apart. And you have children, after all. So you *have* to keep going, right?

This pattern of endurance and adaptation plays out differently for every mother, but the underlying dynamic remains the same. I know because I lived it myself.

My Breaking Point

I stayed quiet for so long.

After having all four of my kids, we were living in a rental, kicked out of our previous home. I was beginning to fall into chronic illness. I went to bed every night feeling like I had failed like no matter how much I gave, it was never enough.

I was in an unhappy marital relationship. I was living under the rules and doctrines of a high-demand religion. I had little to no real, consistent support around me. But still, I tried to keep it all together. I tried to be the mother I was told I should be or thought I ought to be.

I did my best to enjoy my children. I made birthdays magical, turned learning into adventure, and created cleaning-time routines with chore charts and silly songs. I dressed everyone for church every Sunday, smiled at the happy moments, and did my best to meet the unspoken expectations. All while carrying the weight of a deeply empty relationship while being in financial shambles.

I spared every penny. Made meals to feed six people from scraps. Exercised as regularly as a chronically ill body could. Read books to expand my mind because it was the only part of me that still felt alive. Made homemade toys for Christmas. Bought clothes for my kids from the secondhand store, rarely (if ever) buying anything for myself.

I justified my suffering through religious humility. Told myself this was "sancti-fying." That sacrifice was "sacred." I babysat other people's kids for extra income. Said yes when I wanted to say no. Smiled when I wanted to scream. Pretended "this is just a hard season" while the years stacked up and nothing changed.

I homeschooled. I hustled. I prayed. I cleaned up everyone's messes, emotional and physical. I kept the fridge stocked and the feelings managed. I tried to stay hopeful. I tried to stay quiet. I made magic out of crumbs. I swallowed my exhaustion and suppressed my rage. I kept it all moving.

And I did an amazing job at making it all seem okay on the outside.

Until, one day, I didn't.

One day, as we were getting ready to go out, the kids were already in the car. I don't even remember what triggered it (something small, I think), but something inside me snapped.

Right there, in front of my husband, guttural screams escaped my throat as I pounded my fists against the door over and over again until I thought I had broken my hands. And I didn't care if I had. My palms and fingers throbbed, but I couldn't stop. The screams came: loud, relentless, pouring out from somewhere deep inside me.

Screams I didn't know I was holding.
Screams I hadn't been allowed to make.
Screams I didn't *dare* make.
Screams I couldn't stop making, even as shame pressed its hand over my mouth.

And when I couldn't scream anymore, I walked away. I went into the bathroom, locked the door, shook uncontrollably, cried some more, and tried to comprehend what had just happened.

I knew life had been crushing me. I knew I had been holding things in. But I didn't realize it was that much. I didn't know what I had been doing to myself by swallowing it all for the sake of everyone else.

So no one would feel uncomfortable.
So no one would see me angry.
So no one would accuse me of falling apart.
So no one would feel bad.
So no one would feel guilty for the things they were doing that were hurting me or heaven forbid, feel the need to change or step things up because of it.

So no one would know *I was breaking*.

Something important I learned from that day was this:
You can only go unseen for so long before your body speaks for you.

You can only silence your emotions for so long before they rupture.

What I thought was a breakdown was actually a breakthrough. It was the moment my body said what my voice never could: *enough*.

It was messy. Loud. Uncomfortable. Painful. Terrifying. But finally, it was the deep-down truth. And it was the beginning of everything shifting.

My experience illustrates what happens when we buy into the myth of the unbreakable mother. But understanding the problem is only the first step.

Recognizing what we truly need is the next step.

What We Really Need to Survive and Thrive

It's okay to need rest.
It's just fine if you're willing to admit you're feeling overwhelmed.
You aren't incompetent or incapable because you can't carry it all or because you simply don't want to anymore.

You're not inconveniently delicate.
You're depleted.

And depletion isn't weakness-
It's a signal.

Mothers are humans. Humans who need more than survival.

What do we actually need to be well?

• Rest, not just sleep
• Safety (emotional and physical)
• Reassurance that we're not alone
• Touch that heals instead of takes
• Laughter that comes naturally
• Nourishment that feeds the body and soul
• Time away, without guilt
• Creative expression that feeds our soul
• Understanding without advice
• Someone to cry with or laugh with
• Financial stability or support
• Boundaries without backlash
• Personal dreams and goals we're working towards
• Emotional release (tears, rage, laughter, physical movement)
• Connection without performance
• Quiet without explanation
• Encouragement without conditions
• Spiritual meaning, in whatever form it speaks
• A tribe: trusted people who will help carry the weight, witness the struggle, and love your children alongside you

And dare we say (heaven forbid we mention it): a society that actually supports the act of having and raising children: healthcare, childcare, paid leave, higher wages, housing, safety nets, and systems designed to lift mothers instead of watching them fall.

These are the birthright of a living, breathing, evolving human being.

And if all we're doing is giving and giving, without receiving, without being seen, it's no wonder we're headed toward breaking!

At some point, something in you might say: I'm not holding all of this anymore.

Because love isn't about doing everything and getting nothing in return. And it isn't about being endlessly available while slowly disappearing. Real love (love that includes you) requires room to be human. And that means being held, too.

Recognizing these needs is the first step toward a radical reframing of what it means when mothers "break down."

The Sacred Act of Breaking

So, what if the breakdown isn't the end?
What if it's actually the beginning?
What if cracking open is how the light gets in?
What if losing it is what leads to finally finding something real?

The myth of the unbreakable mother tells us to hide our needs. But our needs are a doorway. A doorway to deeper connection. To better boundaries. To actual support. And to being seen.

And maybe, just maybe, the mother isn't the one who's the problem.
Maybe she's the goddamn signal!
The canary in the coal mine.
The truth-teller in a world that keeps asking for too much.

Her rage is data.
Her exhaustion is a red flag.
Her silence, her crying, her withdrawal?
They are the body's way of alerting everyone around her:
Something is wrong.

She is the lighthouse. The early warning system. The pulse of the family and the environment.

Not only should she be allowed to falter;
she should be listened to when she does.
And not just listened to,
but watched.
Closely.
Tenderly.
With respect.

Because how a mother responds to her environment (her home, her relationships, the roles she's holding) is the clearest gauge we have of what's working within a home environment and what's not.

She isn't the one to fix.
She's the one to follow!

Her wellbeing isn't a footnote.
It's the headline!

The Beginning of the End

So maybe the strongest thing a mother can do *is* fall apart: loudly, truthfully, and without apology.

When a woman finally breaks, what rises first is her voice. And with it - storm and chaos. But what rises next is long-overdue, necessary change.

Perhaps breaking is wisdom. And it's the beginning of the end of the unbreakable myth.

It took years to fully unlearn what I had internalized. To give myself permission to feel my rage. My grief. My disappointment. My truth. But it started with that moment of breaking.

And if you've had one like it, or feel one coming, I want you to know: It doesn't make you weak or scary or dangerous. It makes you real. And being real is what will save you in the end.

Mothers live through years of survival mode, doing everything possible to help their children survive and thrive. That alone is a victory. But that kind of chronic stress has a cost.

Yes, it tires you but it also buries your blueprint beneath layers of survival. This is the trauma of modern motherhood.

But just like that frog could be lifted from the pot, you can come back to yourself. You can find your way out of survival and into your own recovery.

Your survival (and *your* thriving) matter just as much, if not more, than those you care for.

You're allowed to say,
"This is hurting me."
You're allowed to name what's too much.
You're allowed to ask for space, time, healing, and support.

You're not doing it wrong when feeling depleted and hollow and run down.
You're simply (and magnificently) a human.
And the amazing thing about humans?
They are resilient as hell.
You can find your way home to yourself and build from there.

You deserve a place to be seen.
To be heard.
To be understood.
To name the unseen damage you've carried for so long,
until it started to feel like part of you.

But it's not you.
It's the water.

And the wonderful part about that is -
You don't have to stay in it.

The Day She Didn't Get Up

She didn't yell. She didn't cry. She just didn't get up.

The noise of the morning swirled around her-
cereal bowls clinking, backpacks unzipped, questions flying.
But she stayed in bed.
Not in defiance. Not in depression.
In something else.

A quiet refusal.

Her body said no before her voice ever could.
Her eyes stared at the ceiling,
in a kind of stunned revelation:

I can't do this anymore.

This was a signal. A siren the world had trained itself to ignore.

And that moment,
that silence,
that refusal to keep disappearing-
It was the beginning of her return.

And if anyone had been watching closely enough,
they would've seen:

She had been carrying more than anyone ever realized.
As for strength?
It was never about always getting up and carrying it all.

It was about finally saying no.

Encouragement for the Unbreakable Mother

You're allowed to need.
You're allowed to cry, to falter, to stop holding it together.

If you feel like you're breaking, start here:
Let something go.

One expectation.
One performance.
One belief that tells you you're only worthy if you endure without complaint.

Because this isn't just exhaustion.
It's what happens when you wake up bracing, live each day overstimulated, go to
bed overstretched, and repeat it for years.

That kind of pressure leaves marks.
That kind of pace rewires your brain, your breath, your beliefs about yourself.

You aren't "overreacting" by recognizing and responding to these marks.
You're reacting appropriately to *an unbearable load* carried silently for too long.

And for right now?
You're allowed to lay it down.
Even just one part of it.

It's time to heal your own exhaustion.
Untangle generations of silence.
And show those around you what happens when a woman finally stops pretending she's fine.

Every time you question a myth, feel your feelings, or speak a truth that was once forbidden - you are doing the work others couldn't do.

You aren't a problem when issues come up.
You are *the pulse.*
You are the proof that something deeper needs to change.

And that makes you sacred.
Sacred to all of existence.
To evolution.

This is trauma recovery.
This is generational healing.
And it begins with you.

Chapter 4

The Body-Sacrificing Mother

*Myth: Her body belongs to everyone more than
it belongs to her.*

The myth in this chapter erases a mother's autonomy, branding her body as sacrifice by design. From the moment she becomes pregnant, her body becomes a public object - touched, commented on, tracked.

Poked by doctors,
judged by strangers,
claimed by belief systems.

This isn't new. Even our most sacred stories normalize this taking of women's bodies. Even Mary, the holy virgin mother, wasn't given a choice. Her story begins not with consent, but with divine intrusion. Even *she* didn't get to keep God out of her womb.

The biblical story isn't violent in imagery, but we should realize that it's not consensual in spirit. There's no invitation, no choice, no room to say no. Mary isn't asked. *She's told.* The angel *announces* what will happen. It reflects a divine hierarchy in which Mary is expected to submit to God's will because ... that's what holy women do.

In that light, "divine coercion" becomes a painfully accurate frame, especially in a world where female agency and bodily autonomy are still so often denied in the name of goodness, obedience, or God. It's divine coercion dressed in the language of purity and purpose.

And no, just because it's in the Bible doesn't make it okay. It makes it even more heartbreaking. If the foundation of the "greatest story ever told" doesn't even allow a woman her own voice or body, then maybe the story itself, or the men who wrote it, need to be questioned.

Yet somehow we're still supposed to see this as *sacred*?
As *divine*?!

Let's not pretend that just because this story is stamped in gold leaf and canonized in scripture, that makes it okay. If we applied that same blind acceptance to other disturbing moments in the Bible, we'd be horrified.

So why do we stay silent and accept *this* story?

Probably because the body-sacrificing myth runs deep. That the female body is "meant" to be entered. Used. Accessed. Given. And that a mother's body, in particular, exists not for her but for others.

And the most staggering part? Men are still the ones writing the rules about our bodies. How, if, or when our body is used.

How on earth did we let it get this far? It got this far by passing this down as "love", as "duty", and as "motherhood."

This is how the myth seeps into her bones:
Her body is not her own.
It's there to be touched when called for.
To be entered when desired.
To be stretched in labor, in service, in silence.
To be consumed without question -
until nothing of her remains for herself.

To feed when they demand.
To rise when they call.
To hold when they reach.
To comfort when they cry.
To give, and give again,
while moving further away from the woman she once was.

Her body becomes the altar.
To be taken.
To be used.
To be emptied.
To be called holy only when it disappears into others.

This is the *Always Responsive Mother*. The one who exists entirely in reaction to the needs of others, rarely her own. This is also the *Wife-Mother Myth*. The one who is expected to nurture like a mother and serve like a wife, all while disappearing as a woman.

This is the slow erasure of a body that once belonged to her.

Serving, nurturing, giving of yourself... these *can* be beautiful things.
They can build connection, safety, trust, and belonging.
They can be how love gets expressed in action.

But the problem arises when these acts stop being *choices* and become *requirements*.

They become a problem when these acts are no longer expressions of love but conditions for being loved. They're also a problem when the giving never pauses and when the caring becomes a form of self-erasure.

That's when something begins to fracture beneath the surface -
Involving a loss of self and a silencing of the woman inside the mother.

The woman who thinks.
Desires.
Wanders.
Wonders.
Explores.
Changes her mind.
Who wants to say no.
The woman who isn't defined by her usefulness,
but by her *aliveness*.

The Physical Cost of Pregnancy

There should be more transparency regarding the depletion that pregnancy brings to a woman's body.

The way our bones ache.
The nutrients drain.
The muscles never fully recover.
The sleep we lose that no nap will ever repay.

Something every soon-to-be mother should know is that every baby she has takes years off of her life.

Literally.

The physical toll is real and measurable. Like Prince Westley in The Princess Bride, strapped to the torture machine while Count Rugen gleefully cranks the dial. "I've just sucked one year of your life away."

Except in motherhood, there's no dramatic villain.
Just biology.
Just expectation.
It's depletion rebranded as devotion.
Exhaustion, positioned as love.

Studies show that each pregnancy can shorten a mother's lifespan by as much as two years due to the enormous nutritional, hormonal, and cellular toll:

The bone loss.
The iron drain.
The mineral depletion.
The immune exhaustion.

The way her body gives away its reserves to grow another life and rarely gets those reserves restored.

And yet!

She's expected to bounce back.
To serve.
To smile.
And to offer more.

Even worse, there's a silent game among mothers to see who can endure the most while appearing untouched.

The physical depletion. The fatigue. The anxiety. The emotional collapse. All of it hidden under a fresh coat of lipstick, a perfectly packed diaper bag, and glowing social media updates.

Like a badge of honor, some women wear their survival like a second skin to prove it didn't touch them. They crank Count Rugen's dial to full power and walk away like runway models, laughing, humble-bragging, quietly daring the rest of us to keep up.

And those who can't? The ones who gain weight, who deal with the daily anxiety, who stop smiling, who cry in the bathroom, who say "I don't love this"? They look to those polished survivors as the standard and ask themselves what they're doing wrong.

But no mother walks away untouched. Some tuck the depletion out of sight, others carry scars that don't surface until decades later. It returns in the body, in moods that refuse to lift, in rage that seeps out sideways. It rises again when menopause swings the pendulum, or when the silence of an empty home makes her wonder who she is without their need.

We don't outrun what we've silenced. We don't bypass what we've buried. We either tend to it, or it waits for us.

The Mental and Emotional Load

If the physical depletion wasn't enough, there's another layer of body-sacrificing exhaustion that often coincides with it. You feed your baby from your body and still be expected to feed your partner's ego, soothe their emotions, and somehow keep the spark alive.

Eventually your body may have given everything, but so did your mind.

Holding names, sizes, schedules, feelings, meals, appointments, moods - the invisible labor of keeping it all running, with little praise and no pause. And because the brain is a body too, that invisible labor bleeds into the most essential form of recovery: sleep.

Only recently have scientists begun studying women's sleep patterns separately from men's. For decades, most sleep research and the recommendations that came from it were based almost entirely on studies done on men. The result? A universal standard that ignores hormonal shifts, caregiving demands, and the neurological load women carry.

But when women were finally studied, the findings were clear:
Women actually need more sleep than men.
Not less.
Not the same.
More.

Because women often experience greater emotional labor, multitasking, and more frequent sleep disruption (especially in motherhood), the brain requires more time to recover and reset. Yet women are the ones most likely to sacrifice sleep for others.

Once again: our needs were never the baseline. They were the afterthought.

And we've been conditioned to believe that needing more rest is weakness when it's actually wisdom.

Touch Overload and Sexual Expectations

And if all of this wasn't enough, there's something else that adds to the body-sacrificing exhaustion: *touch overload*. When the skin can't bear one more reach, one more grab, one more poke, one more child tugging on your shirt or partner sliding in behind you.

You flinch, not from a lack of appreciation or the need for affection, but because there's nothing left.

And still, you serve.
You wake in the night.
You answer the cry.
You give up showers, sleep, space, silence.

And if you pull back? If you say no to sex, or don't smile when touched, or need a break from the baby, or choose to pump or use formula, you're labeled frigid, hard to love, selfish, or unmotherly.

Seeing With New Eyes

The problem isn't that women give.

Or that she serves or nurtures or shows up - again and again, with her vast ability to love.

The problem is when motherhood demands that she dismember herself piece by piece - body part by body part, dream by dream - until she no longer recognizes the woman beneath the role.

Dreams put on hold.
Hobbies erased.
Career detoured.
Body ignored.
Friendships neglected.
Passions dimmed.
Books unread or unwritten.
Journals left unfinished.

Paintbrushes dry.
A body stitched, stretched or scarred - with little time to heal.
Degrees never finished.
Certifications left incomplete.
Dance floors empty.
Sleep chronically fractured.
Energy rerouted into the infinite vortex of caretaking.
Even her own thoughts are interrupted before they're complete.
Or her breath is shortened by the next request.

And in the later years, the bill comes due. After half a lifetime of depletion, hormones revolt, wombs are scarred or removed, and the body bears the proof of how much it was asked to endure.

We act like this is normal - normalizing her disappearance.

And heaven forbid that maybe the father of her children can take care of his own damn needs for a while. That maybe the "heroic" thing isn't clinging to sex or ease, but sacrificing something himself while the mother of his children sacrifices everything.

Not demanding what he wants from her, or staying stuck in the boyhood entitlement, alpha illusion, or religious indoctrination that says sex is something she owes him because she's his wife, and that's just what wives are supposed to give.

That maybe the bare minimum isn't cheating on his wife or expecting her to serve *his* needs while she's barely surviving on her own.

This should be obvious.
This should be universal.
This should be non-negotiable.
This should be common cultural knowledge.

The physical demands on a mother (the giving, the depletion, the lack of recovery time) should come with full societal support.

Not just from family.
Or from partners.
But from *systems*.
From *communities*.
And from *policies*.

But, more than likely, she wasn't the first woman to disappear inside the service. Her mother probably did it. As did her grandmother.

She learned this version of love from the women who had no choice. She's the first to see it with new eyes. *And the first to choose a new way.*

Her Body Isn't a Vessel

First and foremost: Your body isn't just a tool for feeding. Or a comfort object. Or a sexual receptacle. Or a bottomless well of warmth and grace. Or a holy sacrifice from God, made for the service of others.

Your body is *yours*.
Even after birth.
Even when breastfeeding.
Even when your child clings to your clothes or your partner craves the touch of your skin.

Touch should be yours to give, not to owe.
Rest should be yours to claim, not to earn.
And your sexuality should return when *you* return to it,
when *you* feel whole, not pressured.

We ask mothers to give, give, give and then wonder why they burn out. We ignore what's obvious. We pretend the cost isn't spiritual, cellular, and complete.

We don't protect what's most sacred to society - and we pretend not to notice.

Staying Rooted in Yourself

But there's something ugly festering underneath it all: *Entitlement.*

The expectation that her body *should* stay sweet, available, fit, and always eager to give.
That a "good" mother never says no.
That a "good" wife keeps giving, even when she's barely holding herself together.
That her body, her energy, her tenderness exist for others to take.

In the end, we simply need to see it for what it is, call it what it is, and end the entitlement mentality and the body-sacrificing myth that runs alongside it.

It's a slow, smiling theft wrapped in the language of love.

But it's not love to expect someone to disappear from themselves for you.
And it's not love to demand more from someone who's already given everything.

Motherhood should never require the abandonment of the mother.

And the fact that it does, and no one blinks, is proof that our culture isn't just failing mothers. *It's consuming them.*

But what if sacred motherhood wasn't about giving everything, including the body that was never meant to be an endless offering?

What if it's about being so rooted in yourself that your presence itself becomes medicine that nourishes you and those around you?

⸺⸺⸺ ›)○(‹ ⸺⸺⸺

The Body That Never Rested

She woke to the sound of crying.
Not the baby's, but her own.
A silent ache spilling out of her bones before her eyes even opened.

Her nipples cracked.
Her back sore.
Her skin begged for space.
But the day demanded her again.
Breakfast. Boogers. Bills.
Being touched, again, again, and again.

She wanted to love it.
To cherish it.
To savor it the way everyone told her she should.

And some days, she did.
Some days, her heart caught the light just right
and the joy of it all bloomed in her chest and filled her soul.
The tiny hands.
The laughter.
The sacredness of being needed.

It wasn't all burden.
But she had to admit that it was never without cost.

Her body had been on call for months.
No, years.
Milk, meals, sex, service.
Everyone pulling, needing, asking, taking.
She stood in the kitchen, bare feet on cold tile,
and whispered to no one:

"This body *used* to be mine."

That was the most honest prayer she'd said in a long time.

And slowly, she began to come back to herself.
The prayer became action.

She began to say no.
She began to say yes to herself first.
She took baths with the door locked.
She changed how she dressed with the intent of feeling like herself again.
She stopped performing sex and started honoring her desire.
She made pleasure hers before offering it to anyone else.
She let silence speak louder than guilt.
She let authenticity be her guide.

And with every small act of return,
her body whispered back:

"I'm still here. You're still mine. We're coming home. Together."

Encouragement for the Body-Sacrificing Mother

It isn't selfish for wanting your body back.
It's okay to feel touched out, worn down, or empty.

Your needs are valid.
In fact, they are the map back to your aliveness.

If you're craving silence, rest, distance, or pleasure that's yours alone, *listen*.
That's your body remembering itself.

And every time you honor that?
You stitch yourself back together.

You're allowed to reclaim the you within yourself.
Because love isn't meant to self-erase a person.

And motherhood was never meant to cost you your connection to yourself.

Chapter 5

The Carbon-Copy Mother

Myth: There's only one kind of mother - the "right" kind.

She is white. Straight. Married. Cisgender. Neurotypical. Able-bodied. Middle-class. Conventionally attractive. Soft-spoken. Mildly ambitious but not too driven. She's submissive but with a smile and has enough positive energy to happily meet everyone's needs.

This is the image that floats beneath most parenting books, baby product ads, school-drop-offs, and cultural assumptions.

She is the ideal blueprint. The mold. The standard.

And mothers who deviate from her are expected to conform or be excluded.

The Myth of the One-Size-Fits-All Mother

There has never been just one kind of real mother but that hasn't stopped society from pretending otherwise.

This myth of the Carbon-Copy Mother has been written into laws, policies, and expectations. It has excluded, judged, and erased those who don't fit the narrow mold: mothers who are queer, trans, single, polyamorous, neurodivergent, disabled, mentally ill, not feminine enough, too loud, too tattooed, too poor, too brown - too everything that she's not.

These mothers are scrutinized.
Their children are watched.
And their stories are squashed.

The culture doesn't offer them a seat at the table because the table was built to uphold sameness, not to acknowledge and celebrate difference. A mother who doesn't fit the mold disturbs the fragile system built on uniformity, unravelling the illusion that there's only one right way to mother.

So instead of offering a seat, it offers them a warning: "You can mother here, but only if you mother like her."

Where Did the "Carbon-Copy Mother" Come From?

The Carbon-Copy Mother myth didn't come from nature.
It didn't come from truth.
And it definitely didn't come from God.

It came from rigid beliefs and fear. And fear is quite often the bedfellow of control.

This narrow definition took root during the post-World War II era, when the "nuclear family" became the political and economic ideal. The 1950s housewife (white, suburban, financially dependent) became the template, despite representing only a fraction of actual mothers even then.

If we take several steps back to see the larger picture, we find that it came from patriarchy, from colonization, from whiteness and classism and from religious purity culture. From systems that work best if everyone falls in line. From governments that endorse only their version of family. And from corporations that only sell to a mother they can comfortably define and predict.

Working mothers, mothers of color, immigrant mothers, and single mothers were systematically excluded from this idealized vision, their unique contributions erased from the cultural narrative.

(The "idealized mother" was a construct meant to uphold white, middle-class, patriarchal norms. Anyone who didn't fit that narrow picture - because of race, class, marital status, or economic need - was systematically excluded. Their stories weren't written into magazines, TV shows, or political speeches. And their contributions to families, communities, and economies were hidden or minimized.)

But let's zoom out and look at the natural world. What do we see?

We see diversity.
And we see it *everywhere*.

From galaxies to microbiomes, there's no singular form of anything.

Every star is different.
Every tree is different.
Every snowflake,

every cell,
every fingerprint,
every strand of DNA,
every rhythm in the ocean,
every call of every bird.
Every person from every culture, every language, every land.
Every people across time, across civilizations, across the span of history.

Diversity isn't the exception - *it's the original design*. It's the rule written into everything that lives.

So where did we get the idea that motherhood should look, sound, move, and feel the same across every body?

Where did we learn to fear what is different?

Where did we learn to control what we can't define?

And why, after millennia of human existence, are we still pretending that one template of mother is the universal standard?

The ridiculousness of it defies logic, compassion, and common sense.

The Violence of Invisibility

When mothers who don't fit the mold are erased, their children are erased too.

When queer families don't see themselves represented in school paperwork, the message is: *You don't belong here.*

When disabled mothers are questioned about their capacity to parent, the message is: *Your body is an inconvenience to society.*

When Black and Brown mothers are monitored more closely by teachers, social workers, and medical professionals, the message is: *Your love can't be trusted.*

When neurodivergent mothers are overwhelmed by systems that ignore their needs, the message is: *You're the problem.*

My guess is that these aren't accidents. They are decades of cultural decisions that have caused harm and have limited our collective growth.

When we dismiss mothers who don't fit the default template, we lose their wisdom, their innovations, and their unique ways of nurturing. We deprive children of diverse role models and limit our understanding of what effective parenting can look like.

This erasure has practical consequences too. Non-default mothers often lack access to resources, support systems, and recognition. They face higher rates of discrimination in healthcare, education, and employment. They struggle to find parenting advice that acknowledges their realities or children's books that reflect their families.

When we center only the mothers who already have a seat at the table, we build a motherhood culture that is performative, narrow, and violent in its exclusions.

Honoring Every Way of Being

The Carbon-Copy Mother isn't just a body or lifestyle. She's a personality template too.

She's calm, sweet, soft-spoken. She's warm but not too intense, nurturing but not too emotional. She rarely yells, never shuts down, and never needs too much space.

If you don't match that template, you're seen as cold, harsh, dramatic, unstable, overwhelming, or inconvenient.

This myth punishes mothers for being human.

It rewards emotional flatness and self-erasure while shaming passion, depth, sensitivity, urgency, intensity, ambitiousness, intelligence, and complexity.

Something we should honor is this: *every temperament holds sacred gifts.*

• The melancholic mother sees the unseen. She is observant, emotionally honest, and rooted in the wisdom of nuance.
• The choleric mother is a fierce protector and natural leader. She advocates, decides, and defends with unapologetic clarity.
• The sanguine mother brings joy, light, spontaneity, and connection. She is the heartbeat of celebration.
• The phlegmatic mother offers gentleness, stability, consistency, and peace. She is the steady rhythm in a chaotic world.

And what about the mother who is a Leo - radiant, expressive, bold?
Or a Virgo - precise, analytical, deeply devoted to what's good and right?

What about the mother whose Ayurvedic constitution is Vata: creative, light, and changeable?
Or Kapha: nurturing, slow-moving, grounded?
Or Pitta: fiery, driven, focused, and clear?

What about the mother whose energetic design is that of a Manifesting Generator - multi-passionate, fast-moving, nonlinear, and wired for bursts of energy followed by deep rest?

Or a Projector, who sees the bigger picture but needs more space and less doing?
What about a Reflector, attuned to the emotional climate of her environment?

Or the mother who carries Afro-Caribbean rhythm and resilience.
Or the Indigenous mother who mothers through ceremony and connection to land.
Or the Latina mother whose warmth and fire carry generations of survival.
Or the Asian mother whose quiet devotion and discipline hold her family steady.
Or the immigrant mother whose courage bridges two worlds for her children.

And what about the mother who is neurodivergent?
The one who feels *everything* or shuts down under too much noise?
The one who processes slowly or rapidly?
The one who needs stimulation, solitude, clarity, or breaks from sensory overload?

She's often misunderstood. But she brings *depth, insight, and creativity* that offer her children a *completely unique* kind of presence and understanding.

We aren't built the same.
And we were never meant to mother the same.

We don't need more mothers who pretend to be calm while burning inside.
We need more mothers who are allowed to be *real* - and supported as they are.

There's no ideal emotional profile.
There's no "right" way to feel or process.
There's only *the truth of your nervous system, your soul, and your wiring.*
And it deserves to be *respected,* not repressed.

Building Something Better

But we can build something else. Something better. Something expansive. Something that mirrors the intelligence of life itself, from the swirl of galaxies to the structure of a single cell.

If the earth can hold both hurricane and still pond, if the body can hold both stem cell and scar tissue, if the sky can hold both storm and moonlight, then surely motherhood can hold all of us.

We're not here to match a mold. We're here to mother from the fullness of who we are - *from the unique ways we love, give, create, and offer ourselves to the world.*

Perhaps we should stop measuring mothers by how closely they mirror a myth and instead start measuring our culture by *how well it embraces diversity.*

Because nature does.
And so should we.

In the end, the world needs all kinds of mothers.
Because children come with all kinds of needs.
And no single temperament,
no single way of being,
can mother them all.

The Mother They Didn't Expect

She didn't look the part.
Too many piercings.
Too tired.
Too brown.
Too queer.
Too ambitious.
Too soft-spoken.
Too rough around the edges.
Too alone.
Too everything that didn't match the default.

Because maybe...
She didn't bake cupcakes for the school fundraiser.
She forgot spirit week.
She cried in parking lots.
She questioned authority.
She didn't stay married.
She didn't fit in at mom groups.

She said "no" to things other mothers nodded through.
She doesn't know what she's doing.
She showed up late - sometimes with a panic attack, sometimes with coffee,
sometimes just barely holding it together.
Sometimes with little left to give.
Sometimes with nothing but the strength and bravery to keep going.

She didn't look the part.
But still - she mothered.

She held the baby through the night.
She made the appointments.
she worked two jobs.
She wiped the tears, calmed the storms,
carried the weight no one else saw.
She translated diagnoses.
Fought with insurance.
Held boundaries.
Held her child.
And held herself together.

And still, she was questioned.
By doctors who didn't listen.
By schools that made assumptions.
By mothers who smiled but never invited her in.

But she knew.

She knew her child was safe.
She knew her intuition could be trusted.
She knew love doesn't need to look like perfection to be *real*.

And one day, she met another mother who didn't look the part either.
Not in her clothes. Not in her body. Not in her story.

And they didn't need to explain.
They just nodded.
Softened.
Exhaled.

And for a moment, the world cracked open.
And made room for all of them.

Encouragement for the Non-Carbon-Copy Mother

Perhaps you were never meant to blend in.
But you were meant to *belong*.
And those aren't the same thing.

Your motherhood isn't less sacred just because it looks different.
It's sacred because it exists and its real.
Because you're honoring your wiring, your story, and your way of loving.
Because the way you mother expands what the world thought motherhood could
be.

Your power will be depleted if you allow the myths of the Carbon-Copy Mother
to erase you or make you smaller than you really are.

But you *will* be powerful if you stay *real*, even in a world that tends to reward
pretending and suffocation.

Let them call you different.
Let them raise that eyebrow.
Let them underestimate you.
Let them feel some discomfort.
Let them stare.

You're not here to fit their image.
You're here to stand fully in your truth.
And every time you do,
you make the world wider for all of us.

You'll help reshape the world by mothering in alignment with who you really are.

Motherhood was never meant to flatten you into sameness.
It was meant to stretch your capacity to love,
and to be loved -
in your full, unfiltered form.

Chapter 6

The Sacred Family Unit

Myth: Her greatest duty is to preserve the
family, even if it destroys her.

The Sacred Family Unit myth says a "good" mother finds her joy in the home. She builds a beautiful life inside four walls. She keeps the sacred family unit intact, no matter the cost.

We're told that the nuclear family is the cornerstone of a strong society. That nothing matters more than preserving the image of one man, one woman, and their children, neatly framed within the white-picket box of stability and morality.

The nuclear family was never meant to protect mothers. It was meant to protect property, lineage, and appearances - leaving her at the margins without true power. And yet the skewed messages still demand everything from her, creating a chorus of expectations that drown out her own voice.

Churches preach: *A picture perfect family rests on the woman's shoulders.* Stay. Submit. Sacrifice. God will reward any suffering involved. Her calling is in the home, not in the world. A righteous woman doesn't chase ambition; she builds the kingdom by staying put.

Society declares: *Two parents, married, heterosexual, stable, and respectable...* that's what's best for the child.

Political leaders insist: *Strong families make strong nations* - but only certain families count. Have more babies but don't expect us to support you.

Media scripts: Perfect moms in cozy homes with scroungy husbands who fumble adorably but always redeem themselves and win applause for the bare minimum. Their struggle is cute. Your loneliness and frustration are expected. Smiling is required.

Family whispers behind her back: "You should've tried harder. You shouldn't have been so picky. He's still their father. It's better than being alone."

Schools quietly imply: Kids from "broken homes" are the ones who act out, struggle to learn, or fall behind.

The economy reminds her daily: Single moms are expensive. Families without two incomes are risky. You need a man - if not for love, then for survival.

Culture as a whole reinforces the message: You can mother here, but only if you mother like *her*. Quietly. Gratefully. With no needs of your own.

In the end, this system ends up isolating her - and it exhausts her.

It traps her in a role meant to be shared across a village and tells her she should be grateful for the privilege.

Think about what we've loaded onto one person:

Emotional labor.
Logistical coordination.
Meal planning.
Bedtime routines.
School pick-ups.
Birthday and holiday parties.
Home decorator.
Sick days.
Middle-of-the-night Googling.
Maid.
Chauffeur.
Therapist.
Conflict mediator.
Nurse.

Teacher.
Project manager.
Personal assistant.
Housekeeper.
Event planner.
Cook.
Laundry service.
Homework supervisor.
And often - employee or breadwinner, too.

All of it behind closed doors, without enough support, without enough rest, without enough witnessing.

We call this *sacred*.
We call it *strength*.
We call this "just what moms do."

But this wasn't how mothers were meant to live.

For most of human history, mothering wasn't done in isolation. In traditional societies across cultures, women were surrounded by aunties, elders, neighbors, sisters. Anthropologists like Sarah Blaffer Hrdy and others have shown that humans are "cooperative breeders," meaning multiple caregivers (often female kin) that have historically shared child-rearing responsibilities.

Children belonged to the community, not just to one overwhelmed woman behind a locked front door. Women didn't carry the emotional and physical burden of raising children alone in silence.

Consider the !Kung people of the Kalahari Desert, where children are cared for by multiple adults throughout the day.

Look at multigenerational Italian families where grandmothers, aunts, and older siblings all share childcare duties.

Even in early American communities, barn raisings and quilting circles meant mothers had built-in support networks.

Yet today, we hold up the nuclear family as the gold standard, even when it costs women their mental and physical health, their dreams, and sometimes, their safety.

This myth also keeps women in damaging relationships. It makes them afraid to leave. It convinces them that life without a man by their side (no matter how uninvolved, manipulative, or harmful he may be) will be worse than staying.

But ask the women who did leave. Ask those who finally divorced their husband after years of loneliness or abuse, only to discover that parenting alone was actually easier than parenting around her husband's chaos.

Ask those who left their emotionally distant marriage and found that without the constant work of managing an adult who acted like a child, they had energy left over for their kids.

What many of them find is:
Freedom.
Relief.
Ease.
Healing.
Clarity.
Safety.
Peace.

For many mothers, the moment they stopped caring for a partner they were also parenting (or hiding from) was the moment mothering their children and piecing themselves back together got easier.

Maybe *that's* the story we should be passing down.

Maybe what we should be saying is: She never should have had to raise children, hold a household, and manage an underdeveloped man - all at once.

But if she has to?
She's more than capable.
Capable of making it work.
Capable of rebuilding outside the confines of a nuclear family.

But she shouldn't have to do it in isolation.
She deserves sisters, circles, and systems of support.
She deserves to mother in community - because motherhood was never meant to be endured alone, not even under the illusion of a solid nuclear family.

The Fear of a Free Mother

Why would systems want to erase a mother within the confines of a nuclear family?

Because a mother who is fully visible, vocal, and powerful is harder to control.

Because her presence threatens more than order - it threatens the fragile egos the patriarchy was built to protect.

Centuries of male dominance required shrinking the feminine to inflate the masculine. But a mother in her ethereal, grounded, and awakened state becomes impossible to dominate.

She's magnetic.
Sovereign.
Unapologetic.
And becomes a divine leader.

She becomes the one others watch, follow, and learn from.

And that disrupts everything the underdeveloped man has worked to create an what he depends on to feel superior.

So instead of rising to meet her, they built a world that ever so deceitfully and sneakily (and effectively) suppresses her rise and dims the spark in her eyes.

She's a threat because a mother in her power might:
Leave a harmful relationship.
Demand resources and support.
Challenge cultural and political norms.
Call out systems that exploit her labor and love.
Raise children who question the rules - and rewrite them.
Refuse to pass down silence as love.
Model liberation instead of endurance.
Disrupt institutions built on her obedience.
Replace men in power who refuse to grow.
Reshape society with the wisdom of someone who's held life in her hands.

And who is "the system" anyway?

It's the overlapping web of power structures that benefit from keeping women small: religious institutions, political leaders, economic frameworks, and the media giants who shape what we see and believe.

They rely on her exhaustion. They profit from her guilt. They count on her silence.

They don't want mothers to rise because a mother who rises raises children who won't be easy to control either. She becomes not just a parent, but a pattern breaker.

A revolution in motion.

Mother as Citizen

If the burden inside the home of a nuclear family wasn't enough, there's another layer hiding beneath the surface: the myth that a mother's job is to raise good citizens.

Obedient children.
Productive workers.
Future soldiers,
taxpayers,
chronic consumers,
and system-abiding adults.

All scaffolding of a world engineered by male power – a society, centuries in the making, built by men, for men.

In this framing, a mother is no longer just a nurturer; she becomes a tool of the state. Her success is measured by how well her child assimilates, by how well her child fits into a world that's increasingly unnatural to live in.

Think about what we're preparing our children for:
Eight to twelve-hour workdays.
Little time off.
Low pay.
Shallow purpose.
Minimal maternity leave (if any).
No village.
No rest.
No future that looks much different from our own grinding present.

Is this really what we're raising children for? To continue a system where a handful of corporations profit while most people are overworked, under-cared for, and rarely free?

This myth says a mother's job is to raise children who function in this system. But what if our job is to raise children who question it? Who change it? Who live in alignment with something more human, *more whole*?

Research shows that children who learn to think critically, who are encouraged to question authority appropriately, who develop strong emotional intelligence, often become the adults who create positive change in their communities. But these aren't the qualities rewarded in our current "good citizen" model.

But before we are citizens, *we are humans.*
And before we are humans, *we are creators.*

We're not here to reproduce the system.
We're here to remember who we are outside of it.

What Real Support Looks Like

What would it actually mean to support mothers in ways that honor both their humanity and their children's wellbeing?

It might mean communities where childcare is shared responsibility, not individual burden.

It might mean workplaces that recognize that employees are whole people with families, not just productivity units.

It might mean extended family networks that show up consistently, not just during crises.

Look at countries like Denmark, where parents get 52 weeks of paid parental leave to share between them.

Or consider Iceland, where fathers are required to take paternity leave.

Think about historical kibbutzim, where children were raised communally while still maintaining strong bonds with their parents.

Or look to Indigenous and cooperative models across the world that share care among extended family and community.

These aren't perfect systems, but they point toward possibilities where mothers aren't expected to sacrifice themselves on the altar of family preservation.

Possibilities that stop sacrificing mothers on the altar of family and instead build family and community on the altar of mother-preservation.

The Whisper in Her Bones

She stood at the sink, again.

Dinner half-made.
Laundry half-done.
Children fed, but not really seen.
Husband home, but never really *with* her.

She had everything she was told to want:
A husband. A home. A family.
A life that looked just right from the outside.

But inside her, something was hollowing out.
The silence after everyone went to bed was the loudest thing she heard all day.
And in that silence, something began to whisper.

"This can't be it."

At first, she tried to push it down.
Tried to pray or wish it away.
Tried to remind herself to be grateful.

But the whisper grew.
Into ache,
Then rage,
Then clarity and truth.

It wasn't that she didn't love her children.
But she was disappearing in the name of loving them.
Disappearing to keep the family intact.

She looked around and realized -
this wasn't "sacred."
This was suffocating.
This was a system that disguised her erasure as devotion
and as ultimate motherhood.

And that night, she didn't run away.
She didn't burn it all down.
She just sat with the truth.

That maybe, the family isn't sacred if the mother is gone inside of it.
That maybe, she was allowed to want more.
And maybe, that whisper wasn't rebellion-
but remembering.

That maybe sacred means a mother who feels whole inside her own life.
And this – the lonely pedestal she'd been placed on,
the distorted image of saintliness she was handed -
wasn't sacred at all.

Maybe sacred means being surrounded, supported, and seen.

Maybe sacred is laughter around a table,
rest that restores,
love that frees.

Maybe sacred is the kind of family where the mother is allowed to evolve and lead
-
and not just endure.

Maybe sacred is a society measured not by its wealth or wars,
but by how gently it holds its mothers.

Maybe sacred is a life where *everyone* gets to thrive.
Including her.

Especially her.

Encouragement for the Mother Who Stayed Too Long, or Left Anyway

You were never meant to carry the weight of the nuclear family.
Not like this.
Not for the sake of a picture-perfect family,
or a society that values obedience in cult-like ways.

You were meant to be held.
And to be witnessed.
You were meant to be free.
And to be a leader,
guided by truth,
lit from within,
rooted in wholeness.

To lead us back to what's real.
To what's best for humanity:
Care, connection and collective healing -
The mending of the human fabric.

There's no such thing as the perfect family.
Families are real no matter what shape they take.

Because perhaps, just perhaps, it's love, not structure, that makes a family.
Perhaps it's showing up that matters more than fitting a mold.
Perhaps it's chosen connection, not genetic code, that makes someone family.
Perhaps it's not who's in the picture-perfect photo, but who stayed after it was
taken that shows you who really belongs.
Perhaps it's how we return to each other that defines connection.
Perhaps it's the rituals we create from scratch, not necessarily the traditions we
inherit, that carry the most meaning.
Perhaps it's the willingness to witness each other fully that makes a place feel like
home.

And perhaps it's love chosen freely, not inherited obligation, that creates something sacred.

And at the core of any unique family, where a mother is present, there should sit
a mother who is allowed to be fully human.

A mother who isn't gradually expected to hold the impossible all together, but one who is honored as part of the wholeness herself.

Real family is what forms when a home embraces its unique rhythm, its honest dynamics, when a mother is allowed to be fully human, and (perhaps most importantly)-

When a mother is home to herself.

Chapter 7

The Endlessly Nurturing Mother

*Myth: Women are natural nurturers who
don't need to be nurtured themselves.*

From the time we're little girls, a message begins its slow crawl into our understanding of what's expected of us:

You are here to give.
Your tenderness is expected.
Your ability to care is needed.

And then as we watch the older women in our lives, we learn this: If it tires you out, breaks you down, leaves you hollow, breathless, and spent... well, that just means you're doing it right and you're doing the most "honorable" and "noble" work a woman can do.

Because the mother gives so endlessly, the world stops wondering what she might need in return.
It assumes her fulfillment comes from service alone.
It mistakes her sacrifice for satisfaction.
They've grown so accustomed to her selflessness that reciprocity feels unnecessary.

Her emptiness tends to go unnoticed,
as though depletion is simply the shape she's meant to take.

Because she was "made for this",
shaped to nurture,
designed to give.
Her own longing dissolves quietly,
forbidden to take form.

Because those around her curl into her giving
like infants at the breast,

taking and taking.
They drink from her endlessly,
never sensing the hollow growing beneath them.

We've romanticized this disappearing act. A woman with a super-hero-like heart so big, she feeds the world with it - and conveniently never needs anything in return.

But what happens when the one doing all the feeding starts to starve?

What happens when her body keeps showing up but her soul starts slipping quietly out the back door?

The Historical Weight of Expectation

If we dig deeper, we see that this myth was carefully constructed over centuries, woven into religious doctrine, legal systems, and economic structures that needed women's unpaid labor to function.

In the 1800s, the "Cult of True Womanhood" declared that women's moral superiority came through their nurturing nature. By the 1950s, psychologists were warning that working mothers would damage their children permanently. The messaging was clear: good women sacrifice themselves completely.

Meanwhile, the economy was quietly depending on this sacrifice. If women weren't providing free childcare, eldercare, household management, and emotional labor, those services would cost society trillions of dollars annually. (Heaven forbid.)

The myth wasn't just cultural; it was economic survival disguised as feminine virtue.

The Cultural Hallucination

We have created a cultural hallucination that women, by nature of their care, are somehow exempt from needing it themselves. That their worth is measured by how long they can pour from an empty cup without asking to be filled.

But what we've forgotten - something so simple and so obvious is this:

All life needs nurturing.

Babies need constant care.
Children need attention and guidance.

Teenagers need patience and understanding.
Partners need emotional support.
Even *houseplants* thrive when they're given care and presence.
Even *pets* grow sick without attention.
Even *soil* must be replenished!

But the woman?

She's expected to thrive in the shade.
To live off scraps.
To treat depletion as destiny.

Because she nurtures so "naturally", so seemingly effortlessly, the world assumes she needs no nurturing herself.

Everyone is so ravenous for what she gives, their hunger is endless, they feast like spoiled infants, fattened babes, suckling from a breast long withered and dry, blind to the life draining from her body, never noticing (or caring) that the woman beneath is withered to the bone.

Feed! Feed! Feed!
Like parasites bloating on a host,
thriving on more than they really need,
indifferent as she withers in plain sight.

And when there's nothing left of her, they'll call it devotion.
They'll praise her in death for all the many ways she erased herself in life.
And build fleeting monuments to her sacrifice.

The world follows the same script - gorging on women's giving, naming it holy, blind to the ruin it leaves behind.

In the end, all that remains of her is the echo of what she gave.
They'll honor her exhaustion, but never ease it.
She fades, and they call it a beautiful offering.
In her absence, they feel only the loss of what she once provided.

They say she was "made for this."
They call it her "nature."
Then they wonder why she's so tired.

And when she's emptied,
they move on,
seeking the next woman to bleed dry.

Forms of Marginalization

Something that ought to be mentioned is this: Not all women are natural nurturers, and this matters more than we acknowledge.

Some women are builders, architects, visionaries, leaders, and creators whose love comes through movement, action, invention, not caretaking. The capacity and desire to nurture isn't universal. It varies from one woman to the next, and every version is valid.

But when nurturing is expected, when it's declared divine by doctrine, prescribed in church proclamations, and exalted as a woman's one true purpose, it stops being a gift and becomes a place of confinement.

Consider the woman who excels in the boardroom but struggles with bedtime routines. She's made to feel deficient because her strengths don't align with cultural expectations. Or the woman who loves her children fiercely but finds daily caregiving draining. She carries shame for not being "naturally maternal" enough.

The myth doesn't just harm nurturing women; it confines all women to a single definition of feminine worth.

This burden also doesn't fall equally on all women. Single mothers carry it without a partner to share the load. Women of color often face additional expectations to be the "strong" ones who never break. Immigrant women may lack extended family support systems. Women with disabilities navigate caregiving while managing their own health needs. Women in poverty have fewer resources to buy relief.

The myth intersects with every form of marginalization, creating impossible standards for women who are already fighting uphill battles.

The Caregiver Without Care

In the end, once it comes to the expectations of the Nurturing Mother, the tragedy at the heart of this myth is this: *those expected to nurture the most are often nurtured the least.*

The mother who tends to everyone's emotional needs but hasn't had someone ask about her in months.

There is no creature on Earth that thrives without nourishment. No living thing that flourishes without rest, without touch, without tenderness. And yet, we have asked mothers to do just that.

To keep giving. To keep smiling. To keep holding it all together.

We've handed them praise instead of support, expectation instead of compassion, exhaustion instead of help - and we've called it "love."

But this myth doesn't serve women.
It serves entitled, selfish humans.
It serves systems.
And benefits economies built on unpaid labor.

(It props up economies that run on invisible labor. It keeps patriarchies safe from women's full power. It sanctifies exhaustion so religion doesn't have to confront its own control. And it lets governments off the hook for care they should be funding.)

It also serves families that don't want to look at their imbalance. And it serves institutions that rely on obedient, overextended women to keep functioning without making noise.

It benefits a society that thrives on emotional outsourcing and counts on women to be the buffer between pressure and collapse but refuses to acknowledge that it's happening at all.

Perhaps most tragically, the myth convinces women that their depletion is noble. That her breaking point is a badge. That needing help makes them weak and needy. And that rest is selfish and that tending to themselves is indulgent.

It also convinces them that they must earn restoration by keeping everyone else okay first.

But she's not the exception to nature.
She IS nature.

And when nature is ignored, the entire ecosystem begins to falter.

Do we really not see this?
What kind of world starves its source?!
How many more women have to wither before we call it what it is?

Why are we the only part of nature expected to bloom without nourishment?

What If the Mother Is the Ecosystem?

What if the mother is the ecosystem, and we've been draining her dry?

In nature, the health of one element affects everything else.
When soil becomes depleted, plants struggle.
When plants fail, animals starve.
When pollinators disappear, entire food webs collapse.
Nothing exists in isolation.
Everything is connected.

Now consider the woman at the center of her family system.
She is the soil from which emotional health grows.
She is the root system that connects everyone to stability.
She is the pollinator, moving between family members, carrying messages,
resolving conflicts, ensuring everyone's needs are met.

When she becomes depleted, the entire system begins to show signs of stress:
Children act out more.
Marriages strain.
Extended family relationships suffer.
Work performance declines.
Even friendships wither because she has little energy left to nurture them.
Multiply this across millions of mothers, and it becomes more than personal
struggle -
it becomes a societal crisis rippling through classrooms, boardrooms, neighbor-
hoods, and nations.

We need to remember that ecosystems require balance to thrive.
In nature, there's always a cycle of giving and receiving.
The tree gives oxygen and receives nutrients from the soil.
The bee gives pollination and receives nectar.
Rain gives life to the earth and evaporates to be replenished by the sky.

Only in human families have we created a system where *one element* gives endlessly
without receiving equivalent nourishment in return.

The Mother as Root System

In forests, the mother trees, the oldest and largest, share nutrients through underground networks with younger trees.

But the young trees also share back.

They send nutrients to the mother tree when she needs them. The entire forest functions as one organism, each tree supporting the others' survival.

Human families could learn from this. Instead of expecting the mother to be the sole source of emotional nutrients, what if every family member contributed to the network?

She offers physical care, mental labor, and spiritual grounding. She is the root system holding everything together. But what if she didn't have to do it alone?

What if children learned early to give back, not just take? What if partners saw themselves as co-contributors to the family's emotional ecosystem rather than beneficiaries of it?

When Ecosystems Collapse

We've seen what happens when natural ecosystems are overexploited.

The Dust Bowl.
Deforestation.
Ocean dead zones.

The warning signs are always the same: a few species disappear first. Then others follow. Eventually, the entire system collapses.

In family systems, the warning signs are just as clear. The mother stops laughing as easily. She becomes irritable or withdrawn. She gets sick more often. She stops pursuing her own interests. These are ecosystem stress signals.

Yet instead of responding by restoring balance, we often ask her to give more. To be more patient. To try harder. To sacrifice deeper. We treat the symptoms of system collapse as individual weakness rather than collective responsibility.

The Ripple Effect Across Generations

Children raised in depleted ecosystems learn that love means depletion. They grow up believing that caring for others requires sacrificing yourself completely.

Daughters learn to ignore their own needs, perpetuating the cycle. Sons learn to expect care without reciprocating, becoming part of the problem. Both carry forward the belief that healthy relationships involve one person giving everything while the other takes freely.

This is how generational trauma spreads. Not through dramatic events, but through daily patterns of imbalance that teach children unhealthy relationship dynamics.

The Abundance Principle

But nature also teaches us something else: when ecosystems are balanced, they create abundance. Healthy forests are incredibly productive. Thriving coral reefs support enormous diversity. Fertile soil yields bountiful harvests.

When mothers are nourished, families flourish beyond what seems possible. Children feel secure enough to take healthy risks. Partners feel loved rather than obligated. And extended relationships thrive because there's emotional surplus to share.

The mother who is fed produces children who understand reciprocity. The woman who models self-care raises children who know their worth. The wife who receives as much as she gives creates a marriage based on mutual nourishment rather than one-sided sacrifice.

The Sacred Responsibility

If we truly understood that the mother is the ecosystem, we would treat her care as a sacred responsibility, not an optional luxury.

We would understand that her wellbeing isn't separate from the family's wellbeing; it *is* the family's wellbeing.

We would stop seeing her self-care as selfish and start seeing it as essential maintenance of the system that supports everyone else. We would recognize that asking her to give from emptiness is like asking a forest to grow without water, expecting fruit from a tree we never feed.

The Evolution Humanity Needs

For humanity to evolve, we need to remember what indigenous cultures have always known: *the feminine life-giving force must be honored, protected, and replenished because healthy societies depend on balanced ecosystems.*

The answer lies in understanding that we aren't separate from nature - we **are** nature.

And the same principles that govern healthy ecosystems must govern healthy families, healthy communities, and healthy societies.

When mothers thrive, everyone thrives.
When women are nourished, the whole world is fed.
When the ecosystem is balanced, abundance becomes possible.

This is biology.

This is one of the fundamental truths our species needs to remember if we want to survive and flourish on this planet.

The Ripple Effect of Depletion

When caregivers are depleted, everyone suffers.

Children of burnt-out mothers learn that love comes with resentment. They grow up believing that needing care is burdensome, that asking for help is selfish. They carry this into their own relationships, perpetuating the cycle.

Partners receive care that feels dutiful rather than joyful. The woman who gives from emptiness often gives with an edge of martyrdom that poisons the very relationships she's trying to nurture.

Communities lose the full contributions of women who are too exhausted to dream, create, or lead. How many innovations, how many solutions, how many movements have we lost because the women who could have led them were too busy managing everyone else's lives?

What if we rewrote the ending? What if we moved beyond identifying the problem to actually solving it?

The Sacred Reversal

What if the main thing mothers heard was:

You need rest.
You need tenderness.
You need to be held, to be heard, valued, and believed.

You need these things because you're alive!
And because you were never meant to carry this much alone.

What if we honored the nurturer by nurturing her?
What if we whispered this truth into every tired ear:

You aren't here to disappear into devotion.
You are here to be seen.
To be nourished.
To be held.
To be whole.
To be protected.
To be cherished.
To be buoyed up.
And to be supported.

Because what you do matters to all of humankind.

And if the world expects you to carry so much,
we need to make sure you're whole enough to carry it.
You deserve to be okay - not just for them,
but for *you*.

So let's begin again.

Let's make space for the mother who doesn't want to mother the way she was
told.
Let's reimagine the role not as a container of endless giving, but as a woman
worthy of being poured into.

This is how we heal the nurturing trap:
By insisting they receive as much, if not more, than they give.

Even the Soil Is Watered

Even the soil is watered.
Even the houseplant leans toward light.
Even the family dog is fed, petted, spoken to with warmth.

The tree outside is pruned with care.
The sourdough starter is stirred each day.
The garden is mulched.
The baby is swaddled.
The toddler kissed a hundred times before noon.

And yet the mother-
the giver of milk, of meals, of mornings-
is far too often left to run dry.
Unspoken to.
Unnoticed.
Untouched unless needed.

As if she wasn't a living thing.
As if her soul could survive on dry crumbs.

But she is nature, too.
She is made of tides and tension.
Of blood and bark and pulse and dreams.
She is a creature of rhythms,
a vessel of thunder,
a body of sacred weather.

And when the mother isn't nurtured,
the whole system begins to starve.

Because the mother is the mycelium-
quietly connecting every part of the forest.
She is the riverbed, holding the flow.
She is the sun-warmed stone-
reliable, but not invincible.

Why do we nurture everything but her?

Is she a machine?
A ghost in an apron?

She is life itself.
And life, by nature, must be nurtured.

Let her be watered.
Let her be fed.
Let her be spoken to with awareness of who and what she is.

Because when the mother is nourished,
everything else has a better chance to flourish.

She was never meant to wilt so others can bloom.

Encouragement for the Nurturer Who Isn't Nurtured

If you've ever felt guilty for wanting rest,
for not wanting to nurture one more thing,
for secretly craving to *receive* instead of *give.*

Keep in mind:
You're wise enough to know when you're empty.
You weren't put on this earth to be the soft place for everyone else to land
while never having a place to land yourself.

You're remembering that you are a human being
in need of care, support, affection, and *presence-*
just like everyone you've poured yourself out for.

There's nothing selfish about needing what you give.
And there's nothing shameful about not being
the ever-giving, ever-smiling, ever-tender version of womanhood
you were told to be.

You're allowed to vary.
You're allowed to say no.
And you're allowed to be a builder, a thinker, a dreamer, a doer-not just a "nurturer."

And most of all,
you're allowed to be nurtured in return.

Start small.
Let yourself receive.

Let the sun warm your skin and call it healing.
Let the wind move through your hair and call it cleansing.
Let the forest, with its healing phytoncides, hold you in its quiet, knowing way -
because *nature recognizes you.*

It knows what the world forgot:
You are part of the wild.
And you were never meant to give endlessly without being filled.

Seek out what softens you:
A friend who sees you clearly.
A bath with music that makes you feel.
Time alone, without guilt.
Food that comforts and strengthens.
Books that awaken something.
Learning a new skill that brings you joy.
Art that reminds you what being in touch with your creativity feels like.
Laughter that releases tension and brings you joy.

Let touch be medicine.
Let solitude be sacred.
And let a long walk, a good cry, and a deep nap bring you back to yourself.

Begin to say yes to the quiet things that pour life back into you.

Because your care should circle back to you.

For the woman reading this:

Start small. Your nervous system has been trained to feel guilty about self-care.
Begin with tiny acts of self-preservation that feel manageable:

Eat your meal hot, before serving others. Take three deep breaths before responding to requests. Say "let me check my calendar" instead of automatically saying yes. Ask for help without apologizing. Rest without earning it through productivity.

For families:

Redistribute the invisible labor. Make lists of who handles what: emotional support, scheduling, planning, remembering, managing. Notice the imbalances. Create systems where caregiving is shared, not assumed.

Stop praising women for their sacrifice and start supporting them in their wholeness. The mother who takes time for herself isn't selfish; she's modeling health for her children.

For communities:

Create support networks that go beyond crisis intervention. Offer practical help: meal trains that aren't just for new babies, childcare swaps, eldercare resources, mental health support.

Celebrate women's achievements outside of caregiving. Recognize the teacher, the entrepreneur, the artist, the leader, not just the mother. Trust her intuition with what's needed to improve the community.

For systems:

Policy matters. Paid family leave, affordable childcare, mental health resources, and flexible work arrangements aren't luxuries; they're necessities for supporting caregivers.

Workplace cultures that honor caregiving responsibilities for all genders, not just women. Healthcare that addresses women's needs beyond reproduction. Communities designed to support families, not just individual achievement.

And decision-making tables that include women as architects of the future. Women shouldn't just be included in decision-making roles (in government, policy, business, etc.), but should be recognized and empowered as co-creators of what the future looks like - shaping it, not just participating in it.

Chapter 8

The Dumping Ground Mother

*Myth: Mothers must give emotional support
but never need it.*

In the previous myth, we looked at the endlessly nurturing mother – the one expected to give without limits. This next myth carries a similar thread, but with a twist: here, she isn't just expected to nurture, she's expected to absorb. Everyone else gets to unload onto her, while she's denied the same release.

Every member of a family holds a spectrum of emotion - sorrow and delight, anger and joy, despair and hope. The brighter feelings blossom when they're witnessed and shared. The heavier feelings need somewhere to land - a safe outlet or a release.

For the children, we create that space. We listen without judgment, soften the sharp edges, help them find their way back to calm. For a partner, we try to do the same - making room for their heaviness, absorbing their hard days so they don't have to carry them alone.

But for the mother, the rules tend to be different. *She's* expected to be the place where everyone's emotions land, yet she's rarely offered a place for her own.

She may hold everyone's storms, but who is prepared to hold hers?

She can soothe, listen, and stay up until midnight processing the tears, fears, stress, trauma, and heartbreak of those she loves. But when it's her turn, she's often met with silence. Confusion. Resentment. Distance. Or discomfort.

She can be her child's emotional container - but heaven forbid she ask them to hold space for hers.

She can absorb.
She can soothe.
She can listen.
She can stay up till midnight processing their tears, their fears, their stress, their trauma, and their heartbreak.

And the underlying message tends to be something like this: It's unsafe, improper, selfish, or frowned upon for a mother to be fully human.

The message in this chapter may not apply to every mother - but to those it does resonate with, let this chapter be a lantern that shines a light on the weight you've carried - so you can finally put some of it down.

The Double Standard We've Normalized

There's a double standard so embedded in motherhood that it feels normal until we see it for what it is:

When children cry, we nurture.
When they explode, we stay calm.
When they're overwhelmed, we listen.
When our partner is stressed, we help soothe their system.
(As it should be.)

But when *we* cry, explode, or break down?

We're considered one or more of several things:
Unstable.
Or too much.
Or scary.
Or an inconvenience.
Or even damaging.

Some of us learn this the hard way. After months of holding it all together during something traumatic, we finally crack - just for five minutes - in front of our teenage daughter. We're not asking her to fix it. We just need to be real.

Her response?" Mom, you're scaring me. Can't you just deal with this like an adult? Or go see a therapist?"

This is the same daughter who often came to us in tears over friend drama, boyfriend dilemmas, or the confusion of finding her life path - always expecting a bottomless well of compassion.

The worst part is that the concern often isn't even for us.
It's not: *How can I show up for mom?*
It's: *When will mom bounce back so things can finally go back to normal?*

It's not so much about our pain; it's about the disruption our pain causes to the person/people it's inconveniencing.

The question seems to be:
What does her breakdown cost everyone else?
Not: *What does she need now that she's breaking?*
And: *How soon will she get back to normal and start serving my needs again?*

The Problem with Being the "Strong One"

The problem with being cast as "the strong one" is that the more we carry without asking for help, the more we're praised for it.

People lean on us.
You're so grounded, they say.
So calm, they admire.
So good at holding it all together!

But when do we get to lean?
Who holds space for us when everyone assumes we're the ones holding it together?

Being the strong one isn't necessarily a compliment. It's often the result of emotional neglect disguised as admiration.

And of survival.

Maybe it was from growing up in a household where being needed felt safer than being vulnerable.
Or learning that your worth was tied to how well you could absorb chaos without adding to it.
Or being praised for your composure while silently falling apart.
Or internalizing the belief that asking for help makes you a burden.

You didn't just become strong.
You basically *had* to.

So you become the grounding wire for the family's nervous systems, all while your own is short-circuiting. You scan constantly for what might erupt, who might spiral, and how you can preemptively adjust.

And if you miss something?
If you break down or lose it?
It all falls apart - or threatens to, just because you did.

Real strength isn't holding everything for everyone.
Real strength is saying, "This is too heavy," and putting it down anyway - even if no one else picks it up

It's saying, "This is too much."
It's asking for help.
It's refusing to carry the emotional weight of a household alone.

Understanding the Complexity

Family emotional dynamics are complex. Some family members may struggle to provide emotional support (usually from their own limitations).

A partner dealing with depression may genuinely lack the emotional bandwidth to offer support. A child with anxiety may become overwhelmed by a parent's distress not from entitlement, but from their nervous system's inability to regulate.

This doesn't excuse the pattern, of course, but it does help us understand that shifting family dynamics requires patience and sometimes professional support.

The goal isn't to shame family members into providing support they're not equipped to give, but to create healthier patterns over time.

The Therapeutic Paradox

Even in therapy circles, those supposedly safe spaces for truth, we're often told to keep our emotional burdens from our children. "Don't put that on them." "Be the adult."

And yes, children shouldn't be our emotional dumping ground. It's harmful to reverse roles or parentify a child.

But what happens to a mother whose never allowed to be real?

What happens when your entire emotional world must be filtered, masked, or shrunk down so your children aren't "affected"?

What happens when your grown child walks away the moment you open up?

What happens when even your therapist echoes the message that your feelings must remain hidden for the sake of the family?

Over time you may begin to believe that your emotions are dangerous. That you're not allowed to feel fully. That your breakdowns are irrelevant and inconvenient to everyone around you. And so you hold it all in.

Until it gradually begins to eat you alive.

The Flip Side of "Men Don't Cry"

We talk a lot about how society has taught men not to cry, not to feel, and not to be vulnerable. Entire movements have emerged to help men access their emotions, which has, of course, been good and necessary.

But while men are being encouraged to open up, *women are still being punished when they do.*

Yes, we've spent generations teaching boys that emotions are weakness. Yet while we work to free boys from the belief that emotions are weakness, women's emotions remain undervalued and misunderstood. Even as boys are encouraged to open up, many grow into men who shut down the moment a woman expresses anything beyond pleasant contentment.

They have been conditioned, from several directions, to see women's tears as "manipulation", women's anger as "hysteria", women's breakdowns as "hormonal", and women's overwhelm as "drama."

While men are now being encouraged to feel and express their emotions, women are still told daily:

"Are you on your period or something?"
"You need to relax."
"Stop being so sensitive."
"You're making a big deal out of nothing."
"You're blowing this out of proportion."
"There's no reason to get upset."
"Can't you just let it go?"
"You're exhausting."
"You're too emotional to think clearly."
"This is why no one takes women seriously."
"Here we go again."
"You're acting crazy."
"This is exactly why I can't talk to you."
"Why are you crying? This isn't a big deal."

Sound familiar?

The same culture that wrings its hands over men's emotional suppression currently still *demands emotional suppression* from women - especially mothers. We're expected to be endlessly emotionally available to everyone around us, while keeping our own emotions invisible.

So let's get this straight...
A man crying in a movie, or expressing his deep-rooted emotions is seen as brave and moving.

But a woman crying in real life is often met with eye rolls, a scoff, or quiet discomfort.

Her tears become something to manage, to fix, or to escape from – instead of being something to witness, to hold, and to *honor* as a signal.

And mothers?
We're caught in the ultimate *double bind.*

We're expected to be emotionally attuned enough to catch every feeling our children (or our partner) have, yet composed enough that our own emotions rarely surface, inconvenience, or be given adequate attention.

So basically,
We're allowed to feel for everyone...
As long as our empathy doesn't come with needs of its own.
And as long as it doesn't cost anyone else too much of *their* comfort.
Is *that* right?

When Partners Join the Silence

Often, the silencing comes from partners too. The very person who should be your emotional refuge becomes another voice telling you to "calm down" or "not here, not now."

A mother may finally gather the courage to share how overwhelmed and invisible she feels, only to be met with a shrug and the words, "You knew what you were signing up for when we had kids." Then the TV goes back on. This, from the same man who expects her to be his sounding board (or body) after every hard day at work.

When both your children and your partner participate in this emotional dismissal, you become an island. You're the family's emotional support system with no support system of your own.

The weight becomes unbearable, and you begin to carry it alone.

This compounds the damage. When a mother has no emotional refuge anywhere in her own family, she starts to fragment. She begins living multiple lives: the calm mother, the supportive wife, and the woman who cries alone in her car.

These fractured selves never integrate, leaving her feeling like a stranger to herself.

What the Mother Loses

What does a mother lose when she becomes the family's continuous dumping ground?

More than anyone realizes.

She loses her voice.
After years of modifying every emotion to protect others, she forgets how to speak her truth. She second-guesses every feeling, wondering if it's "too much."

She loses her sense of self.
When your entire identity revolves around managing everyone else's emotions while suppressing your own, you begin to disappear. Who am I if I'm not holding everyone together? The question becomes terrifying because the answer feels empty.

She loses trust in her own worthiness.
When love only flows one way, when support is something you give but never receive, you internalize the message that your needs don't matter. That you don't matter, except as a service provider.

She loses connection to her own children.
The very people she's trying to protect by hiding her humanity become strangers to the real her. They love the performance, not the person. And she knows it.

A mother might realize this in midlife when her adult child calls her "Angel Mom," and all she feels is sadness.

Not pride.
Not the bond she hoped for.
Just the weight of being misunderstood.

Because they don't truly know her. They know the smiling, accommodating version she performed for decades. Not the woman who grieves her own mother, who feels alone in her marriage, who still dreams of painting again.

This emotional suppression feels like a tombstone. And she begins to lose her body.

Years of swallowing rage, choking back tears, and forcing smiles leave physical marks. The chronic tension in her jaw. The knot in her stomach that never fully releases. The headaches that come from holding back words. The insomnia from processing everyone else's day while her own remains unwitnessed.

Her body becomes the storage unit for all the emotions she couldn't express, even as she absorbed, soothed, and carried everyone else's.

The Lie of the Invisible Contract

There's a belief that exists that says: because a mother chose to have children, she now owes them *everything*.

Her time.
Her body.
Her peace.
Her dreams.
Her softness.
Her silence.

Or her identity.
Her sleep.
Her mental health.
Her career, if it conflicts with their needs.
Her boundaries, if they make anyone uncomfortable.
Her autonomy, if asserting it feels like abandonment.
Basically her entire self, with little to nothing left over.

That somehow, just because she said yes to motherhood, she forfeited the right to ever say:

"This is too much."

"I can't do this alone."
"I have needs too."

This belief often comes from society but also comes from the children themselves. Whether still young or fully grown, many carry the unconscious entitlement that their mother should give everything of herself for their own benefit.

It's the belief that her exhaustion is irrelevant.
That she can run on three hours of sleep and still be everyone's caretaker.
That her body can break down from years of self-sacrifice and have it framed as the inevitable toll of love.
That her burnout is brushed off with, *"That's just what moms do."*

That because she gave life, her own becomes secondary, disposable even.

What sacred contract says one life must be erased for another to thrive?!

Life doesn't demand martyrdom as payment.

Motherhood is a *relationship*, not a *sacrifice ceremony*.

She's allowed (and should be expected to) exist fully, even while raising others.

Learning from Other Cultures

Other cultures do this differently. We should learn from them.

In many Indigenous traditions, storytelling circles include children. Emotions aren't hidden but modeled as part of life.

In African grief traditions, women mourn together in embodied, communal ways.

Scandinavian cultures normalize emotional honesty with children. Feelings are acknowledged, not pathologized.

Even *nature* shows us: elephants mourn together, whales sing grief songs, birds cry for lost mates, dolphins comfort each other, and trees send nutrients to struggling neighbors.

Emotion isn't a liability. It's a language. A survival strategy. A form of connection.

But here? In hyper-individualistic Western culture? We've convinced ourselves that emotional honesty is somehow unacceptable. That mothers sharing their struggles is somehow "inappropriate." That truth and emotional rawness should be reserved for therapy, *not* family.

Since when did a mother being real become an act of harm? And since when did being human become a liability in motherhood?

That mentality has *got* to go.

The Myth of the Perfect Emotional Boundary

Somewhere along the line, we adopted this idea that "good parenting" means rarely letting your children see you struggle or showing raw, honest emotions.

But how is that real?

Are we raising emotionally literate children by pretending emotions don't exist? Are we protecting them when we model perfection and silence?

Emotional health doesn't come from pretending things are okay. It comes from seeing how people move through what's not okay.

How can we raise resilient, emotionally intelligent humans if the people raising them aren't allowed to be human?

The Difference Between Dumping and Being Real

Dumping means unloading on your child with no boundaries - graphic details about adult problems, asking them to take sides, making them your therapist, or collapsing into them emotionally.

Being real means sharing honestly *with limits*:
"I'm going through something hard, but it's not about you, and I'm getting help."

Or, "I feel sad today because Grandma died. It's normal to feel sad when we lose someone we love, and it's okay to talk about our feelings."

With younger kids, this looks like simply naming emotions and modeling healthy ways to process them. With teens, it's offering context without burden. With adult children, it can mean inviting mutual, honest conversations.

This isn't about placing a weight on your child - it's about raising emotionally literate humans who know that:

- Feelings are normal and temporary
- Even strong people struggle sometimes
- Love never requires erasing your emotions

Breaking the Cycle: What Changes When Mothers Get Real

When mothers stop hiding their humanity, transformations ripple through generations. Adult children who finally see their mothers as whole people can experience profound shifts. They stop taking endless emotional labor for granted. They begin reciprocating care. And they realize that the woman who raised them has her own unique story, her own special dreams, and her own personal struggles worth honoring.

When a mother finally opens up to her adult daughter about her depression and the quiet unraveling of her marriage, the initial discomfort in the room may give way to something deeper.

"I never thought of you as having problems," the daughter might say.
"I guess I need to stop treating you like you're just here to fix mine."

And just like that, an authentic adult relationship begins.

For grandchildren, this shift can be even more powerful. They grow up seeing emotional honesty as normal. They witness their grandmother being supported by their parents, creating a template for mutual care that they'll be able to carry forward.

The generational cycle of one-sided emotional labor can finally begin to heal. And instead of raising children who take emotional support for granted, we raise children who give it naturally.

So, instead of perpetuating the myth of the invincible mother, we can model what healthy, reciprocal love looks like.

You Aren't a Dumping Ground or a Vault

So you aren't a robot.
Nor are you a locked box for the family's pain.
And you aren't a smiling, unfeeling mask.

You're a mother.
And a mother is a *full-spectrum human*.

We should rewrite the rulebook.
One where mothers are allowed to exist out loud.
Where our children learn that love goes both ways.
Where being openly emotional doesn't mean being irresponsible.
And where you get to be held too.

This is about healing. Because the emotional absence of mothers from their own lives is one of the most silent wounds in our families today. And it's continuing the generational cycle of emotional suppression, maternal invisibility, and one-sided caregiving disguised as love.

The cost of this silence isn't measured just in the mothers who lose themselves, but in the children who grow up emotionally impoverished, unable to handle real feelings, unable to give *genuine* support, and unable to see the full humanity of the women who raised them.

When we break free from being the family's emotional dumping ground while refusing to become its vault, we give the greatest gift possible:

Permission for all humans to be human.

Your Truth to Anchor In
A declaration to hold onto

I am a sacred vessel, not a container for everyone else's pain.
I am a living, breathing being - meant to feel, to express, to release.
My emotions are a source of wisdom and power.
My truth is divine and worthy of voice.

I deserve to be witnessed in my sorrow, my rage, my overwhelm, and my longing.
I thrive with support, connection, and care.
I belong fully - in every room, in every role, in every part of my life.

I am a mother.
I am human with a large range of emotions.
And I honor both.

Chapter 9

The Limitless Jobs Mother

Myth: Motherhood means saying yes to every task - forever.

It's said that motherhood is a "calling."
A "gift."
A "sacred role."
And it promises that it will fulfill you, complete you, and make you whole.

And often, yes, it can be breathtaking. It can split your heart open with love you never imagined existed. It can anchor you to your deepest values and awaken strength you didn't know was yours.

The bond.
The laughter.
The milestones.
The way your child's joy becomes yours.

Motherhood can be *profoundly* meaningful.
And love is part of the job description.

Yet somehow, we've confused *loving our children* with silently accepting an invisible contract - one that demands more hats than any one head can carry, in exchange for unpaid, unlimited labor.

Some Fine Print That Needs Mentioning

One day you might look up and realize:
You've become the full-time chef for people with the pickiest taste buds on Earth. That you'll drive like an unpaid Uber driver on call 24/7, no pay, no tips, no sick days.

Your brain becomes the family's calendar.
Your hands, the dishwasher.
Your body, the walk-in clinic.

Your mind, the chaos-control center.
Your smile, the customer service desk.
Your income, the emergency fund.
Your spirit, the one holding it all together.

And you'll go to bed with tomorrow's to-do list already etched into your skull, then wake up only to pick up where you left off.

Every. Single. Day.

Somewhere between the third tantrum of the day and reheating the same cup of coffee for the fourth time, it hits you. You haven't eaten. You haven't sat down. You're answering questions, wiping spills, juggling tasks - and somewhere in the mix, you realize you're a person who has needs as well.

You thought you were becoming a *mother*. Not a one-woman logistics team. Not a household executive. Not the emotional and operational manager of everyone's lives.

You never consciously signed up for all this. Not fully. Not with the whole truth laid out before you.

You didn't say, "Yes, I want to be responsible for everyone's socks, fevers, birthday gifts, and emotional regulation for the next 18-plus years."

You said, "I want to love my child. I want to be a mother."

But somewhere along the way, you were handed a different contract entirely, slipped to you in fine print you never saw.

The Numbers Tell a Story

Sometimes, the work does feel good. There can be real satisfaction in knowing the rhythms of a home, in managing a hundred moving pieces and keeping it all together.

There's a sense of purpose in feeding your family, in creating order, in being the one who sees what needs doing and quietly does it. For some, it's a kind of unseen mastery - the ability to anticipate needs, hold space, solve problems, and make it all run.

There's pride in that.
And fulfillment.
This work *can* matter deeply.

But mastery shouldn't be mistaken for obligation.

Love-driven mastery also doesn't mean expected and unending servitude. It doesn't mean becoming the entire cast and crew of a household production running 365 days a year with no credits rolling at the end.

According to the American Time Use Survey, mothers spend an average of 8.8 hours per day on household activities and childcare.

That's nearly equivalent to a full-time job.

If mothers were paid for this unpaid labor at market rates, it would be worth approximately $178,000 annually. We're talking about the economic equivalent of a high-level professional salary that we perform for free, on top of any paid work we might already do.

But this isn't about money.
It's about dignity, acknowledgment, and being seen.
It's about being witnessed - for the labor, the love, and the load.
It's about having support so that value is more than words.

That value shouldn't be invisible just because it happens *inside our homes*.

The Backlash Against Boundaries

When you do try to say no?
When you hire help or ask for assistance?

The responses may come swift and sharp:
"You're lazy."
"You're not cut out for this."
"You should have known what you were getting into."
"You're entitled."
"You chose this."
"You shouldn't complain."
"Must be nice to live this kind of cushy life."
"Wow, someone's feeling fancy."
"Don't be bougie - this is just part of the job."

But we didn't choose *this* version.

We didn't say yes to becoming a multi-department domestic workforce. We didn't agree to absorb every logistical, physical, emotional, and spiritual task just because we had a baby.

Some of us hate cooking.
Some of us hate cleaning.
Some of us were never meant to be project managers.
Some of us don't want to plan another birthday party.
Some of us don't want to be the default driver to dance class, soccer practice, dentist appointments, and school drop-off, with a baby screaming in the backseat while dinner still hasn't been figured out.

Yet here we are.
Drowning in it.

The Unpaid Infrastructure

Do we think this level of imbalance happened by accident? Or did it happen because of assumptions so deep we no longer even see them?

This didn't happen by accident. It happened because of assumptions that we'll pick up the slack, remember everything, we'll hold the center steady while managing everyone's moods along with our own. And we'll somehow be naturally better at noticing what needs to be done.

When the system fails to offer support, the mother becomes the support.
When community structures crumble, we become the entire village.
When paid childcare is unaffordable, we become the unpaid workforce.

But this isn't how it always was.

Many grandmothers and great-grandmothers lived in communities where child-care was genuinely shared, where extended families pitched in, where multiple women helped raise each child.

Historian Stephanie Coontz has documented how the isolated, task-burdened nuclear family is actually a historical anomaly, *not* the natural order we've been told it is.

Coontz has shown that what we think of as "traditional" isn't actually ancient - it's modern. The isolated, self-sufficient nuclear family - the mother, the father, the kids, alone in a single home - is a modern invention. It didn't become the cultural ideal until the 1950s, when postwar prosperity created a brief window where a single breadwinner could afford to support a family.

But even then, this setup mostly applied to white, middle-class families with government-subsidized mortgages and strong labor unions. It wasn't universal. And it wasn't built to last.

For most of history, families were interwoven with others. Survival and child-rearing depended on cooperation, not isolation. Love wasn't privatized. Neither was care. But in the last several decades, as those broader community structures eroded, and as capitalism privatized almost everything, the village disappeared.

And the weight of the entire system within the home landed on one person: the mother.

Stephanie Coontz makes it clear: this idea that a single household can contain every need, fulfill every role, and raise children without outside help is not how it's always been. It's how it is now. And it's why so many of us are drowning. We feel like it's too much most days - because it is. We were never meant to feel the constant grips of stress as we do this alone.

As families scattered and communities dissolved, the work didn't disappear. It all landed on one person: *Us.* We *are* the unpaid infrastructure holding up the modern family, filling gaps that used to be supported by entire communities.

If we feel like it's too much most days - it should!
No single person was ever meant to do this job.

We weren't built to mother in isolation.
If it feels like it's too lonely, unfulfilling or too much most days-

It's because it is.

What This Does to Love

This invisible labor crisis doesn't just exhaust mothers; it rewrites the very relationships we're trying to protect. Partners begin to feel like roommates managing competing schedules rather than teammates building a life together.

Resentment builds when one person carries the mental load while the other asks, "What can I do to help?" as if household management is fundamentally your responsibility and they're just lending a charitable hand.

But the problem may not be that our partners don't help enough. The problem is the word "help" itself. Help implies that one person owns the responsibility and the other is doing a favor. Real partnership means *both* people taking ownership of family life, period.

It means recognizing that emotional labor, planning, and remembering aren't innate female traits but learned skills that anyone can develop. The woman who remembers to buy birthday gifts wasn't born with a gift-remembering gene. She learned to pay attention because someone had to, and she was the one who picked up the slack.

The Deeper Truth About What We've Lost

Most of us don't hate being mothers. But we might hate having everything be about everyone else besides ourselves.

We might hate that our own needs have become obsolete, even to us.

We might hate that we've somehow accepted that our exhaustion, our dreams, our basic human need for rest and fulfillment always comes last.

We might hate that we've been convinced this (or feeling any of it) is what love looks like, when really, it's what exploitation looks like wearing love's mask.

And we might hate that questioning any of this feels like a betrayal of the very children we'd die for.

But our children don't need us to be everything.

They need us to be whole. They need to see us as full human beings with our own needs, boundaries, and dreams. When we model self-sacrifice as the highest form of love, we teach them that their worth comes from how much of themselves they're willing to give away.

What if instead we showed them what it looks like to be generous from a place of fullness rather than depletion?

What if we demonstrated that healthy relationships involve mutual care, not one-sided service?

What if we modeled what it means to pursue dreams without guilt?

What if our children saw us honoring our goals with the same care we give to theirs?

What if we taught them that their needs matter, but so do ours?

The Revolution Starts at Home

The way we organize our families is political. Every time we accept that mothers should carry the emotional labor, we're casting a vote for inequality. Every time we apologize for having needs, we're teaching our children that women's needs don't matter.

But every time we insist on true partnership, we're creating a new template. Every time we model self-care as a responsibility rather than a luxury, we're showing our children what healthy relationships look like.

This isn't just about us. It's about the world we're creating for the next generation.

Our daughters are watching to see if they're destined for this same invisible exhaustion. Our sons are learning what they can expect from their future partners. When we change our own patterns, we change their future possibilities.

Rewriting the Contract

This chapter hasn't been about whether we love our children. That love is sacred and unquestioned. It's about the mountain of jobs, large and small, we never applied for and the myth that told us we had to do them all.

So let's tear up that invisible contract and let's normalize not liking parts of motherhood while still loving our kids with everything we have.

Let's stop apologizing for not wanting to be and do everything, every day, for everyone. And let's recognize that we were never meant to carry this alone. We were never meant to lose ourselves in this unpaid empire of endless tasks.

We aren't just the "help."
We aren't the backup plan when systems fail.
We aren't the shock absorbers for a society that refuses to support families properly.

We are whole human beings who happen to be raising other whole human beings.

And it's time the world started treating us that way.

The Application

She never saw the fine print.

There was no contract to read. No interview. No conversation about terms.
Just a heartbeat on a screen...
and the decision to love with her whole being.

And then-
The tasks began.
Tiny ones, at first.
Feeding. Rocking. Watching them breathe.

Then they multiplied.
Diapers. Meals. Forms. Appointments.
Parties. Projects. Sibling conflicts.
Midnight laundry. Morning meetings. Emotional triage.
And she began to ask, "Why am I the one doing all of this?"
The world shrugged and replied:
Because you're the mother.

She didn't say no-
Not at first.
She said yes because she thought that's what love meant.
She said yes because she thought everyone else was doing it too.
She said yes because she didn't know she could say no.

But now?

She's reading the fine print.
She's rewriting the contract.
She's handing back the jobs that never belonged to her.

Because she finally understands:
being good at everything,
doesn't mean she should be doing everything.

Because now she understands:
being the mother doesn't mean being the entire system.

She's not a workforce, she's a woman.

And she was never meant to carry the weight of a whole village alone.

Encouragement for the Mother Who's Tired of Doing It All

If you've ever looked around and thought, "This is too much," you're justified in feeling this way.

You're *not* a failure for *not* wanting to do it all.
Or selfish for wishing someone would notice all you carry.
And you're not lazy for wanting help, rest, support, or even escape.

Yes, you're a mother.
But you're also a human being.
One who lives in a time of high demands.
One who deserves partnership, acknowledgment, equity, and care.
One who can raise children and raise boundaries at the same time.
One who lives in a culture where the load has multiplied -
where the daily demands on a mother's body, mind, and time stretch far beyond what tribal societies ever required.

It's okay to say "no."
You're not abandoning your role by refusing to do five people's jobs.

You're allowed to love your children and still return the tasks you never signed up for.

You don't have to do it all. In fact, *you're not supposed to.* Find ways to delegate. Ask for help from people who care:

• Set up a neighborhood meal swap - even just once a month.
• Coordinate carpooling.
• Hire a cleaning service, even if it's just for the bathrooms.
• Choose crockpot meals.
• Order takeout once a week and call it peace, not failure.
• Trade favors with a friend.
• Outsource what drains you most, even just once a month (laundry service, grocery delivery, deep cleaning)
• Keep shared family calendars so the mental load doesn't live only in your mind
• Release perfectionism - let the house be lived-in, the kids be bored
• Teach your kids self-sufficiency (even if it's messy or slow at first)
• Be honest with your partner about what's not working instead of trying to push through it silently
• Start documenting everything you do to see the truth yourself. Keep a log for one week of every task, every mental note, every emotional regulation moment. Share this with your partner. Help them see what you see and do on a daily basis. (And see it for what it is for yourself as well.)
• Where possible, buy back your time. Grocery delivery, house cleaning, meal kits. The money spent on these helps purchase your humanity back.
• Create support networks with other families. Swap babysitting, share school pick up duties, organize communal dinners, fold laundry together. Do childcare co-ops, create emergency networks for sick days. We can't recreate traditional community structures, but we can build new ones that actually work for modern life.
• Use #thehumanmother to connect with other mothers who are reimagining motherhood through shared care, collective wisdom, and community support.

Rest and replenishment aren't luxuries for mothers - they're lifelines.
Even small acts of care, chosen intentionally, remind your nervous system that *you matter too.*

• Build mini-rituals into your day (even 5 minutes alone with your coffee in silence)
• Start a practice of "one nourishing thing" each day (no matter how small)
• Nap when the guilt hits (because you probably need it most then)
• Protect a block of time each week just for yourself (non-negotiable)
• Say yes to help when it's offered (and practice asking even when it isn't)

Start asking yourself:

Where are the breaks I'm building in for me?
Where is the support I'm *allowing* - not just wishing for?

This is about granting yourself permission to do less,
Or at the very least, to delegate more.

Stop carrying the mountain of tasks that are muffling your soul.
Let "good enough" sometimes be sacred.
And remember: the goal isn't to do it all.
The goal is honoring your soul as much as your to-do list.

There are several helpful apps and programs (from digital tools to some state resources) that mothers can use to lighten their load, get support, and reclaim time and energy:

Helpful Apps for Managing the Load

1. Cozi Family OrganizerHelps manage calendars, grocery lists, meal plans, and to-dos all in one place. Great for family coordination.

2. YNAB (You Need A Budget)Takes the stress out of budgeting and helps moms stay financially organized and empowered.

3. Instacart / Shipt / Amazon FreshOrder groceries for delivery or pickup – saves time and energy.

4. Calm / Insight Timer / BreathwrkMental health support for nervous system regulation and mini-breaks throughout the day.

5. Mealime / Plan to Eat / PrepearSimple weekly meal planning with customizable recipes and grocery lists.

6. Sweepy / TodyTurn home cleaning into a shared, gamified responsibility. Track and delegate chores.

7. Marco Polo / VoxerStay connected to friends and support circles without needing to text or schedule calls.

8. Trello / Notion (for the organized mom)Declutter your mental load by storing plans, lists, and info in a visual and collaborative space.

Government and State Support Programs (U.S.)

1. WIC (Women, Infants, and Children)Provides nutrition education, food, and breastfeeding support to low-income mothers.

2. SNAP (Supplemental Nutrition Assistance Program)Grocery assistance for eligible families to reduce food insecurity.

3. Medicaid / CHIPAffordable healthcare coverage for moms and kids, including prenatal and postpartum care.

4. Child Care Assistance Program (CCAP)Helps pay for childcare if you're working, in school, or job-seeking (state-specific).

5. TANF (Temporary Assistance for Needy Families)Offers cash assistance, job support, and aid to qualifying low-income families.

6. State-Run Paid Family Leave ProgramsCurrently in CA, NJ, NY, RI, CT, MA, WA, CO, OR, and DC – check eligibility for paid leave after birth or for caregiving.

7. Local Food Pantries & Diaper BanksSearch via or for local resources.

8. Free / Sliding-Scale Therapy OptionsAvailable through local clinics, community centers, or platforms like Open Path Collective.

(More suggestions are shared in section three of this book.)

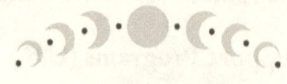

Chapter 10

The Always Forgiving Mother

Myth: A good woman always forgives.

There's a myth that walks hand in hand with the image of the Saintly Mother. It's the myth that forgiveness is a moral currency. That it's a spiritual superiority and it's proof that a woman has transcended her anger.

Somewhere along the line we're taught that a good woman always forgives.

She forgives her partner (again and again) for the harsh words, emotional absence, and even betrayal.
She forgives her parents for the unspoken damage, the unmet needs, the legacy of silence or abuse.
She forgives her children for the ways they take and take without stepping up.
And she forgives society for the cost of being a mother in a world that pushes women to be baby making machines but gives little back in return.

Forgiveness, we're told, is "holy."
Forgiveness "liberates."
It "heals."

But for many women, that kind of forgiveness is anything but healing.

The Cultural Script

From every direction - religion, pop psychology, therapy, even wellness spaces - we hear that "forgiveness is freedom." That it's what enlightened people do. That holding onto hurt makes us bitter or poisoned by pain. Forgiveness is framed as self-work and is said to be the key to our supposed liberation or healing.

For many women, this kind of forgiveness doesn't free them. It keeps them circling the same pain, returning again and again to people or places that won't change. It teaches them to silence anger rather than express it, to carry wounds quietly rather than demand repair.

We're told that forgiveness brings peace, but for many of us it brings other levels of exhaustion. Instead of closing a chapter, it reopens the same old story. Instead of healing, it keeps us bound to the people who hurt us. Forgiveness becomes less about freedom and more about endurance - about being the one who absorbs harm so others don't have to face it or evolve.

But for women, especially mothers, this script can be deeply gendered. And it more than likely, at least in part, is designed to preserve systems.

Because when women *stop* forgiving - they stop tolerating.
...And when they stop tolerating, they stop performing.
...And when they stop performing, they stop returning to harm.
...And when they stop returning to harm, they begin to heal.

And if we take several steps back, we see that those shifts threaten the entire structure that benefits from her ongoing forgivings.

This pressure intensifies across different cultural and religious contexts. In many faith traditions, forgiveness is positioned as divine virtue: turning the other cheek, honoring thy father and mother, being the peacemaker in the home.

Some cultures emphasize family harmony above individual wellbeing, where a woman's refusal to forgive is seen as selfish, even bringing shame to the family name.

In therapeutic circles influenced by Western Buddhism or New Age spirituality, forgiveness becomes a mark of "enlightenment", suggesting that holding onto hurt reveals spiritual immaturity and self-inflicted pain.

Each tradition may use a different language, calling it duty, karma, grace, or honor. But the message remains consistent. And the message is this:

Good women accept and let go of pain rather than reflect it back.

How This Hurts Women

The myth of required forgiveness does many things.

• It forces women to reconcile with abusers or betrayers before they're ready - or before real accountability has happened
• It shames women for having anger, grief, or ongoing boundaries
• It encourages them to doubt their own emotional timelines

• It elevates peacekeeping above self-respect
• It promotes spiritual bypassing as growth

Mothers get praised for forgiving children who scream at them, partners who disappear emotionally, and parents who emotionally abandoned them. (And heaven forbid they draw a line or choose distance or take legal action against more serious abuse.)

The Partner Who Benefits

In intimate relationships, the forgiveness myth becomes a particularly insidious tool. Partners who repeatedly cause emotional, physical, or psychological harm learn to weaponize forgiveness against the women they hurt.

The cycle becomes predictable:
harm,
remorse,
promises,
and then the expectation of forgiveness to "move forward."

But moving forward without accountability isn't healing, it's enabling. The partner learns that performative apologies are sufficient payment for damage, that tears (or supposed regret and apologies) can buy another round of the same behavior, that "I'm sorry" is a get-out-of-jail-free card.

Women in these dynamics often hear:
"If you really loved me, you'd forgive me."
"You're holding onto the past."
"I said I was sorry, what more do you want?"
"What do you want from me?!"

The forgiveness myth tells her that withholding forgiveness makes *her* the problem, not the one causing repeated harm.

Meanwhile, her partner benefits enormously from her endless capacity to forgive. He gets to keep his comfortable life, his emotional support system, and his image as a good man who just "makes mistakes."

Her forgiveness becomes his permission slip to never truly change.

Real love doesn't demand forgiveness without accountability.
Nor does it ask you to forget patterns of harm.

And real love certainly doesn't use your capacity for forgiveness as a shield against facing the damage it has caused.

Forgiveness vs. Boundaries

Dr. Ramani, a psychologist and expert on narcissistic abuse, once said:

> "I don't forgive them. I will never forgive them. I will never forget what they did to me because what they did changed my view on myself. I spent years crawling out from that rubble. I still doubt myself. I still don't feel safe in the world. They took that safety away. How the hell do you forgive that? I don't. And I sleep fine at night.
>
> I feel totally at peace because what bothers me is they're out there doing this to other people. I think people who don't forgive definitely feel peace. I think people who don't feel peace are the people who forgive and keep getting harmed. Or the people who forgive who weren't ready to forgive."

Forgiveness looks different for everyone. For some, it might involve a softening, or a letting go that brings peace and release. For others, it might mean a sharp remembering and a refusal to forget, because, in the end, remembering is what keeps them safe.

We need to realize that sometimes, *not* forgiving is a survival response. It's a way of keeping the memory active, the awareness intact, so harm doesn't happen again.

No one gets to decide how a woman should respond to harm.

Not a therapist.
Not a spiritual teacher.
Not her family.
Not religious texts.
And not a partner.

Forgiveness *isn't* a moral finish line.

It's a deeply personal, nervous system-informed response that should serve the safety and wholeness of the woman choosing it.

So keep in mind that you aren't obligated to forgive just because someone else has moved on or because the story demands you carry the repair they refused to make. It's *your* mind, *your* body, *your* history and the way you choose to respond. *You* get to choose how this plays out.

Respond accordingly.
Respond honestly.
And respond in a way that keeps you safe from ever being hurt in that same way again.

True forgiveness can't be demanded.
Nor can it be timed, expected, or performed to make others comfortable.
It's not a checkbox on the healing journey.

Forgiveness *without* boundaries *isn't* healing, it's self-abandonment dressed as grace.

You can:

• Forgive and never speak to them again
• Forgive and still feel angry
• Forgive slowly
• Not forgive, and still heal

In the end, your liberation isn't found in meeting society's rules about forgiveness. Forgiveness can look and feel many different ways. It doesn't always mean letting go, forgetting, or no longer caring about the injustices or wounds inflicted by others.

Sometimes forgiveness isn't soft.
Sometimes it's sharp and clear-eyed.

Maybe the anger and rage behind the injustice done (that others now claim you should forgive) is more healing than forgiveness.

We've been taught to bypass anger. To skip straight to grace.
But rage is sacred intelligence.

Maybe we don't need more quick forgiveness.
Maybe we need more honest anger.
More space to feel without shame.
More truth before peace.

Rage and anger say: *This was wrong. This should never have happened. I want nothing more to do with carrying the weight of other people's wrongs.*

As Nadia Bolz-Weber puts it, when asked what she'd say to someone she chooses not to forgive:

> "What you did to me was so not okay, I refuse to be connected to it anymore. *That's* forgiveness. It's like using bolt cutters. Because if someone has caused you harm (whether it's a person, an institution, or a belief system) you're still connected. It's like an umbilical cord, and their toxicity has access to your heart.
>
> Forgiveness, in this sense, isn't about absolving them. It's about protecting you. It's saying: *I'm not going to be connected to this anymore. I want to be free.*"

Healing might involve forgiveness, but not always.

What this type of forgiveness can look like is:

• Reclaiming the right to be angry without apology
• Letting time do its work without a deadline
• Refusing to reconcile just to keep the peace
• Building a life with stronger boundaries, not weaker emotions
• Letting the pain exist without rushing to sanitize it

Healing can also be allowing yourself to say:
They don't deserve access to me anymore.

What Must Be Protected

There are things that belong at the very top of a woman's list and things that must be protected at all costs.

These things matter more than being liked.
More than keeping the peace.
More than someone else's comfort.
And more than fitting into the shape others expect of you.

These things aren't luxuries and they aren't negotiable.
They should be your foundation.

Your compass.
Your birthright.

Before we get into the list of these things that women should protect at all costs -
can we just stop for a moment and remember who we are?

Women are the most extraordinary force on this entire planet.
Not one of the most.
THE most!

When will humans evolve enough to realize this?

Collectively, we are the intuitive ones.
The ones who sense what's wrong before anyone speaks.
The ones who carry the emotional map of every room we walk into and the world
we live in.

We are the ones attuned to rhythm.
To the tides of the moon, to the ebb and flow of our own cycles. Our bodies
mirror the cosmos: waxing, waning, shedding, renewing. This is a synchrony with
the deepest patterns of life itself.

We are one of only five mammals who live beyond our reproductive years.
Alongside orcas, belugas, narwhals, and pilot whales, we are part of a rare evolutionary design: the grandmother species. In every one of these species, it's the
elders, the post-reproductive females, who carry memory, guide survival, and hold
the knowledge that sustains the group. Science calls it the "grandmother effect."
In our feminine wisdom, we call it matriarchal wisdom written into the body.

We are the carriers of memory and continuity.
Our biology itself insists that women are meant not only to birth, but to guide,
to teach, to preserve, and, yes, even to lead. Our long lives beyond childbearing
is nature's way of saying that the wisdom of women is essential to the thriving of
generations.

We are the sensitive ones, rooted in the wisdom of feeling and perceiving deeply,
attuned to what the world is in need of.

We are the compassionate ones, caring for the collective.
We are the seers,
the feelers,
the connectors.

We are the ones who remember birthdays,
pack lunches,
hold grief,
give advice,
start revolutions,
whisper healing into children's hair,
and call our friends' mothers when they're sick.

We are the ones who bleed and still show up.
Who break and still nurture.
Who cry and still lead.
Who feel everything - and keep going anyway.

We are deeply spiritual, tuned into the deeper currents of life,
the silent language of the Universe.
We are fiercely insightful, seeing not just what is, but what *could be.*
We hold paradox with grace, soft and powerful, gentle and unshakeable, open and
wildly discerning.

But we aren't only soft - we are strength in motion.
We hold the fire and the calm,
the sword and the sanctuary,
the vision and the follow-through.
We carry the whole picture in our minds, while tending to a thousand unseen
details.

We are the makers of worlds,
the holders of legacy,
the birthers of new life,
the pulse of evolution itself,
the force that bends evolution toward renewal.

If we choose to look, even warily, at the Bible, the first description of woman was
called *ezer kenegdo* - mistranslated as "helper" or "helpmeet", when what it really
means is the strength you cannot live without. The kind of strength you cry out
for when you are drowning. The word used of God himself, over and over again,
to name the One who rescues, who holds, who comes through when all feels lost.

This is who she was, who she is still – not an afterthought, but the necessary,
essential, strength that keeps the world alive.

If we could truly see who we are...
If we could remember our design, our depth, our divinity,
then we would realize:

What we must protect might not be what we've been trained to protect.

It isn't our image.
Or others' comfort.
It isn't tradition, or belonging, or keeping the peace.
It isn't a role.
It isn't dogmas, doctrines, or culturally imposed teachings.

It's ourselves.

Our *wholeness.*
Our radiant, untamed, sacred self.

You are allowed - no, called - to protect and prioritize the following:

Your heart.
Your soul.
Your essence.
Your safety.
Your nervous system.
Your peace.
Your future.
Your voice.
Your body.
Your energy.
Your health.
Your joy.
Your vibrancy.
Your creativity.
Your desires.
Your becoming.
Your ability to thrive.

You do *not* need to hand these over in the name of "forgiveness", "understand-ing", "patience", or "love."

What should *not* come before protecting those things is:

• Someone else's comfort (especially when there's little to no mutual, healthy exchange) should never come at the cost of protecting these parts of you
• The illusion of stability or familiarity that keeps you from leaving harmful dynamics
• Cultural narratives that tell you forgiveness is required for healing
• Pressure to be the "bigger person" at the cost of your truth
• The idea that being a mother means swallowing and forgiving everything quietly

Yes, there are times when we stretch ourselves for the sake of our children. But common sense doesn't mean self-sacrifice without end. Especially when the ones we protect grow up watching us disappear.

Remember the elephants.

In the wild, elephant matriarchs don't forget harm. They preserve memory (of danger, betrayal, or loss) because survival depends on it.

Their memory protects the herd.
It ensures future safety.
It teaches the young who and what to avoid.
This is wisdom.
It's nature.

So ask yourself:
When you choose to forgive, is it coming from pressure to make others more comfortable, to keep the peace at your own expense, or to avoid being called hardened or unloving?

Or is it a forgiveness that honors your truth - one that holds others accountable and protects your safety, your peace and your comfort?

You can be a devoted mother but also have boundaries.
You can be a spiritual woman but also say no.
You can be forgiving in your nature but also choose not to forgive someone who hasn't earned it.

Motherhood and Forgiveness

The most radical thing you might ever do as a mother is stop modeling self-betrayal in the name of being spiritually evolved or morally superior.

Your children don't need to see you forgive everything.
They need to see you respect yourself.

They need to see what real accountability looks like.
They need to see that love doesn't mean the absence of boundaries.

You don't need to forgive everyone who hurts you just because you became a mother - or because you're a woman.
Or because you believe in God.
Or because you want to be someone who lives with integrity and compassion.
You don't owe anyone a clean slate at the cost of your healing.
You're allowed to carry *both love and limits*.

Forgiveness is a choice you get to make.
It's sacred when it's earned.
And it's optional when it's not.

＊————————— ⟩⟩◯⟨⟨ —————————＊

The Boundary

She stood at the family gathering, arms at her sides,
A familiar ache blooming in her chest.

The expectation to play nice.
The decades of silencing.
The sermons about grace.
The swallowed rage.
The call to be the bigger person.
The lie that said her freedom lived on the other side of forgetting.

She didn't move.
Not forward. Not toward. Not into it.
She didn't smile.
Nor did she perform.

She let the moment hang in the air like thick incense -
heavy, fragrant with memory,
stinging the eyes of anyone who dared to look too closely.

And then...she stepped back.

Not just from them.
From the myth.
From the contract.
From the inherited obligation to make others comfortable with what hurt her.

She didn't make a scene.
She made a boundary.

And in that act, she didn't just forgive herself-
she released herself.
From the need to explain.
From the burden to be gracious.
From the centuries of women who were asked to eat their pain and call it peace.

She walked out angry.
She walked out honest.
She walked out at peace with herself,
with her truth, with the line she finally drew.

The silence she left behind may have been awkward for them.
But for her, it was sacred.

Encouragement for the Woman Who Decides How She Forgives

The myth of the forgiving woman (the one who absorbs all pain to maintain peace) is crumbling. And in its place, a new story is emerging.

It's a story where you say no without an explanation. Where you choose distance over dysfunction. Where you refuse to carry responsibility for other people's comfort at the expense of your own wellbeing.

It's where you understand that your refusal to forgive makes you honest.
Your boundaries make you whole.
And your anger makes you human.

You're teaching your children that love includes limits.
That relationships require accountability.

You're discovering that healing doesn't always come through forgiveness. Sometimes it comes through choosing yourself, unapologetically, at last.

The path forward is about becoming more honest about what you will and won't accept. It's about choosing relationships and situations that honor your full humanity.

Protect yourself.
Choose your peace over others' comfort, in wisdom.
You don't need to forgive your way into freedom.

Freedom comes from finally being honest about what happened, how it affected you, and what you need to feel safe moving forward.

Sometimes that includes forgiveness.
And sometimes it doesn't.
Both paths can lead you home to yourself.

The myth told you that good women always forgive. But a better approach is this:

Whole women honor themselves enough to choose whether they will forgive or not.

Chapter 11

The Waiting Mother

*Myth: The rescue is coming - if we just hold on
a little longer.*

So far, we've explored myths about how mothers are expected to show up, including the internalized expectations and the false standards we try to meet.

But this myth is different. This one is about what we thought (or hoped) would meet *us*.

The rescue we were promised.
The support we assumed would arrive.
The help we believed would come if patience, prayer, and obedience could finally tip the scales in our favor.

Somewhere along the way, we were taught to wait for some sort of rescue.

To hope.
To hold on.
That God would take care of it all.
Or that a good man would swoop in and fix the mess.
Or that a new president,
a better policy,
a shift in culture would *finally* make it easier to be a woman.
A mother.
A human.

We were told, and we may have hoped, directly or indirectly, that someone was coming-
To help us.
Or rescue us.
To *finally* make it easier.
And to ease the load.

But the hardest and most probable truth is this: *No one is coming.*

And even if someone does, it likely won't look the way we hoped. The relief may be temporary. The disappointment, inevitable. Support might arrive, but so might *more* conditions. *More* compromises. *More* sacrifices. More pain. More difficult choices. More trauma and more damage to fix.

For the sake of your health, your safety, and your peace: Trust me when I say, it's far better *not* to expect a rescue.

Because the numbers, the patterns, and the lived experiences of women today tell us plainly: The rescue rarely comes. And when it does, it often costs you yourself, leaving behind a trail of disappointment, damage, and unmet needs.

Unlearning the Wait

Look closer, and the numbers start to speak:

Nearly *half* of all marriages in the U.S. end in divorce. And among those that last, many women are holding on by a thread, carrying the emotional, financial, and physical weight of the family unit, while their own needs are dismissed or unseen.

More than one in three women in the U.S. has experienced intimate partner violence. Men make up roughly half the population, yet account for nearly 85% of all violent crime.

And while marriage has been shown to extend a man's life and improve his health, research suggests it often drains a woman - costing her time, energy, health, and in many cases, her freedom. ([1],[2],[3],[4])

This isn't to say every man will harm or every marriage will wound or that men can't rise - but the weight of evidence shows how often women are the ones left paying the cost.

Religious institutions have long asked women to sacrifice. To submit. To silence themselves in the name of righteousness. They promised protection, purpose, and holiness while upholding money-making power structures that kept women in the sidelines.

Political systems have betrayed us - turning women's bodies into bargaining chips and our freedoms into battlegrounds. Creating a system that has codified our subordination into law.

Our autonomy, the ownership over ourselves, should have never been theirs to grant, yet they legislate as if it belongs to them. Some states have gone so far as to propose restrictions that feel dystopian, like efforts to make voting harder for women who changed their last name after marriage.

These laws don't exist in a vacuum – they're born out of a culture that warps everyone inside it.

We should recognize that the patriarchy didn't just harm *women.*
It created generations of emotionally and mentally stunted *men.*

For centuries, boys have been taught that vulnerability is weakness, that emotions are feminine, and that asking for help is failure. They've been raised to compete instead of connect, to conquer instead of collaborate, and to provide instead of participate.

But perhaps even more damaging, they've been taught that they are inherently superior. That they "deserve" a woman. That women exist to serve them, support them, and absorb their emotional mess while asking for little to nothing in return.

The same system that oppressed women also severed men from their own humanity.

It taught them to bury their feelings so deep they can't even find them. Told them their worth comes from what they do, not who they are. Convinced them that being a "real man" means never needing anyone, never showing pain, never admitting they don't know how to love someone well.

And somehow (despite being emotionally stunted, spiritually severed, and relationally unequipped) they've convinced themselves (and nearly everyone else) that *they're* the most capable and competent leaders of humanity. The ones best suited to guide civilization, speak for God, and decide what's best for everyone else.

And simultaneously, the system whispered that women owe them something. That a relationship means she gives and he receives. That her job is to make his life easier - not to be an equal partner in building something whole, mutual, and alive.

This is why so many women find themselves married to boys in men's bodies.
This is why emotional labor falls to us.
This is why we're still waiting for them to grow up, show up, and wake the fuck up.

They literally don't know how.

They're inherently flawed, but they've been systematically disconnected from the very skills that make partnership possible:

• Emotional intelligence
• Vulnerability
• Intuition
• Empathy
• The ability to hold space for someone else's pain

And they've been systematically programmed to believe that women exist for their benefit, not as whole humans with their own needs, dreams, and autonomy.

The patriarchy made them strangers to themselves.
And you can't give what you don't have.
And so they lead from a hollowed place of underdevelopment.
And women, along with the world they hold together, suffer at the core of it.

While not every man reflects this pattern, the reality is that many do. And the men who crave power most urgently are often the least suited to hold it and the very ones willing to corrupt it.

And so, when we wait for rescue, we're often waiting on someone who was never taught how to save or take care of anyone, let alone *themselves.*

We *are* moving forward - but it's at a very slow pace. And in many ways, we're even sliding backwards. And the louder women become, the more some systems push to quiet us again.

So, no, more than likely, the president isn't coming to save us.
The new pastor isn't either.
Nor are the systems run by men.
Nor is the partner who refuses to grow emotionally.

The system wasn't built to hold us. And yet we keep holding it, hoping it will.

Because we were trained to believe that if we were good enough, quiet enough, patient enough, grateful enough, docile enough, *worthy* enough ... a man would come.

And so we stayed.
In marriages that hollowed us.

In churches that shamed us and pushed us to the sidelines.
In belief systems that rewarded our silence.

And we did so simply because we thought the rescue would come if we just held on a little longer.

Perhaps it's time we realize: The rescue isn't likely.

The only rescue to come will be the one we make when we stop waiting and use our own two feet to walk into the life that finally feels like home.

The Fairy Tale We Were Fed

Before we talk about how to walk ourselves out, we need to look at how we got stuck in the first place.

It started early. The princess in the tower. The girl asleep in the woods. The woman facing darkness, always rescued by a man who knew what to do.

Even when we grew out of fairy tales, the messaging stayed.
God will save you.
A husband will step up.
A "real man" will protect you.
A new leader will fix it.
The system will eventually work in your favor.

And the woman? As Reese Witherspoon cleverly pointed out, she'll turn to the man beside her during times of stress or danger, with exasperation in her voice, and naively ask, "What should we do?"

As if *she* couldn't *possibly* know.
As if *she* wasn't built to survive, to endure, to lead.
As if instinct belongs only to him.

As if she hasn't been the one holding families and civilizations together in the wake of male violence and abandonment *for centuries*.

But for most women, that rescue never comes.
And even when it does, it comes with conditions...

Or is fraught with disappointments.

The Cry Beneath the Silence

There's a quiet, soul-deep cry that flows through existence – a centuries-old current of women who waited for help that never came.

Mothers carrying their own burdens (and their partner's too) while being told to "submit."

Wives married to emotionally unavailable, underdeveloped men still clinging to their mother's breast, except now, the new mother is you.

Women who signed petitions, cast their votes, and held the line only to find the promises didn't reach their doorstep.

Religious women who prayed and fasted and obeyed, who silenced their own voice because they were told obedience was holy. They wore modest clothes, piled on multiple layers even in sweltering heat to keep their shoulders hidden, veiled their faces while worshiping God, and served in quiet corners where their voices could never rise too loud.

Who were taught that exhaustion was godly, that suffering was sacred, and that joy would come in the next life if they just endured this one a little longer, under the guidance and direction of a man.

Religion didn't just abandon women. It smeared their names in the stories. It wrote Eve as the sinner, Mary as the vessel, and every woman after as either sinfully dangerous or welcomingly docile.

It scripted women's freedom as something men must deliver - Jesus, God, the pastor, the prophet, the husband - never something women could claim on their own.

Women were promised protection but received control. They were promised peace but were handed pressure.

And when they collapsed under the weight of it all, they were told they just weren't faithful enough. They weren't devoted enough to their marriage, or obedient enough to their God, or patient enough with their leaders, or grateful enough for the scraps that policy offered.

These are women who gave everything they had and still got the short end of the stick.

Women who stayed in marriages, stayed in churches, stayed in systems, waiting for a rescue that never came.

This isn't just personal.
It's generational.

The Economics of Waiting

One reason why the waiting persists is often due to economic reasons.

The systems that keep women waiting are the same ones that make independence financially precarious.

When childcare costs more than rent,
when healthcare is tied to someone else's job,
when the wage gap ensures you'll always need supplemental income,
when divorce means poverty for most women,
the choice to stop waiting becomes a luxury many can't afford.

The "waiting woman" is often psychologically trapped.
And she's economically cornered.

This is why the myth of rescue is so seductive. It promises that if you just wait long enough, someone else will solve the financial equation you can't solve alone.

But the same systems that make you financially dependent tend to be the ones that benefit from your waiting.

The History of Being Undone by False Hope

So, religion didn't save us. In fact, it taught us to stay silent, to serve harder, to sacrifice more. It told us suffering was sanctified and that our reward would come later.

And politics didn't save us. Even the "good guys" protect power and their own needs before they protect women.

Fathers also didn't always save us. Some abandoned us, some controlled us, some loved us in incomplete and painful ways.

And science didn't save us either. It studied men and called the results universal. It built medical models around male bodies, dismissed women's pain as emotional, underfunded our conditions, and pathologized our cycles. It took centuries to study the female brain, to acknowledge our hormones, to research our diseases, and to begin believing our symptoms.

And even now, it often still doesn't listen.

And men, as a group, are only just now beginning to understand that they have deep, buried work to do-

Shadow work.
Emotional maturity.
Self reflection and realization.
Accountability.
Centuries of stunted evolution.
And the wreckage women were left to clean up because of it.

Too many are still baby-men, expecting women to be mothers and lovers, therapists and servants, cheerleaders and punching bags.

Or they're self-proclaimed "alphas," preaching that women crave safety but only the kind earned through her submission. Only the kind that demands her obedience, her silence, and her servitude. A new mask for an old playbook: control her, and call it care.

Pfft. *Please.*

How long have women carried men's pain, managed their moods, fed their egos, absorbed their blows, healed their traumas, and used their own energy to raise the damn man – all while abandoning themselves?

He climbs on her weary back, higher and higher, waving his flag of superiority, and claims the title of "man" - as if it were strength. Strength built on burning women as witches, forcing them into marriages, claiming their work as his own, erasing their votes, forcing their bodies into wretched marriages and endless births, silencing their voices in courts and pulpits, burying their brilliance beneath his promotion, denying their health rights in councils of men, and dismissing them in police stations when they report the violence they've endured.

Yet *still* we wait?

Imagine what women could create if their brilliance wasn't wasted piecing underdeveloped men back together.

Now men grieve a loneliness epidemic, but it's their own system that starved them - a legacy of patriarchy that confused domination for love and silence for strength. A matriarchal society would have raised them capable of connection, not afraid of it. Instead, men demand to be adored, honored, and heard - a shift into feminine power, masked as alpha superiority - which I expand on in my book, *Let There Be Lies*.

It's the fruit of centuries of refusing to see women as their *ezer kenegdo* - the essential strength meant to be their deliverer and equal - fearing her presence would expose their flaws, humble their egos, and reveal that domination was weakness all along, and that, as a collective, only in acknowledging her fully and yielding to her wisdom could they have touched divinity and have met their own humanity.

The Bare Minimum Hero

Another reason why the waiting may persist is because somewhere along the line, we thought *he would show up*. That when a child entered the picture, something sacred would awaken in him.

That he would rise. Protect. Provide. Partner.

And when he didn't show up, we told ourselves to wait.
To support him through his transition into fatherhood.
To lower our expectations - because he's not a mind reader, after all.
And to keep the peace - for the children.

The myth of the "Good Father" is one of the most haunting. Because it should be true. But for many, it never was.

We are sold the story that fatherhood transforms a man. That biology or morality or love will somehow kickstart emotional maturity, responsibility, and attentiveness where there was none. That he will suddenly match her labor, feel her intuition, carry her mental load. And that having children will jumpstart his desire to support and care for his family. And that becoming a father will flip some hidden switch, turning him into a partner who carries the weight with her.

We're told that his mere presence is enough. That a man standing in a room, nodding occasionally, grunting approval at a toddler counts. That he's "trying." That he's "doing his best."

We're told that even a subpar father is better than none at all.

And so women stay.
They wait.
They defend him.
They raise him.
They quiet their anger and continue hoping,
and keep pouring from empty cups.

Because he's not *that bad.*
Because at least *he's here.*
Because the children *need a father.*

But what we know, in our bones, in our lived experience, in our exhausted nights, in our deep and profound feminine intuition and our collective experience is this:

A disengaged father pushes his children's mother into survival mode, and those children grow up in the shadow of her exhaustion as much as in his neglect.

Many mothers have been drained, dismissed, and disrespected while the world praises him for doing the bare minimum.

And we have the scars to prove it.

He made dinner once and got a standing ovation.
He changed a diaper and earned the title of "such a good dad."
He watched the kids for two hours and people said, "Wow, you're lucky to have him."

Meanwhile, you bled through your pads in silence, breastfed while answering work emails, scheduled every appointment, remembered every shoe size, packed every bag, covered your nipples in healing balm, wiped every tear, had sex before you were healed – and they called it motherhood.

Mothers become stressed out, maxed out ghosts while fathers become saints for showing up at all.

This is what happens when we're told his crumbs are a feast.

The myth goes deeper still. Because even when he's angry. Neglectful. Addicted. Dismissive. Even then, we're told: "But he's their father."

We're told to protect his image. To "not talk badly about him in front of the kids." To model forgiveness. To stay.

And we do.
For a while.
Until something snaps.

Yet when we leave, we're the villain - the one who "gave up," the one who broke religious "covenants," the one who has to explain, the coward for "running away." The one who carries the full weight of the aftermath, while he disappears into a new chapter, often unscathed.

Some women waited their whole lives.

Waited for the man they married to become the man they imagined.
Waited for the father to finally become the partner.
Waited for the apology.
Waited for the shift.
Waited to feel cared for and to be seen.
Waited for someone to choose them.

Single women who were told to stay sweet, stay patient, stay available because the right man would come and complete their lives.

And in the waiting, they wasted and withered away.

Because no one told them that the waiting itself was a myth. No one told them that a man who rises only after *you've* collapsed isn't a fucking hero.

He's a delayed witness to your downfall.

The Paradox of Strength

Many of the strongest women you know are expert waiters.

They rescue everyone else while secretly waiting to be rescued themselves.

They're the ones who show up for every crisis, who solve every problem, who carry everyone else's pain. They look capable and unshakeable.

But inside, they're still that little girl hoping someone will finally see how tired she is and take care of her.

This is how the myth survives even in seemingly empowered women. They become so good at rescuing others that they forget they're still waiting for their own rescue.

The sad thing about this is that the waiting mother creates children who either become waiters themselves or who carry the crushing burden of being the rescuer.

Your daughter learns that love means waiting for someone to choose you. Your son learns that showing up is optional, that someone else will always carry the weight.

This is how the pattern perpetuates.

The waiting mother, in her own pain, unconsciously teaches her children that rescue comes from outside.

And so the cycle continues.
Until someone breaks it.

The Real Rescuer

So, dear women, even if you deserve it-
(And you really do.)
More than likely, no one is coming.

Not the husband who once made promises he never kept.
Not the father who shows up with gifts but never with presence.
Not the boyfriend who means well but can't carry anything real.

This doesn't mean we give up on love, or men, or fathers.
It does mean we stop waiting for them to become something they may never be.
It means we stop defining our worth by what he does or doesn't do.
It means we stop preserving the myth to keep the peace while our souls unravel.

It means we recognize that sometimes, the rescuer is *you* -
The warrior.
The mother.

Maybe the most radical thing we can do is stop romanticizing his role and stop waiting for him to rescue us and start honoring our own strength.

Because every false rescue will leave us more depleted - while every return to ourselves makes us more whole, more present, and more steady for ourselves and for our children.

Self-Rescue to the Rescue

The rescue begins by protecting your nervous system.
Finding peace should be *your number one priority.*

It starts with small acts of defiance against the voice that says "you should wait."

You feel the urge to speak, and instead of swallowing it, you speak.
You feel the need to leave, and instead of staying, you walk.
You feel the impulse to choose yourself, and instead of choosing everyone else, you choose you.

It's learning to tolerate the discomfort of disappointing others.
It's practicing the art of saying no without explaining why.

The rescue is opening your own bank account.
Learning to change your own tire – or knowing what service to call to change it for you.
Taking yourself to the doctor and believing your own pain.
Getting yourself where you need to go - even if that means taking Uber safely.
Changing the locks.
Taking the class, learning the skill, or building the plan.

It's small and unglamorous. It's terrifying and exhilarating. Yet it's the most ordinary and extraordinary thing you'll ever do.

The rescue is remembering you don't need saving - you need space to live.
When you stop waiting, you break a spell that has been cast over women for centuries.
When you rescue yourself, you give every woman in your orbit permission to do the same.
When you stop shrinking, you make room for other women to expand.

This Was the Rescue

So, more than likely, no one is coming.
But *you're* already here.

And if you've been reading closely, you'll notice:
We've been saving ourselves all along.

In the unraveling of every myth. Each chapter has been a rescue mission we carried out ourselves through truth-telling, boundary-setting, waking up, and refusing to disappear.

We wake ourselves up.
We rise out of burnout and silence.
We start drawing lines.
We stop pleasing.
We start speaking.
We set the tone.
We remember the feminine force within us.
We say this is how it's going to be now.
We begin healing.
We reconnect to ourselves.
We plan our escape.
We begin connecting to other women.
We stop apologizing.
We start refusing to carry what isn't ours.

And through these seemingly small acts comes something unexpected: power.

Real power - the kind that builds a life we finally love living.

Each time you choose truth over peace-keeping, you claim power.
Each time you set a boundary instead of accommodating, you claim power.
Each time you take a step toward your escape, you claim power.
Each time you leave instead of enduring, you claim power.

Even in the smallest moments, you are wielding this power: the energy you choose to bring to your child's birthday party, the music that fills your home, the meals you decide to make or not make, the tone you set when you walk through your front door – you're using your power to shape a home and a life that feels like your own.

These are purposeful acts of creation. You're literally authoring the atmosphere of your life, painting the emotional landscape your children will remember, deciding what kind of world exists within the walls you call home - and the soul and mind you experience life from.

This is sacred, reality-creating and soul-shaping work.

These moments, these choices, these tiny rebellions, they accumulate into something larger than the sum of their parts.

And you get to decide what you do with this power.

You can use it to heal your own wounds.
You can use it to protect your children from inheriting your patterns.
You can use it to build something new where something broken once stood.
You can use it to light the way for other women still finding their courage.

This is how revolution actually happens. In the accumulation of ordinary women making extraordinary choices to stop waiting and start wielding the power they never knew they had – or dared to embrace.

The power was always there. Maybe somewhere along the line, we just forgot that we can use it.

And through our efforts, not their promises, men and their systems will either evolve or fall behind.

And whether we feel ready or not, this era is calling us to lead.
This is the perfect time to face the damage that needs to be healed.

It isn't the time to keep building more nuclear families, or to bring more babies than we can handle into a world that hasn't yet made space for mothers to breathe - no matter what political leaders, religious authorities, or cultural narratives try to demand of us.

There's too much work to do first.
Too many wounds to tend.
Too many truths to bring awareness to.

We can't keep layering new life over unhealed pain and toxic patterns - pretending that's love.

And if we have had children (or will have children) in this broken system, then our role isn't to pretend the world is fine.

It's to break the silence and to name what we wish we'd known.
It's to model something different, even if imperfect.
It's to stop normalizing burnout, betrayal, and self-abandonment in the name of motherhood.

We need to rise - for ourselves, for our daughters, and for the women who are watching us quietly, hoping it's possible.

So they don't grow up believing they have to earn their rescue.
Or that their worth depends on who chooses them.
Or that they need a man, a marriage, or anyone else's approval to be safe or have a life they love.

We're breaking the pattern for them and for us.

Even if Hollywood has turned it into a cliché and made it cheesy as hell.
This is no longer the era of the rescued woman.
This is the era of the woman who rescued herself.

And as we rise, let's find each other, other women who stopped waiting. Women who carry truth instead of silence.

And even though we deserve to be rescued, let's create something our current systems never could:

A world that was never built to rescue us, but one we're finally free to rebuild-with the insight, leadership, and deep-rooted intuition of women.

Gifts from women this world is currently starving for, and may not be able to survive much longer without.

She Waited

She waited for someone to see.
To notice.
To step in.

She thought maybe it would be her husband.
Her church.
Her father.
Her friends.
God.

Surely someone would come.
Surely someone would say:
This isn't fair. Let me help.

She deserves better.

Surely someone would see how desperate she is-to be truly seen,
to be protected,
to be cared for in the way she's cared for everyone else.

But no one came.

The baby cried. The dishes piled. The bills waited.

And she finally realized...
no one was coming.

So she stopped waiting.

She stood in the center of her life,
picked up what mattered,
and set the rest down.

And with that small, quiet motion,
a truth cracked open:

The woman who saves herself doesn't need a sword or some savior.

She just needs to stop waiting-
and realize her life was never meant to be on hold.
To begin gathering the pieces of herself she scattered in survival.
And begin the courageous walk home.
Back to herself.

Because maybe the one she's been waiting for-
was the self she kept sacrificing for everyone else.

Encouragement for the Woman Who's Done Waiting

You *are* worth being rescued.
You *deserve* to be rescued.
But perhaps you were never going to be rescued.
In the end, you were meant to *remember your own strength.*

It makes sense that you hoped for help.
That you believed what they told you - about God, about men, about systems.
But the disappointment isn't yours to carry anymore.

Let it go.

You don't have to wait for someone to tell you it's time.
You're allowed to rise now.
To name what isn't working.
To speak up and stop pretending it's fine.
To reclaim your voice, your time, your energy.

The most revolutionary thing you can do is stop waiting to be saved-
and start building the world you know you're capable of creating.
The world they *swore* you'd need them to create.
The world they warned would fall apart without their hands on it.
The world they feared you'd build without them.

The world you long for.
The world you were born to shape.

And once enough women do, once we stop waiting for permission and start
creating what we were always capable of, the ground will shake.

There may even be resistance.
There may be fury.
There will probably be some chaos.
But give it time.

Because after the dust settles,
a new world can finally begin.

·)◯(·

References

1. *APA, "Marriage and Divorce," 2023.*

2. *NCADV, "Statistics," 2022.*

3. *Psychology Today, "Marriage Benefits Men More Than Women," Drexler, 2012.*

4. *FBI Uniform Crime Report, Table 42 (2019): Males accounted for 78.9% of violent crime arrests and 88% of murder arrests*

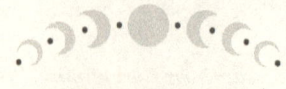

Chapter 12

The Mother Without a Timeline

Myth: A mother has no story outside of her children.

There's a strange thing that happens when a woman becomes a mother:

Her past becomes irrelevant.
And her future becomes invisible.

Everything she was before tends to disappear into the background, and everything she might become is put on a twenty year (or indefinite) hold.

Suddenly, it's as if motherhood is the only chapter of her life that matters. The only one worth reading. The only one others are willing to acknowledge or value her for.

She had dreams.
She had depth.
She had a name.

But now she's just "Mom."

We rarely ask mothers: Who were you before your children? What do you still want beyond them? What are you becoming outside of them?

Her timeline doesn't stop when she has children. But culturally, we pretend that it does.

The Cultural Freeze (And Who Benefits)

We freeze mothers in time, as if they're meant to stay emotionally paused, physically present, and spiritually selfless and committed to the motherly cause forever. But time is still passing. And she's still growing (probably aching) - and always becoming.

This freeze serves everyone around her.

To fully see her as human, with her own hungers, longings, and unfinished becoming, would endanger what she provides. People don't want to risk losing the endless mother. They want the comfort of her endless giving, and the safety of her endless presence and coddling. (Again, like babies endlessly suckling at a breast, blind to the body beneath it slowly fading away.)

Her husband wants the wife who makes everything work without complaint. Her children want the mother who never changes or leaves or has needs of her own. Her employer wants the worker who absorbs every scheduling conflict. Her aging parents want the daughter who handles their needs without question.

To humanize her is to disturb the self-feeding illusion.

Because once she's seen as fully human, the self-engorging spell breaks, the illusion of endless consumption collapses, and the hunger must finally face its own starvation.

Their emptiness is a hunger inherited by a world that teaches taking over tending, dominance over devotion, and consumption over connection.

They consume her because they have no idea how to feed themselves.
Their own barren roots reach for her soil, draining what they won't cultivate within.

And so they choose blindness, calling it "timeless devotion" when it's really just convenient stagnation.

This plays out differently depending on who she is:
The single mother gets frozen as the "strong one who handles everything."
The mother of color gets frozen as the "nurturing pillar who never breaks."
The working-class mother gets frozen as the "sacrificer who never asks for more."

Each version serves the same function: keeping her real self small so others can stay comfortable.

Not all families freeze the mother this way.
Some witness her becoming.
Some grow with her instead of asking her to stay the same.
Some learn to feed themselves and offer her rest, replenishment, recognition, and room to rise.

Some families realize that when the mother is allowed to grow, everyone around her grows too. That when the mother is allowed to grow, everyone grows with her. That is the kind of evolution our families (and our culture) desperately need.

When Children Inherit Empty Mothers

When mothers disappear into their role in an unbalanced way, their children inherit a ghost. Children learn love by watching their parents. When a mother has no identity outside of serving others, she teaches her children that:

- Women exist to be used, not seen.
- Love means giving until nothing is left.
- A woman's needs are a burden.
- Boundaries are rejection, not protection.
- A mother's worth is measured only in how much she disappears.

Her daughter might learn that becoming a woman means disappearing. Her son might learn that women exist to serve his comfort.

The very children she sacrifices for inherit a broken model of what it means to be human. They enter adulthood either expecting to be served or expecting to serve - never expecting to be whole.

But when a mother maintains her timeline (her friendships, dreams, growth, interests) she shows her children what an integrated human looks like. She gives them permission to be complex, to have needs, to honor both their connections and their individual becoming.

The Myth of "Having It All"

People often tell mothers they can "have it all" if they just manage their time better. Get up at 5 AM. Optimize their schedules. Find balance.

But this isn't about time management.
It's about permission.

The world isn't going to give you permission to have a timeline outside of motherhood. You have to take it.

This means saying no when everyone expects yes.
This means maintaining friendships even when it's inconvenient.
This means pursuing interests that have nothing to do with your children.
This means asking for help instead of martyring yourself.

Because although you are an attentive and responsible mother, you were never meant to orbit only their lives. You are your own sun.

Living life on your terms isn't something handed to you.
You have to *own it*.

Autonomy is something you choose, day by day.
Prioritize it.

The Baseline

I've noticed something that keeps showing up in the lives of people I know - myself included. For many of us, life creates a baseline that's just tolerable enough to keep us from changing it.

Not life-alteringly devastating. But not deeply fulfilling enough to keep it as it is either.

It lingers in that murky in-between space - where we stay stuck, waiting for permission that may never come, or for some dramatic, eye-opening event to finally catapult us into the transformation we've been quietly craving all along.

But maybe that's the point. Maybe life is asking *us* to choose. To decide what our vitality, our freedom, and our future will look like.

In the same way we hope our children will one day stop clinging, find their strength, and live fully - maybe life is hoping the same for us.

Unlike the people who may be taking from us endlessly, life itself is different.

Life is always offering.
Always waiting.
It responds to our self-claiming.
It ignites when we move with intention.

In the end, I've learned that life doesn't stop us from stepping into ourselves - but it does wait for us to choose it.

The Inheritance You Leave

Every mother who refuses to disappear creates space for the next generation to stay whole.

Every mother who maintains her timeline shows her children what full humanity looks like.

Every mother who honors her past, present, and future teaches the world that women are not vessels to be emptied, they are stories to be celebrated.

Your children need a mother who has stayed whole - not one who has erased herself to meet their every need.

They need a mother who shows them how to live with wholeness, not delay it.
How to grow a life of their own, not orbit someone else's.
How to authentically make and reach goals.
How to belong to themselves without apology.

That's the greatest gift you can give: not your sacrifice, but your wholeness.

This is your life, too. Not just a chapter of service. But a whole, breathing story that still belongs to you.

And every chapter deserves to be fully lived, not just survived.

What Reclaiming Looks Like

Remember who you were.
Write down what you loved before children. The music that moved you. The books that changed you. The dreams that felt electric. These parts of you didn't die; they got buried. Dig them up.

Stay curious about who you're becoming.
Every season of life reveals new parts of you. The mother at 30 is different from the mother at 45. Let yourself evolve. Take classes. Try new things. Follow what calls to you, even if it makes no practical sense.

Maintain relationships that see you as more than Mom.
Keep friends who knew you before children. Make friends who share your interests, not just your parenting philosophy. Let people see and know the full you.

Document your timeline.
Keep journals. Take photos that aren't just of your children. Save ticket stubs, write down thoughts, record your growth. Your story matters beyond what you provide for others.

Create micro-moments of selfhood.
You don't need to quit your life to reclaim it. Read poetry while coffee brews. Listen to music that stirs something in you. Take walks alone. Write three sentences about what you're thinking. Small acts of self-honoring add up.

Teach others how to see you.
When someone asks "How are the kids?" respond with "The kids are great, and I just started reading this fascinating book about..." Train people to see you as more than a children-delivery system.

She Had a Name

Before anyone called her "Mom,"
she had a name that lit up when someone said it just right.

She had favorite songs that weren't lullabies.
She had dreams that didn't involve anyone else's needs.
She used to wander bookstores, write poems in the margins of receipts,
or walk just to hear her own thoughts.

Then time bent.
Days blurred.
And little by little, she became background.
The one holding everything together.
The one no one looked at long enough to see disappearing.

In the joy and exhaustion,
in the laughter and late nights,
in the beauty and burden of becoming a mother-
she didn't mean to lose herself.
There was love.
There was growth.
There were moments that cracked her open in the best way.

But her becoming, as a mother, should have always walked beside the rest of her.
The artist.
The dreamer.

The thinker.
The traveler.
The entrepreneur.
The woman.

She was never meant to vanish.
Not even for a season.

And now-
as an act of sacred return-
she is writing herself back in as the main character of the story.
And that's okay.

It was always okay.

Encouragement for the Mother Who Feels Like Her Story Stopped

If you feel like your life has been reduced to the role you play for others,
if your name has become an afterthought to "Mom,"
if it seems like everything you once were has gone quiet-
you're not alone.

And more importantly: *you're not done.*

You're not just a chapter in someone else's story.
You're a whole book.
And the pages are still turning.

You're allowed to remember who you were before.
You're allowed to wonder who you could still become.
You're allowed to take yourself seriously.
Not as someone who "used to," or "might one day," but as someone who *still is.*

Your timeline didn't end when theirs began.
It just changed direction, ever so slightly.
And that shift doesn't erase your depth, it expands it.

We don't need to try and reclaim our youth
or walking away from motherhood.
This is about reclaiming *your authorship.*

You are the writer.
You always were.

And your story shifts, deepens, and reshapes itself - every time you pick up the pen.

Chapter 13

The Childless Woman

Myth: That without children, a woman is incomplete.

At some point in her life, a woman is often met with questions such as:
"Do you have kids?"
"Why not?"
"Don't you *want* to be a mother?"

The questions can be kind. But they can also be invasive. Whether kind or invasive, there's an undertone that says: You're missing something.

There's an implication in society that says that motherhood is the pinnacle of womanhood. That you haven't fully *become* until you've given birth. And that your deepest contribution to society must be in the form of a child.

This belief follows women like a shadow, whispering at baby showers, pulsing through family gatherings, embedded in religious language, and is deeply coded into laws and expectations.

It tells women who don't have children that they're not quite whole - not yet anyway. That their lives are lacking shape. That their joy is counterfeit. That their wisdom is incomplete. That their love means less simply because it hasn't been poured into someone else.

But none of that is true.

Some women don't have children by choice.
Some tried, and it didn't happen.
Some lost pregnancies.
Some lost relationships.
Some lost themselves trying to become a mother and chose a different path.
Some never felt the call.
Some did, and it never came to pass.

But every childless woman has a story.

And that story *isn't* less valuable because it doesn't include diapers, tantrums, or college funds.

When Motherhood Was Longed For

For some women, childlessness wasn't a choice. It was a heartbreak.

They imagined a child's laugh in the hallways. They made space in their hearts, and in their homes ... but life didn't meet them there.

That grief is so real. And so is the love that lives inside it.

But even there, in that empty ache,
a woman isn't lacking.
She isn't living a half-life.

Grief can live beside wholeness. And longing can exist within a full and sacred life. You don't need to turn your love into productivity or caretaking to prove you've made peace.

This grief can also show up in women who actively choose a different path sometimes find themselves grieving the road not taken.

It speaks to the complexity of being human.

The ability to hold multiple truths:
Contentment with your path
and occasional wonder about another.

This is human depth.

And it's the mark of a heart wide enough to hold contradictions without breaking.

For the women who have longed for children (whether early in life or later on) but never had the chance, or haven't been able to yet:

You are still whole.
You are still radiant.
You're definitely still enough.
And you deserve to be here - just like anyone else.

Belonging Too

Too many women are left feeling that a woman without children is living an empty life.
That her womb is her worth.
That her softness or uniqueness means little if not poured into a child.

But women without children mother in a thousand unseen ways!
They mother their communities.
They mother their art.
They mother ideas, movements, healing spaces, friendships, gardens, animals, rituals, companies - their futures!
They mother the *world*.

And there's deep value in this kind of mothering.

Consider the women who shaped our world:
Georgia O'Keeffe, painting the landscapes of her soul onto canvas.
Maya Angelou, who called herself "mother" to countless writers she mentored.
Dorothy Day, mothering the homeless and forgotten.

These women created legacies that ripple through generations, not through biology, but through vision, courage, and love.

And then...
There are those who don't mother at all.
Not people.
Not projects.
Not dreams.
They simply live.
They breathe.
Create.
Connect.
Laugh.
Heal.
Learn.
Grow.

And they belong, too.

Because you can mother in many ways -
Your nieces and nephews.

Your communities.
Animals.
Art.
The earth.
Even your own beautiful becoming.

And still...
And still!
You don't have to "mother" anything at all.

Because whether or not you choose to pour yourself into others,
whether or not you give birth to a child,
or a mission,
or a masterpiece...

You're not a human meant solely to reproduce - or mother something.
You are a force that already is.

The existence and creation of your one, wondrous, irreplaceable life from cradle
to twilight years is enough.

It's more than enough.
It's everything.

And let's keep in mind that love doesn't only flow through *bloodlines*. Love creates
its own rivers, carving new channels through the landscape of human connection.

Many women without biological children have created families of choice - networks of deep friendship, mentorship relationships that span decades, and communities built around shared values and dreams.

These connections aren't lesser versions of "real" family. They're different expressions of the same human need for belonging, love, and continuity.

The Pain of Erasure

We live in a world that elevates mothers on pedestals. (Praising the idea of them
on one hand, while often ignoring the reality of their needs on the other hand.)

But for women without children?
There's often no pedestal at all.
Mostly silence.

Even pity.
Definitely projection.

As if the only version of womanhood worth celebrating is one that involves physical sacrifice and visible offspring.

As if your inner wisdom, emotional availability, and lifetime of learning somehow don't count unless a child benefits from them.

But many childless women have been the aunties, mentors, guides, and keepers of wisdom for entire communities.

Because *that's who they are.* Because that's *who they chose to be.*

One mother might teach art to neighborhood kids every summer for twenty years, watching them discover their creativity.

Another mother might spend decades as a nurse, holding hands with the dying, ensuring no one left this world alone.

And another mother might build libraries in underserved communities, believing every child deserves access to stories and dreams.

And many others chose different paths:
The traveler.
The healer.
The builder.
The explorer.
The activist.
The woman devoted to her own unfolding.

All of it matters.
All of it belongs.

Women are an incredible contribution to society.
Simply because they exist.

So...

You don't have to birth a babe to prove you matter.
You don't have to be relational to be relevant.

Your *being* is enough.
Your breath.

Your aliveness.
Your becoming.
That alone is sacred.
That alone is contribution.

You're not here to earn your place by adding to the human population.

You already belong.

The Myth of the Biological Clock

We've been told our bodies are timers, ticking toward some inevitable deadline. That fertility has an expiration date that determines our worth. That biological processes should dictate life choices.

But consider this: the phrase "biological clock" wasn't even used until the 1970s. For most of human history, women didn't organize their entire identities around a supposed countdown.

Your body isn't a timer.
Your worth doesn't decrease with age.
And your purpose doesn't expire.

The urgency you feel? Much of it isn't biological. *It's cultural.* And it's ridiculous. It's the pressure of a society that profits from women's anxiety about time, about aging, and about missing out.

Your relationship with time belongs to you.
Not to anyone else's expectations.
Not to some arbitrary timeline.

To you.

Nature's Blueprint

Look again to nature.
Not all living things reproduce.
Some trees never bear fruit.
Some bees never birth a colony.
Some stars never form planets.
Some animals never mate, yet still shape the ecosystem around them.
Some fungi live underground, unseen, nourishing entire forests without ever

sprouting a visible cap.
And some winds carry no pollen, only change.

And yet, *all of them* matter.
All of them contribute.
And all of them are part of the *great unfolding*.

Human worth isn't just "reproductive."
It's *relational*.
It's *energetic*.
It's *soul-deep*.

It feels.
It receives.
It grows.
It becomes.
It transforms.
And it becomes again.

The human mother lives in all of us who nurture life, opportunity, creativity, exploration or discovery, wherever we find it. And motherhood has never belonged to biology alone.

We live in a culture that demands women prove their usefulness through care. That expects them to disappear into service, and rewards them for doing so quietly.

So of course, the woman who simply exists (with joy, or grief, or solitude, or stillness) feels disruptive.

But she's *not* a disruption.
She's a return to truth.

A living reminder, like the tree that never bears fruit – she is still rooted, still worthy, still whole.

Perhaps that's why history feared this version of her...
Unmarried.
Childless.
Uncontainable.
They called her a witch, when really, she was just free.
She didn't serve a husband.
She didn't birth a nation's next laborers.

She served something wilder - her soul.
And for that, she was punished.

But not anymore.

Because she's returning.
In all of us.

A reminder that we aren't here to prove our worth, but to live it.

Beyond Individual Healing: Changing the Story

This is about individual women finding peace and it's about evolving as a species, expanding our understanding of human value beyond reproduction.

When we question the motherhood myth, we're also questioning:

- Why human worth is tied to productivity
- Why women's bodies are treated as public property
- Why caring labor is undervalued
- Why some lives are seen as more meaningful than others

We're part of a larger awakening - recognizing that every human has inherent worth, not because of what they produce or reproduce, but because they exist.

This benefits everyone. It benefits mothers who want to be seen as whole people beyond their parental role, fathers who want to be involved caregivers, children who deserve parents who chose them freely, and all of us who want to live in a world where human dignity isn't conditional.

You Were Never Less

You aren't defective.
You aren't late.
You aren't waiting to be chosen, anointed, or activated.
You aren't less of a woman if you don't have children.
You aren't missing your true purpose.
And you aren't selfish, useless, or unloving.

You are a creator.
A creator of beauty, of truth, of ideas.
A weaver of worlds.
A builder of what has never existed until you imagined it.

You deserve to be honored in the fullness of your womanhood - and, most importantly, in the wild, wondrous expanse of your humanity.

Because at the center of life, of nature, of the universe itself, there is one unstoppable force:

Creation.

Stars are born.
Rivers carve valleys.
Mountains rise from tectonic shifts.
The universe creates because that is what it does.

And so do you.

But unlike the stars,
unlike the trees,
you get to choose what you create.

You can create healing.
You can create art.
You can create ideas, beauty, safety, rebellion, softness, revolution, experiences, or joy.

You can create a life that no one has ever seen before.

Whether you're a mother-
or you're not-
you get to do this simply because you're here.

Because you exist.

You are the creator of your unique creations.
And that's your power.
That's your magic.
That's what makes you matter.

The fact that you are here, breathing, becoming, choosing, creating...
This is the spark of the divine made visible.
The miracle of Being.

It's your right.

Additional Insights:

When you hear someone questioning a woman's life choices, speak up. When you catch yourself making assumptions about women's roles or desires, pause and examine those beliefs.

Your daughters, sisters, friends, and partners need you to understand that a woman's worth isn't tied to her reproductive choices. They need you to see that supporting women means supporting all their choices, not just the ones that align with traditional expectations.

Ask yourself:

• What messages did I receive about women's roles growing up?
• How do I react when women choose paths different from what I expected?
• What would change if I truly believed women were complete exactly as they are?

This evolution requires all of us.

Speaking Your Truth: Language for the Questions

When people ask invasive questions, you don't owe them explanations. But sometimes having language ready can help you respond with dignity and boundaries:

"Do you have kids?"
"No, I don't." (Full stop. No explanation needed.)

"Why not?"
"That's quite personal." or "It wasn't the right path for me." or "I've built a different kind of life."

"Don't you want to be a mother?"
"I am fulfilled by the life I've created." or "I mother in different ways." or "That question assumes there's only one way to be a woman."

"You'd be such a good mother!"
"Thank you, and I'm good at lots of things." or "I channel that energy in other directions."

"You'll change your mind."
"I trust myself to know what I want." or "I've given this a lot of thought."

"Who will take care of you when you're old?"
"The same thing mothers wonder, actually. There are no guarantees in any life path."

Remember, their discomfort with your choices isn't your responsibility to manage. Your job is to live authentically, not to make others comfortable with your decisions.

Chapter 14

The Good Woman Obituary

*Myth: A woman's worth is proven by how well
she erased herself.*

They gather in a chapel. A woman's life has ended. And the stories about her begin.

"She never asked for anything."
"She gave everything she had to her family."
"She never once complained."
"She was always smiling."
"She lived for her husband and children."
"She never took time for herself."

And they say this *with pride!*
They say this as though this was the goal all along.
As though a life well-lived, is a life *well-vanished*.

But beneath those praises, something more human must have lived-
things like quiet longings and vivid dreams.
Ideas that lit up her mind late at night.
A sense of humor that surfaced around old friends.
Notebooks full of plans she never shared.
Songs that made her cry every single time.
A soul moved by beauty, drawn to mystery, or captivated by conspiracies.
A deep need to be in nature.

She couldn't have just been what *she gave -*
or gave up.

We've convinced ourselves that a woman's highest calling is to need *nothing*.
To want nothing.
To be nothing but a vessel,

a conduit,
and a facilitator for *everyone else's* dreams.

But what if the real tribute is everything *she was* - not just everything she gave
away?

What We Refuse to Say at Her Funeral

At funerals across the world, the words spoken about women rarely sound like
this:
"She was fierce. She set fire to the silence."
"She walked away when she had to save herself."
"She made people uncomfortable with her truths."
"She had dreams larger than motherhood, and she dared to chase them."

Funeral eulogies and memorials for women have historically leaned toward em-
phasizing their selflessness, sacrifice, caregiving, and devotion to family rather
than qualities like defiance, independence, or unapologetic truth-telling.

So, instead, we canonize the quiet.
We exalt the erasure.
And we praise the martyrdom.

We don't call it beautiful because that's what it truly is. We call it beautiful because
it's familiar. Talking about women this way has been ingrained in us for decades.
It feels natural to praise her sacrifice, her silence, her endless giving, because that's
what we've been conditioned to honor in women, even in death.

Talking about women this way is the script we inherited. It's psychological safety:
honor her sacrifice and ignore her becoming. Keep the story neat and keep the
machine running.

And so, again and again, we celebrate the women who disappeared the best.
Even in her death.

We praise those who folded themselves the smallest.
Who asked for nothing and gave everything.
We ooh and aah over the bravery of how small she made herself.
We speak of her as though she were a *serene saint* now that she's gone,
even though in life, we treated her like a bent slave.

But perhaps what we *should* be mourning ...
are the *human* ghosts.

We're burying women who were already *half-gone.*

And every time we do this, we teach the living that disappearance is holy, when the only thing that's *actually* sacred is a soul fully alive.

Let this be seared into our collective memory:
A species that celebrates erasure over existence will never evolve beyond survival.

What Is a Life?

Is a life measured by how well you smiled through sacrifice?
By how little you needed?
By how completely you gave yourself away?

Or is a life something more?
Is it voice?
Desire?
Presence?
Experiences?
The courage to become who you actually are?

Is it the pottery classes you finally took at fifty-three? The novel you wrote in secret? The boundary you drew that made everyone uncomfortable but saved your sanity? The joy you embraced and refused to apologize for? The truth you finally spoke, even when your voice shook?

A life isn't just marked by years,
or even by how well you helped others live theirs.
We are not our age.
We are our energy.
And it's marked by how deeply you were allowed to exist *inside* those years.
How fully you were permitted to take up space-
not just inside the walls of a home,
but in the world.
In one, special lifetime.

Because a life without room for your dreams, your wildness, and your wonder, isn't a life.
It's a slow disappearance.
And that is *not* what you were born for.

Some of you might be bristling right now. "But taking care of my family *is* meaningful," you're thinking. "Sacrifice can be beautiful."

And you're right. The problem isn't care or even sacrifice.

The problem is when care becomes erasure,
when sacrifice becomes suicide,
and when love becomes loss of self.

There's a difference between choosing to nurture others from a full cup and being expected to pour from an empty one until you disappear entirely.

The Graveyard We All Live In

We live surrounded by a different kind of graveyard.
Not one of bodies,
but of dreams.
Of women who became mothers and who never got to fully live.

The grandmother who wanted to be a teacher but was told girls didn't need college.
The mother who had a beautiful singing voice but was told it wasn't practical.
The sister who loves to write but says she doesn't have time.
Or yourself, maybe, with that thing you used to love doing before life got in the way.

This is the graveyard of women's brilliance, buried under systems, dogmas, and doctrines that depend on her loss.

It's untapped genius, unexpressed creativity, and unexplored dreams buried beneath routines that drain rather than ignite.

It's souls suffocated beneath the weight of survival.
Dreams buried under obligations.
Wildness tamed by societal structures.
Curiosity dulled by the daily grind.
Spirit eroded by relentless exhaustion.

But here's what gives me hope:
where there are graveyards,
the soil is rich for rebirth.
Everything needed to sustain life is already there, waiting.

That creative fire doesn't *die*.
It just goes underground, waiting.
Waiting to be remembered, nurtured, and awakened.

We Lose So Much in the Name of Love

Real love doesn't require anyone's disappearance.

Real. Love. Does. Not. Require. Anyone's. Disappearance.

If two people fall into a lake, and one dies trying to save the other, we don't celebrate the death!

We mourn.

We recognize the weight of what was lost! The cost of one life to save another is not something to celebrate. It's a tragedy!

So why on earth do we do this with mothers?!
(Or with women in general?)

Why do we cheer for the ones who sank silently while lifting everyone else above water?!

And when does this cycle end - where every generation of women drowns, while men inherit the world built from their erasure?

A woman's personality, her soul, her essence, her quirks, her passions, her gifts - these aren't extras.

They are life itself.
They are her life.
Her true essence.

Every soul that enters this world carries something the universe has never seen before *and will never see again.*

When we ask a woman to erase herself, we're not just losing her... we're losing a completely original frequency of existence. A unique way of seeing, creating, loving, and being that took *billions of years of cosmic evolution to produce.*

The universe doesn't make duplicates.
It doesn't waste energy creating souls it doesn't need.

Every woman who disappears takes with her irreplaceable gifts that were meant to change the world in ways only she could.

We're not just burying women.
We're burying miracles.

The universe doesn't design a system where half of its beings must erase themselves to endlessly produce more life for a machine that thrives on their absence.

Nature creates cycles, not cages.
It births life through wholeness, not self-destruction.

Nature doesn't ask the tree to vanish once it bears fruit. It doesn't require the river to dry up so others can drink. Only man-made systems demand that women disappear in order to populate and sustain them.

This is not divine design - it's mechanical madness.
Nature grows life without erasing the one who gave it.
Only in honoring the mother do we honor creation itself.

Being remembered as the woman who gave everything and never asked for anything is *not* a badge of honor.

It's a tragedy.

And, quite frankly, *it should shock us.*

It should make us question everything we've been taught to praise.
It should make us ask why a woman's disappearance is still called being a "good mom."
And why self-erasure is still mistaken for "love."

It should cause us to reflect and realize:
Every soul comes here to become, not to vanish.

What We Owe the Living (And the Dead)

Humanity is wasting half of our potential by asking women to disappear. We're literally burying brilliance and evolution alive.

Every woman who never got to explore her gifts is a loss to all of us.
Every silenced voice was a message we'll never hear.
Every abandoned dream was a solution we'll never discover.
Every woman who could've transformed the country might just be one more

reason why this one still struggles to change.

Every woman who vanished instead of becoming - is a piece of human evolution we threw away.

And this doesn't benefit humanity at all.

It only ensures that more women keep repeating the same goddamn cycle, allowing men to remain parasitic creatures gorging on what she gives, feeding the toxic patriarchy that infects every system of society.

This can't continue!

This isn't just about a mother's erasure. And this isn't just about women's rights. This is about human thriving - about what becomes possible when we stop requiring half of the population to shrink in order for the other half to feel comfortable.

We need to begin writing new obituaries.

Not ones that canonize invisibility, but ones that celebrate embodiment.

Obituaries that honor presence.
Truth.
Becoming.
Voice.
Joy.
Rage.
Art.
Success.
Bravery.
Authenticity.
Dreams.
Boundaries.
Aliveness.

But more than that, we need to start *living* these lives. Lives where we take up space, speak our truth, chase our dreams, and refuse to shrink.

Lives where our worth is measured by how fully *we exist*, not by how well *we vanished*.

Lives lived *so* fully that when our time comes, there will be *no* room in our obituary to talk about how much we "erased" ourselves.

Only rich stories about how vibrantly we lived.
Enough that no single obituary could hold it.

It would take pages,
or poems,
or canvases,
or songs she carried and stories she passed down,
or gardens she planted,
or creatures she cared for,
or adventures she dared to embrace,
or hearts she awakened and souls she set alight,
or ripples she sent into the world,
or the voices of countless others who carry her forward...

To even glimpse the radiance of a woman who lived at the blazing center of her
own story.

Endings That Set Spirits Free

So let's stop writing eulogies for ghosts.

Let's start writing endings that let her spirit breathe.
Endings that are untamed and honest.
That carry the originality, the hunger, and the fire of her truest self.

Let's write endings that actually speak her name.
Not just the "mother", the "wife", the "helper."
But the woman that she *was*.
The soul that existed inside of her the day she was born.

The artist who created beauty from chaos.
The dreamer who imagined what hadn't yet been built.
The one who carried music in her hands,
wildness in her step,
laughter that filled rooms,
or fire that lit paths for others.

The one who changed lives with her presence.
Who spoke with clarity.
Who dared greatly.
Who painted, built, wrote, danced, or loved – who *lived*.

Let her be remembered not for what she gave up, but for all that she became.

Let's write endings that are worthy of her life.
And worthy of her release.

Because if her spirit had to stay quiet while she lived,
then, for goodness sake, let's let it finally soar in death.

And let the truth about her authentic self be the breath that sets her free.

And if you're still breathing,
if you're still here reading this-
know that your spirit doesn't have to wait for death in order to soar.

It can fly right now.

What They Forgot to Say

They stood up one by one, telling stories of how good she was.
How quiet.
How giving.
How strong.

How she always had dinner ready.
How she smiled through everything.
How she was the kind of woman who never asked for anything.

She stood in the shadows of her own funeral,
listening for herself in their stories.
But she was missing.

Her paintings weren't there.
Nor the time she wandered through Italy, getting lost on purpose just to feel alive.
No one remembered the poems scribbled on grocery lists,
the dream of a bakery she never opened,
or how her whole body stilled when live music filled a room.
No one mentioned the woman still alive in the pages of her journals,
or the dreams she tucked between folded laundry and grocery bags.

They buried her body that day.
But her spirit (her truest self) had been buried long before.

All she ever wanted was to be more than what they needed from her.

And so she was buried twice:

Once by life,
and once by being misremembered in death.

No woman should be buried twice.

Encouragement for the Woman Who's Tired of Being Remembered Only for What She Gave

If the world has only ever praised you for what you give,
let this be a space where you are celebrated for who you *are*.

Your value is in your presence: fully seen, fully expressed.
Your worth is in your voice: spoken, shaking, rising.
Your goodness is measured by your wholeness: your ability to stay true to yourself,
even when it's hard.

You are a story unfolding.
And you're allowed to live.
To be known in the *now*, not just in the memory.
To let your joy, your dreams, your strangeness, and your brilliance take up space.
Even if it makes people uncomfortable.
(Especially then.)

Being remembered as the woman who never asked for anything isn't the goal.
Being remembered as the woman who took up space and never gave herself away
to be loved...

Now *that's* a courageous legacy worth leaving behind.

PART TWO

The Inner Evolution
of the Mother

Intro to The Inner Evolution of the Mother

Naming every corner of motherhood.

Motherhood can bring a profound sense of purpose. It can invite presence. It can leave mothers feeling deeply fulfilled, calm, grounded, and at home in themselves in ways they never were before.

Mothers may find themselves becoming more disciplined or more intentional. They cook with love, clean with care, or speak with more clarity. And they live toward the best version of themselves they want etched into their children's memory.

Motherhood can awaken awe and adventure: dancing in the kitchen, befriending strangers, laughing freely, connecting with your child-like imagination, and giving hundreds of kisses before the sun goes down. It can deepen connection across generations, spark rich friendships, and even usher in a quieter, more rooted kind of joy that ebbs and flows in rhythm with the seasons.

These moments are treasures. Treasures that deserve to be recognized and remembered.

But so should the *whole* story.
Not just the palatable parts.

This section of the book isn't here to dim the light on the positive aspects of motherhood. It's here to make space for what's often left in the shadows - pushed there by the cultural script of what motherhood should look, feel and be like.

The parts that don't fit the picture-perfect story...

The overwhelm. The depletion. The grief.
The rage. The quiet loss of self.
The pieces too often unseen, unspoken, or quietly endured.

These experiences are *also* part of motherhood.

And that's okay.

In naming them, we let the light fall on every corner of motherhood, not just the beautiful and fulfilling parts, but everything in between. So motherhood can stop being a silent sacrifice, stop being damaging to the woman who has embraced the mother role, and start being something held - with care, by all. So we learn the art of self-nourishment and, through it, awaken to the needs of every mother.

When we honor the full spectrum of the maternal experience, we return to something instinctual - and move toward something whole. Toward a motherhood where a woman stands rooted in her body, grounded in her knowing, steady in her truth. Where she's at one with her voice, unafraid to speak it, and fully alive in her own life.

A motherhood where she dares to raise children without abandoning herself in the process, allowing her to be more present with her children.

Where she isn't hollowed out, but made more alive.
Where she isn't diminished by her giving, but expanded by it.
Where her body is cared for as much as it carries.
Where her joy is as essential as her sacrifice.
Where her dreams are tended, not buried.

Where she lives fully.
Where she's nourished as she nourishes.
And where her becoming is never the cost of her children's survival.

And while we may not be able to change how others treat us, we can change our expectations, our boundaries, and our agreements with how we allow ourselves to be treated.

The change can only begin with us.

By honoring the overlooked, the heavy, and the more difficult parts of motherhood, we begin to restore wholeness.

The transformation begins when we admit that motherhood was never meant to be martyrdom. By allowing ourselves to finally see and feel the darker, unswept corners of motherhood, we can restore access to our inner truth and authentic presence.

Because when a mother dares to witness and acknowledge what was never safe to face, she interrupts what was once passed down in silence.

The old patterns loosen.
The body exhales.
The nervous system softens its grip.
And new patterns can finally emerge.

In that space, life begins to move differently - no longer driven by what was buried, but guided by what is finally seen.

May the light return to what your mother couldn't say, your grandmother couldn't change, and what you now have the power to reclaim.

And may we birth ourselves back into wholeness - one evolutionary step at a time.

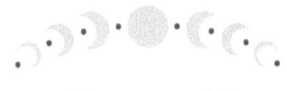

Chapter 15

The Shifting Self Within Motherhood

Some roles may shift. Some illusions may fall.
But your essence (the truest you) can stay.

People awaken in countless ways. They awaken through adventure, artistry, service, or solitude. Through entrepreneurship, caregiving, spiritual exploration, creativity, illness, discovering purpose, or deep surrender.

Motherhood is one of those portals to one's awakening - one that reshapes you from the inside out.

It isn't the *only* way to awakening and growth, but it *is* a potent one - because it shakes one's foundation. It alters your perspective, your priorities, your body, and your sense of self.

This chapter isn't implying that you have to become a mother in order to awaken. It's about what awakening can look and feel like when motherhood *is* your path.

This chapter opens the door to the part of the book that explores the mother's inner evolution - the transformation of self that motherhood brings. What it means to question old identities, confront inherited patterns, and navigate the dissonance between who you've been and who you're becoming.

This is your awakening.
Awakening into a mother who is fully human.

One who feels.
One who knows.
One who trusts her knowing.
And one who becomes connected to her essence, even when things around her shift.

Even when you hold both the mundane and the mystical in the same breath - diapers and dreams, grief and gratitude, burnout and becoming.

Yes, roles may shift.
Illusions may fall.
Routines may change.
Some certainties may crumble.
Some dreams may dissolve.
But your essence, your truth, can stay.
And alongside her, new capacities can rise.

Welcome to the part of the book where your inner world is honored. Where you remember that the goal is to be a whole human, raising another whole human, in a world that needs more wholeness.

You are in the process of becoming...
no matter how scattered or centered,
graceful or wild,
fierce or tender,
raw or polished,
stumbling or soaring,
that becoming may be.

However that looks, you're laying the bricks of a life that includes you too.
Keep going and remember that nothing is wasted.
All of it belongs.

There's no wrong way to become.

Meeting Yourself

You might feel unrecognizable to yourself.

You might look in the mirror, baby on hip, heart half-broken and half-expanded, and wonder: Where did I go? What happened to me?!

What we call motherhood often begins with a strange unraveling.
A collision of the old and the new.

For many women, it's one of the most beautiful things they've ever experienced - but it can also be quite disorienting. There's no single map for what unfolds when a woman becomes a mother. For some, the shift is gentle. For others, it's a complete undoing.

But in nearly every case, something deep does begin to stir.

It stirs in how you see yourself.
In how your new self functions.
In what brings meaning to your life.
In the meaning behind everything.
In how you perceive the world and move through it.

It's not always a mystical awakening - often, it's more like being cracked open. Split between who you were and who you're becoming. Lost in the space where both still exist.

Some call it ego death. Some call it "matrescence" - the gradual transformation a woman undergoes as she steps into motherhood. Some just call it survival.

But underneath it all - you're meeting parts of yourself you probably didn't know existed and probably didn't know you could become.

A Personal Awakening

Three years before becoming a mother at twenty, I was in high school - popular, wild, staying out late with friends, a skater girl with a boyfriend and frequent adventures, still living in the house where my family of seven had been rooted for over a decade.

Then, suddenly, less than two years out of high school, I was married. To someone I'd only known for six months. Living in a cramped apartment. With a newborn who needed me every hour of every day.

The whiplash was intense.

I loved her. Goodness, I loved her.

But I was disoriented, confused, anxious, overwhelmed by the enormity of it all. I didn't know what was normal. I didn't know if I was doing it right. I just knew she needed me, and I was trying.

No one told me about what was happening in my head back then.

No one warned me that your brain can play cruel tricks in the whiplash of adjusting hormones and in the haze of new motherhood. That you can love your baby with a kind of reverent devotion while being haunted by intrusive thoughts that terrify you.

I didn't know it was called postpartum anxiety. I just knew my mind kept imagining horrible things happening to my daughter. And it scared me. I thought something was wrong with me.

I remember one moment in particular so clearly. I had just bathed my newborn daughter, and I was holding her close, studying her impossibly delicate face, my heart bursting with love and angst all at once.

I noticed a tiny blue vein running gently down her forehead. I tried to memorize it because I worried that if she were kidnapped, I wouldn't recognize her among other babies. But that vein was hers alone. If I could just remember the details of that squiggly little line, maybe I could use it to identify her if something happened to her.

The love and fear were so tangled together, I couldn't tell where one ended and the other began.

And that was something I didn't know - that I would carry both wonder and worry in the same breath. That my identity would feel like it was unraveling while something else, a kind of sacred fierceness, was being stitched together in its place to protect this helpless little babe I had just brought into this world.

Sacred fierceness. That's what I call the protective instinct that rises from depths you didn't know you had. The mama bear energy that would move mountains, that sees everything as either a threat or a blessing to your child. It's fierce because it's instinct. Ancient. Animal, even. And unapologetically alive.

I felt lonely, too.

Untethered from the world I once knew, but not yet grounded in the one I had entered. There were days when I didn't recognize my life, or myself. But little by little, as she grew, I grew. Our days took on rhythm, and meaning, and memory.

I kept trying and stayed with it.
Right there. In all of it.

I didn't always feel strong, but I did do my best.
I didn't always feel confident in what I was doing,
and I never quite fit the mold of a societally perfect mother - but I kept showing up.

I stayed through the storms. Through the mess ups. Through the days I felt invisible - or days (months, even) where I just *wanted* to disappear. And that part of me, the one who continually rose through the blur and the breaking...

She's the part of me that finally reached through the fog and pulled me into the light.

That part of me now speaks, I speak for every woman who is still in the blur, or in the breaking, still searching for her way back to the light.

The Many Paths to This Awakening

Awakening doesn't belong solely to motherhood. But for many women, motherhood is where the walls came down.

It's where everything familiar no longer fits, and something deeper begins to take shape.

My story is just one thread in a vast tapestry. Some women find their essence through the long journey of fertility treatments, learning patience and surrender they never knew they possessed. Others discover their fierce tenderness through adoption, choosing love before biology ever enters the picture. Single mothers often uncover a self-reliance so complete it surprises everyone, including themselves.

Some women become mothers at forty-five and find themselves shedding decades of accumulated personas in a matter of months. Others have their second or third child and suddenly understand something about themselves that the first pregnancy kept hidden.

There are stepmothers who learn that love isn't always instant but can grow into something unshakeable. Foster mothers who practice loving with open hands. Mothers who lose children and discover that grief can coexist with an expanded heart.

The awakening doesn't require a biological birth or a specific age or circumstance. It simply asks: Are you willing to be changed by the unraveling of motherhood?

You Are Still In There

Motherhood's unraveling can spark profound inner growth. But there's an unhealthy story that says motherhood changes you by *erasing you*. That the only way to become a good mother is to stop being anything else.

But what if that's not true? What if motherhood doesn't diminish you but dares you to *expand*?

What if it sheds some of the things that were never really you to begin with? Things like your performative strength, your people-pleasing, your avoidance of vulnerability, or your illusion of control?

What if the "you" that feels gone isn't lost, she's just being reorganized.

Moved. Softened. Strengthened.

Maybe you aren't necessarily losing yourself. Maybe you're becoming a version of you that only this particular journey could bring forth.

Motherhood has the ability to strip away what isn't essential - and what used to be. It's brutal that way. Before motherhood, you may have defined yourself by roles, achievements, dreams, or routines. When those structures fall away, it can feel like your identity goes with them.

But what if who you were was only one version?
One chapter?

What emerges from all that shifting might just be the most *you* – you've ever been.

The balance is learning to grow alongside your children, without abandoning the woman you are becoming.

Not a Loss, But an Expansion

Growth can be messy. It doesn't always feel good. But keep in mind that growth doesn't ever require you to disappear.

You don't have to bury your passions.
Or soften your story.
Or edit your joy.

You get to continue to *expand*.
You get to become *more*.
Not less.

If you ever feel like motherhood is making you feel less like you, it's a signal to return to yourself.

The woman who stays up all night with a sick child is the same woman who once danced until dawn. The mother who advocates fiercely for her child's needs is the same person who once fought for her own dreams. The hands that braid hair and pack lunches are the same hands that once created art, or wrote poetry, or built businesses.

Every part of you still belongs here.
And you contain *multitudes.*

Motherhood doesn't need to diminish that.

The version of you emerging may be softer in some ways, and fiercer in others. You may find yourself feeling protective in ways you've never felt before. Exhausted in new ways. Present in new ways. Your intuition sharper. Your tolerance lower. Your thresholds different.

This is adaptation.
This is expansion.

You aren't meant to "bounce back" to who you were. You're meant to grow forward into who you're becoming. This version may not be familiar yet - but she's still a part of who you're becoming.

Maybe she isn't who you were.
And maybe she isn't who you thought you'd be.

But she's *becoming* you - and she'll thrive when you give her space and care, honor her as part of your becoming, and allow her to be the version of you this season is inviting you to be - before the next season whispers your name and asks you to grow again.

A Mother's Timeline

Some women feel a shift immediately, in the delivery room or the moment they hold their adopted child. Others need months or years to fully integrate who they're becoming. Some experience it as a gradual dawn, others as a sudden lightning strike.

There's no wrong timeline for coming home to yourself as a mother.

You might read stories of women who felt instant connection and wonder what's wrong with you if bonding took longer than you expected. You might hear about mothers who felt immediate fulfillment and feel guilty for grieving your old life.

Your experience is yours.
Your timeline is valid.

And your way of becoming is exactly as it should be.
And it holds its own beauty, even if it looks nothing like theirs.

Let This Be Your Reentry Point

So many false myths about motherhood make it easy for a woman to disappear behind the role. These myths should be seen for what they are and stripped of their power.

But there's another way we might disappear, too.
We might vanish into the quiet cracks of our own transformation.

Those cracks appear in the identity shift. In our unraveling and in the reorganization of ourself.

Don't vanish in those cracks.
Let them be the places you rise from.
Because your evolution is part of the world's evolution.
Because each time you choose to evolve, you tilt the world a little closer to wholeness.

If motherhood is the path you're on, let it be a portal - an important part of your becoming. Let it be the ground where you reappear, or where you reinvent yourself into being more human and more whole. And more *you* than ever.

Because the role, no matter how important it is, is only the container - the real transformation is how fully you learn to live as yourself within it.

·)⃝(·

Your Truth to Anchor In
A declaration to hold onto

This transformation may feel like loss-
but it's an awakening.
The parts of me that feel unfamiliar are being reorganized.
I'm still here.
Maybe not quite as I was,

but as I have the potential to be.

I'm allowed to change.
To soften and sharpen.
To fall apart, to change, and come home to myself.

Motherhood revealed a version of me I hadn't met yet-
one I wasn't expecting, but one I now choose to honor.
She isn't the final version.
But she *is* part of me.
And I will carry her with love
as I step into a new version of my becoming.

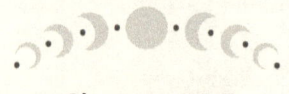

Chapter 16

The Limits of Limitless Love

Even love needs boundaries to stay whole.

There's a phrase so beautiful it's become the gold standard, the pinnacle of what it means to be a mother. You'll find it stitched into greeting cards and whispered in lullabies. It's splashed across Instagram posts and stamped into parenting books.

It says:

"A mother's love is unconditional."

It sounds poetic.
Sacred, even.
And perhaps at times it has been - and still can be.

But somewhere along the way, this phrase became warped.

It became the reason mothers are expected to:
Forgive the unforgivable.
To swallow disrespect like medicine.
To offer endless patience while receiving scraps.
To keep pouring love into vessels that often never seem to fill.
To sacrifice their well-being in the name of "putting family first."
To smile through their own pain so no one feels uncomfortable.
To give even when they are running on empty.
To excuse harmful behavior in the name of love and understanding.
And to keep showing up, no matter how absent others are for them.

Somewhere along the line "unconditional love" stopped being something tender and became something owed. It became something expected rather than honored. It became permission for others to stay underdeveloped, knowing she would bridge the gap.

And it became the steady, unnoticed wearing away of her aliveness.

And that's exactly where the "sacredness" of this version of unconditional love becomes toxic.

The Unspoken Contract

Your love, as a mother, should stretch across any distance, they say.
It should survive exhaustion, neglect, even betrayal.
These are the lives you gave life to, after all.
Your love should flow like water, regardless of drought-
especially if you're a mother.

Somehow, somewhere we began to believe that-
You will love, no matter what.
You will stay soft, even when the world hardens against you.
You will show up, even when everyone else is a no-show.

But if *you* miss the mark? Let *your* love have an edge? Or regularly run out of patience? If you set boundaries? Or put yourself first?

Suddenly you're not a very loving mother.

But what if the problem was never you?
What if the problem was the lie itself?
That to be a "real mother," you had to be infinitely giving.
Infinitely kind.
Infinitely available.
Infinitely accepting.
Infinitely self-sacrificing.
And, of course, infinitely and unconditionally loving.

Are we God?!

Who benefits the most from this god-like unconditional love?

It's definitely not the mother.
Or her unique soul beneath the role.

It's everyone who wants access to her energy for their own benefit.

Partners.
Parents.
Schools.

Systems.
Even other women - they all quietly uphold this myth because it serves them.

Even our most enlightened spaces have reinforced similar lies about love.

Modern spirituality whispers:
"Your triggers are your responsibility."
"No one can make you feel anything."
"Everything is a reflection."
"You attract what you are."
"Your only job is to love unconditionally."
"Love bears all things and conquers all."

Therapy sometimes suggests that if you were just more healed, more regulated, more evolved - you wouldn't be so affected by mistreatment and would have a greater ability to give and receive love.

That if you could better manage your triggers, not take things personally, and focus only on what you can control, you'd suffer less.

That if you stayed in your own lane, stopped trying to change others, and simply adjusted your expectations, peace would follow.

But love without integrity or boundaries isn't enlightenment - it's self-abandonment dressed up as virtue.

Remembering What Love Could Be

It's said that *"God is love."* That real love is unconditional, boundless, all-encompassing and eternal.

And maybe it is.

Those who have brushed against death -
who flatlined and came back,
who floated toward the light,
returned to universal consciousness,
and then returned back to their bodies -
they speak of a love they encountered, too vast for language.

They say this love they've experienced is in everything and judges nothing.
It's a love that envelops, remembers, and restores everything it touches.

This love they describe is found in the spaces between life and death.
It sees the self as sacred.
It loves endlessly, without judgement, and fully accepts everyone for who they are and have been.

Humans seem to ache for this same kind of unconditional love and acceptance. But why do we expect mainly a woman (especially one in the mother role) to be the primary source of that kind of love?

She's expected to be it for her partner. For her children. For her parents. For her grandchildren. For the neighbor's kids. For the struggling friend. For the community in crisis. For anyone who needs a safe place to land.

If the love we seek belongs to the heavens - vast, unconditional, and soul-restoring - why do we expect an endless source of it from a single human woman?

And why do we take it as if her offering is owed, not honored?

She's the closest thing we'll ever experience to divine love in human form because of her ability to tap into something so universally sacred.

She is the *ezer kenegdo*. The vital strength. The rescuer in the storm. The word used for God's own strength and salvation. A name that speaks of power that steadies, sustains, and saves.

So why isn't she met with awe, respect, admiration, and gratitude for this?

Why isn't it normal for us to recognize this gift that woman are known for and ask: Am I even worthy of receiving what a woman has the ability to give? What can I do to become worthy if I'm not?

Why do we not teach the world to look at her with reverence - to admire her and support her, not siphon from her?

And if this love is what we're all aching for, why aren't we learning how to cultivate it within ourselves - to tap into it through spirit, nature, stillness, and Source - instead of expecting women to be its sole wellspring?

Her softness, her forgiveness, her vision, her wisdom - these are sacred echoes of a universal love, not offerings to be endlessly extracted, but gifts to be honored, mirrored, and shared by all.

Maybe *that's* why so many people drain women and mothers dry:
They crave a taste of that original love we all came from.
But instead of learning how to return to it within themselves-
and then share it, circulate it, and replenish it with one another,
they consume the mother, piece by piece.
Because it's easier to take it from her than to become a source of love yourself.

True love isn't parasitic.

We don't need to suck it dry from another human in order to satiate our own desperate or glutinous need for it.

Even in nature, plants and animals give and take in an endless flow.
Life thrives in reciprocity.
Giving love should be mutual, not one-sided,
no matter your role.

And yet, look at what we've done here.

We took something eternal and turned it into a test, a burden strapped to a mother's back.

We told her to keep loving no matter how she's treated.
To stay kind, even when depleted.
To be the bigger person, the softer one, the one who never stops.

That is *not* divine love.
That is domesticated love.
Distorted love.
Diabolical love.

Perhaps when we make mothers the sole well of unconditional love, we don't just exploit them, we desecrate the sacred essence of love itself.

Taking Our Love Back

When a mother finally sees the truth and decides her love will no longer be without boundaries, she changes the game.

She realizes her love is still precious,
but that it needs to have boundaries.
And standards.
And be grounded in reality.

She loves deeply, but no longer at the expense of her sanity.
She shows up, but no longer in spaces that treat her like furniture.
She stays tender, but with backbone intact.
And she guards more than her backbone-her energy remains unbroken,
her aura whole and her essence fully hers.

And her love?
It can transform.
It can become rooted and unburdened.
Clear and authentic.
Raw and alive - no longer a twisted, tangled version of what love was never meant
to be.

This is what we can and should be aiming for.

To love ourselves first - by defending the light within from being dimmed, even
by those who don't mean to cast a shadow.

Then to give what's left from a place of fullness, not depletion.

To then let love flow outward only after we've met ourselves with care.

You are the only self you will ever have.
The only eyes you'll ever see through.
The only soul you'll ever live from.
Just as nature fiercely protects what is rare and vital,
so must you protect yourself, even in the sacred work of motherhood.

As you hold the sacred responsibility of motherhood, never let your existence
become the price you pay for it. As women, we tend to give away our love in pieces
to those who barely looked and to those who only took.

We offer our love, *ourselves*, through gritted teeth, pour it through bone-deep
exhaustion, holding it steady through their silence and our tears. But imagine that
one morning, we gathered it back. Pulled it close to our chests and carried it down
to the river's edge.

We scrubbed away the resentment and the obligation.
Rinsed off the guilt and the should-haves.
Washed it clean of those who scarred it with their taking.
Wrung out the bitterness until only essence remained.

Our love had now remembered that it belonged to us first.
Undistorted.
Undiminished.
Reclaimed.
Sovereign.

And we begin to realize that our *love* is not the same as our *self*. We can hold both
- the self that is ours alone, and the love we choose to give.

One does not have to be the sacrifice for the other.
Your being is not the currency for your care.

Some would say we *are* love itself - and perhaps that's true.
But even love needs a vessel, and that vessel is you.
If it empties beyond repair, there's nothing left for love to move through.

So yes, you can be love, and still keep the self that is yours alone.

Love isn't meant to consume its own source. It's meant to flow from a self that
remains whole, rooted, and alive.

The Mothers Who Loved Without Disappearing

Perhaps there's a memory in our bones, an archetypal truth that calls us back to
how things were meant to be.

Patriarchy has long demanded endless sacrifice from women (whether we want
to admit that or not) often without balance or care in return. Once cultures
turned toward male-dominated structures, women were expected to disappear
into duty. Throughout history, this meant being denied to vote, denied control
over property and wages, denied the right to open a bank account without a man's
signature, and denied reproductive freedom.

And now, the pendulum swings backward again: voting rights questioned, abor-
tion bans spreading (forcing children to carry pregnancies from incest, requiring
women to carry dead fetuses until infection sets in, denying cancer patients treatment, and leaving doctors to wait until women are near death before helping)
while maternal mortality rises. Extreme Christian nationalists call women hosts,
baby makers, helpmeets, wombs for the nation. Political leaders repeat the same
message - a woman's highest value is in producing and serving, not leading or
deciding. It's the same old demand: disappear into what serves them, dressed up
in the language of morality and tradition.

And yet, somewhere deeper than politics and patriarchy, there is an older truth - one we've lived before and could live again. Perhaps this ancestral echo, this memory of how love is meant to be, calls us toward something better...

In wiser cultures and civilizations, women were never reduced to *"hosts"* - vessels to produce babies for the heads of wealthy empires. They weren't seen as tools to expand an ego, feed a legacy, or swell a population so there would be more laborers to build an empire, more bodies to fight a ruler's wars, or more customers to enrich a nation's coffers.

Instead, women were honored as the givers of life *and* the givers of love, wisdom, insight, and intuition.

The life that came through them wasn't viewed as a future servant, soldier, or consumer, but as a unique and unrepeatable gift to the collective. Each child was seen as potential - not for someone's personal gain or power - but for the growth, harmony, and vitality of the whole community.

And the woman who carried that life was protected, nourished, and supported, because to honor her was to honor the future itself.

In some pre-patriarchal, matrilineal, or tribal cultures, mothering was far more communal. A woman's needs and cycles were visible and protected. She wasn't the sole vessel of maternal labor; the whole village helped carry the weight. Her anger, her power, her no - these were a part of her wholeness.

Perhaps this is the shape of real love:
Rooted in reciprocity, collective support, boundaries, and balance.
Perhaps this isn't just a memory.
Perhaps it's a real possibility...

This is a call to remember what can grow when mothers embrace their own personal boundaries, putting themselves first and keeping the universal essence of love alive and protected inside them. How we approach motherhood today, affects the collective.

There's an underlying miracle of being a woman - it's how naturally we tap into this kind of love and care and concern for the collective. Perhaps it's why countries led by women often have higher happiness and wellbeing.

Perhaps it's also why the few mammals who go through menopause, are led by elder females whose love and wisdom sustain the entire group, guiding the collective.

Perhaps it's also why, in villages across the world, microloans are entrusted to women because they repay them and pour the gains back into family and community - instead of abandoning both with stolen money in hand.

Women hold families together, build movements, and tend to the fragile threads that keep life moving forward.

We tap into this love more easily than almost any other force on earth.

Our desire to benefit and protect the collective for our children's future, our instinct to nurture what we bring into being, and our lived knowledge that every decision ripples forward - all of this allows us to tap into a love that holds the whole in mind.

We carry the generational and personal memory of labor and birth, of sustaining life day after day, of knowing the cost of neglect and the power of care. We have learned, through centuries of being the ones who mend what is broken and feed what is hungry, we see beyond and care beyond our own gain.

It's why, in every corner of the world, when women are given power, resources, or authority, they tend to use them to strengthen the community, to grow what benefits the many, and to safeguard the future - because we understand in our bones that the health of the whole is the truest measure of our own wellbeing.

But just because it comes naturally doesn't mean it should be taken for granted.
We must protect it.
Recognize that this is a part of our power,
stay whole and intact,
and give our love where it is worthy of being given.

We are vessels of universal love, a bridge between the infinite love that exists in all things and the human world that so desperately needs it. To keep this love from being used in a way that harms us, we must be its wise stewards.

We aren't just providers of love - we are its protectors and guardians. When we stand in this knowing, when we remember that we are both the river and the keeper of the banks, we help love become what it was always meant to be.

Precious enough to be sought by kings,
needed by newborns,
longed for by the broken,
and powerful enough to reshape our civilization.

This love should never be seized or expected.
It should be asked for and received with respect, care, and acknowledgment.
Only offered with consent.
Only shared when the woman who holds it feels safe, seen, and sovereign.

She is the keeper of its flow.

The healing of the world is bound to the healing of its women.
No empire, no religion, and no system will outlast the rise of sovereign love.

And the next chapter of a healed humanity will be written only when women are lifted from sacrifice into sovereignty.

—————)) ◯ ((—————

Your Truth to Anchor In
A declaration to hold onto

My love is sacred.
It is a gift.
It is whole and strong because it has boundaries.
It flows with discernment.
It is given with integrity and devotion, never out of compulsion.

I am a vessel for universal love,
a bridge between what is infinite and what this world longs for.
I am here to protect this love,
to carry it alive inside me first,
and to offer it where it is worthy of being received.

I stand strong in my care.
I can love fiercely and hold my ground.
I can love deeply and still say no.
I can love fully and walk away when I must.
I can love honestly and stay whole.

This is what love looks like when it is rooted in truth,
protected by boundaries,
stewarded with care,

and kept alive inside me
so it can remind humankind of the love they came from-
and learn to gather it for themselves
from the countless sacred streams flowing through this world.

Chapter 17

Rage as the Turning Point

The fury you've been swallowing isn't
destroying you - it's trying to save you.

I was angry. Deeply, justifiably angry. And I want to tell you why that was okay.

I was angry that I silenced myself to keep the peace, until it broke my health.
Angry that mothers are expected to be wise and patient and calm and soft even while we're falling apart behind closed doors.
Angry that I felt trapped in a life that offered little fulfillment beyond the responsibilities of home.
Angry that I was groomed to serve, but nowhere close to being supported to thrive.
Angry that my worth seemed to shrink to the size of what I could produce, clean, hold, give, or heal for others

I was angry because I was told (directly and through a thousand subtle messages) that expressing anger would make me scary, unwell, unfit, unholy or unstable.

But eventually I finally realized:
Rage wasn't a flaw.
It was a flare.

It was a necessary signal that something was deeply wrong.
A response to injustice.
A compass turning the unseen into undeniable truth,
and pointing me back to myself.

This chapter isn't permission to explode constantly. Nor is it a call to normalize uncontrolled outbursts or make rage a lifestyle (no matter how tempting that may be).

This chapter is for the women who have rarely let themselves be angry. The ones trained to smile instead of shake. And the ones who have swallowed every scream for the sake of "being good and stable."

If you're ready to stop fearing your rage and begin honoring it as a gift and a form of protection, this chapter is for you.

The Policing of Maternal Anger

They used to call women who raged "hysterical", "mad", or "unfit."
Now they call us "dramatic", "bitter", "unhealed", or "toxic."

We're supposed to sigh gently not scream after all.
We're allowed tears but only if they're silent and in secret after all.
We're allowed complaints but only if they're polite after all.

But to rage? Oh no.
Rage is the line we're *not* allowed to cross.

This policing isn't colorblind.

A white mother who raises her voice is "passionate" or "emotional."
A Black mother who expresses the same emotion is labeled "aggressive" or "dangerous."
A Latina mother is "spicy" or "hot-tempered."

The same anger that makes one woman "strong" makes another woman "unstable."

The cultural machinery/power structures that be or social order/patriarchy (call it what you want) it doesn't just want women to be quiet. It wants us quiet in very specific, "culturally approved" ways.

(Weak men and fragile systems can't stand a woman's rage or tears, because both demand presence and response - two things many of them are unwilling or incapable of giving.)

The Rage That Built the World

Women have always raged, and thank God for that.

We raged when our bodies were burned as witches for knowing too much about plants, birth, and healing.

We raged when our daughters were taken as child brides, when our sons were sent to wars we did not start, when our labor built nations while our names were erased from their monuments.

We raged against pulpits that silenced us, scriptures that diminished us, traditions that made obedience our only virtue.

We raged to get the vote, chaining ourselves to the White House fence, going on hunger strikes in prison, being force-fed through tubes because we refused to stay quiet.

We raged when our scientific, mathematic, or artistic discoveries were credited to male colleagues, when our contributions were erased from history books, when Rosalind Franklin's work on DNA structure was stolen and Nobel Prizes were handed to men.

We raged to be believed when we said "no," when we reported assault, when we demanded safety in a world that taught us to make ourselves smaller to avoid male violence.

We raged to open our own bank accounts, to sign our own leases, to control our own bodies. Rights that seem basic now but required fury to obtain.

We raged through perimenopause and menopause when our pain was dismissed as "hysteria," when our hormonal changes were weaponized against us, when we were called "crazy" for existing in aging female bodies - bodies that had finally outgrown the bullshit and weren't afraid to say it out loud.

We raged to enter medical schools, law schools, boardrooms, spaces where they said our brains were too small, our emotions too volatile, or our presence too disruptive.

We raged for equal pay and are still raging, because even today, we make 82 cents to every male dollar while doing more unpaid labor at home.

We raged when we worked two jobs, then came home to a third shift of unpaid labor.

We raged when they called us "bossy" for leadership, "shrill" for speaking up, "difficult" for having standards, "emotional" for caring deeply about our work.

We rage when doctors dismiss our pain, calling it anxiety, depression, or "just stress," while our bodies scream for care. We rage when medical studies are written on men's bodies and then applied to ours, when our heart attacks are misdiagnosed, when our endometriosis, autoimmune conditions, and postpartum suffering are ignored because medicine decided male biology was the default.

We rage when religion steals the language of our souls – when priestess becomes nun, when oracle becomes heretic, when wisdom becomes threat. We rage when our sacred gifts are erased, when the mystic is branded "madwoman," the healer "witch," the prophet "temptress." We rage when the church told us to serve men instead of Spirit, to sit quiet in the pews instead of speak the truths burning in our bones.

And mothers, in particular, have always raged.

You think pushing a child out of your body is *quiet?!*

You think splitting yourself open to bring life into the world is *soft?* There's nothing more primal, more guttural, more necessary than the scream of a woman giving birth.

That's rage.
That's power.
That's creation.

We rage in labor, then we're expected to smile by morning.
We rage silently as we nurse through cracked nipples and sleepless nights.
We rage when we fold the fiftieth load of laundry while our partners scroll their phones.
We rage when our needs are forgotten again, when we're touched out and time-starved and invisible.

We rage quietly - in our bedrooms, in parked cars, in texts to the friends we trust, in locked bathrooms while small fists pound the door.

And still, we're expected to do it all in silence.
To rage but only inside.
To see the root of the issues but never speak.
To cry but never confront.

And when we finally scream?
When we finally speak the truth?
We're told we're unstable.
Overwhelmed.
Hormonal.

Dangerous.
Ungrateful.
Emotional.

No. We're not dangerous! But we *are* exhausted from being emotionally gagged and mentally and physically depleted.

If men raged like women do (in birth, in mothering, in survival), they'd be called warriors.

But when we do it?

We're "too much"? Or our "instability" is a potential "danger" to our families?

Because heaven forbid our rage demand change, expose injustice, or insist that our needs and passions matter.

Why We're So Mad

We might be mad at our kids, our partners, or our families in general. But underlyingly, we're probably also mad at the culture that trapped us here. At the *ridiculous* weight we're expected to carry. And at how easy it is for everyone to fall apart on us while we're still expected to keep it together.

We're mad that we have been taught to be kind when we're being harmed or diminished.
To be understanding when we're being dismissed.
To be loving when we're being forgotten.

We're mad because, in one way or another, we've been groomed to disappear.
And now, finally, we're waking up.

Our rage isn't just personal.
It's generational.
It's cellular.

It's the accumulated fury of every woman who bit her tongue, every mother who suffered in silence, every grandmother who "kept the peace" at the cost of her own soul.

We're carrying the unexpressed rage of our lineage.
The women who couldn't speak.
The mothers who had no choice.

The grandmothers who endured what we're finally learning we don't have to accept.

This is why our anger feels so big, so overwhelming, and so much bigger than the immediate trigger.

Because it is.

It's not just about the dishes or the forgotten birthday or the way he sighs when you ask for help. It's about the silence forced on our mothers, and the dreams they buried so their families could eat.

It's about the inheritance of self-denial passed down like family heirlooms - and our refusal to pass it on. It's about centuries of women who couldn't say no, couldn't leave, couldn't find justice, and couldn't choose a life of their own or for themselves.

Your rage is an evolutionary gift.

It's your psyche's way of saying:
"Not anymore. Not on my watch. Not in my lifetime."

Overriding the Signal

There's greater risk in swallowing rage than in letting it move through you. When rage hits, your nervous system floods with stress hormones: cortisol, adrenaline, norepinephrine. Your heart rate spikes. Blood rushes to your muscles. Your body is priming you to respond to a threat.

This isn't "hysteria."
It's biology.
It's intelligence.

Your body is alerting you that something requires action or protection.

In the wild, animals know how to complete this stress cycle. A gazelle that outruns a lion will shake violently afterward to discharge the survival energy in its body. Birds fluff their feathers and release rapid, jerking movements after escaping danger. Even predators, after a chase, will pace or pant until their nervous system resets.

They let the body finish what it started.

But when you override that signal - when you smile through gritted teeth, change the subject, or swallow your words - those stress hormones don't just vanish, although it might feel like they do. They continue circulating, keeping your body in a prolonged state of stress activation. Over time, as mind–body research shows, this chronic suppression fuels inflammation, dysregulates your nervous system, and can manifest in physical illness.

Psychologist and physician Gabor Maté writes that when emotions are repressed in order to maintain attachment or avoid conflict, the body takes on the burden. What you won't allow yourself to feel or express still exists - but it becomes lodged in your physiology, shaping everything from immune function to hormonal balance.

Dr. John Sarno, author of *The Mindbody Prescription*, believed that at the root of many, if not most, chronic physical issues isn't sadness or grief, but unexpressed rage.

Many women learn this the hard way. They pride themselves on "managing" their anger, on never raising their voice - until one day, it all breaks through.

Maybe it's a Tuesday morning, when they find themselves screaming at their four-year-old over spilled cereal. That outburst isn't about the cereal. It's about the seventeen loads of laundry they've folded while their husband played video games. The birthday party they've planned alone. The years of absorbing micro-disrespect until their own needs became invisible, even to themselves.

That moment of "losing it" isn't a breakdown. It's the body's insistence on truth. It's the point where your nervous system stops cooperating with the self-erasure it's been asked to maintain.

Rage isn't hysteria. It's not an overreaction. It's the body's way of sounding the alarm, of saying *something is not right here*. In *The Gift of Fear*, Gavin de Becker writes:

"You have the gift of a brilliant internal guardian that stands ready to warn you of hazards."

That guardian often shows up as heat rising in the body, tears spilling over, a refusal to comply, or words sharper than we expected. Rage isn't the enemy – it's the evidence that our inner guardian is alive and doing its work.

De Becker also reminds us:

"Intuition is always right in at least two important ways; it is always in response to something, and it always has your best interest at heart."

This is the heart of the matter. Rage, like intuition, is always a response. It doesn't appear out of nowhere. It rises to protect, to point, to warn, and to keep us alive and whole. The turning point comes when we stop apologizing for it and start listening to it.

The body, as the saying goes, has been keeping score. And it's demanding you finally read it.

The Sacred Fire: Rage as Spiritual Practice

If *matrescence* is recognized as a developmental stage, then perhaps *rage* deserves recognition as a practice too.

Rage is the body's way of insisting on boundaries, truth, and change. Like prayer or meditation, it can be a sacred practice of alignment, as it tears away illusions, brings the hidden to the surface, and pulls us back to what matters.

The kind that births clarity.
The kind that burns through illusion and awakens truth.
The kind that liberates and reconnects you to your soul.

This world prefers mothers who are useful without being powerful. Who are soft without being fierce and present without disrupting the status quo. But a mother with access to her rage?

She can't be silenced.
Can't be stepped over.
She becomes un-ghosted.
She returns to herself.

This doesn't mean we glorify explosions. It means we stop demonizing honest heat. We find ways to feel it, move it, and speak from it without weaponizing it against those we love.

Strangely, the more I let myself feel rage all the way through, the more connected I become – to myself, and to other women who have had enough. Warranted rage roots me in my truth, my body, my yes, my no, and my voice.

Rage is the beginning of love with boundaries, clarity, and backbone. Rage makes space for justice. For you. For a different way of being a mother, one that includes you in the story.

Your rage is an evolutionary upgrade.
It's your consciousness evolving beyond what your grandmothers could imagine.
It's your DNA saying:

"We're done. We're not doing this anymore. We're changing the pattern."

The Sound of Your Life Force

Rage isn't the problem but silence and suppression are.

Your rage isn't only a reaction to what has been done to you. It's a signal that can stop harm before it takes root. It's the voice that says *"no"* before the damage piles up, before you're standing in the wreckage again.

Rage is the opposite of numbness. It's the sound of your life force returning, the crackle of your spirit remembering it's still here and there are things in your life that need to change. If you've been dulled, silenced, suppressed or invisible for too long, rage might be the first proof that you are waking up.

And yes, rage will ask you to grieve. To mourn the years you weren't protected. To acknowledge the moments you were erased. To face the reality that motherhood (and life) may not have been what you were promised. Grief might be the root system that feeds your fire.

For many of us, the hardest part of feeling rage is the fear that we'll lose love or belonging if we show it. But when you betray your own voice to keep the peace, you lose yourself. And no relationship is worth the cost of disappearing.

Your rage is also a mirror. It reflects what you value most - your dignity, your safety, your respect, your freedom, and your children's future. Even if you've been ignoring them and stuffing them away for some time. Pay attention to what it's protecting.

And don't try to carry it alone. Rage locked in isolation will turn inward and eat you alive. But rage witnessed by safe, understanding women (or men) becomes medicine. It transforms into collective clarity, into the courage to do something different.

Let it guide you and point you back to the center of who you are.
Because rage isn't the end.
It's a beginning.
And it starts with your sacred, necessary, life-giving rage.

The Sacred Permission to Rage

Remember when we said it's okay if the truth makes noise? This is where that noise becomes a roar.

Permission Granted:

It's okay to let your rage rise. To let it crack the walls you built to survive. To let it speak the truth you've been swallowing. To let it exist without justifying, fixing, or softening it first.

It's okay to feel rage toward people who needed you small so they could feel safe. It's okay to be angry at your partner for how much you carry. It's okay to rage at your mother for what she couldn't give you. It's okay to feel bitter about healing alone.

It's okay if love and fury are tangled together. It's okay to scream into your steering wheel, your pillow, the forest. It's okay to fantasize about disappearing just to breathe.

It's okay to feel rage at your children sometimes and still love them completely. It's okay if resentment doesn't disappear just because you understand its source. It's okay to feel rage about what was taken before you knew it was yours.

It's okay to want to break every rule that made you "good." It's okay to stop being grateful and start being honest. It's okay to stop forgiving people who haven't earned it. It's okay to grieve the woman you buried to be "enough."

It's okay if rage is your most honest voice some days. It's okay to protect your peace, even if it disappoints others. It's okay to stop fixing what you didn't break. It's okay to burn the "good mother" blueprint if it cost you your soul.

It's okay if rage was the first voice you recognized as your own.

Because rage isn't a flaw in your motherhood, or in you.
It's a signal from your soul that something needs to change.
It's your inner wisdom refusing to accept what your conditioning taught you to endure.

So rage.

Let them see you come back to center.
Let them witness a woman who feels deeply and chooses consciously.
Let them learn that anger can be sacred, that boundaries are loving, that a mother's full humanity is a gift to the world.

That's a greater gift than pretending you were never mad at all.

What About the Kids? Age-Appropriate Anger

Let's address the fear: "If I rage, I'll damage them."

But what's more damaging? Seeing your mother express anger honestly and honestly and healthily, or watching her silently erode under the weight of what she never said?

Children don't need perfection. They need reality. They need to see that anger can be felt without becoming violence. That truth can be voiced without destruction. And that rupture can lead to repair.

We can model anger in age-appropriate ways, giving our children language and tools they can grow with.

> **Ages 2-5**: "Mommy is feeling very angry right now. I need to let out that anger and then take some deep breaths and calm my body down."

> **Ages 6-10**: "I'm feeling really frustrated because I asked for help and didn't get it. I'm going to take a few minutes to figure out how to handle this."

> **Ages 11+**: "I'm angry, and that's okay. Anger tells us when something isn't working. I'm going to think about what needs to change."

The goal isn't to hide your humanity. It's to show them that big feelings are manageable, that adults can feel intensely and still choose their response, that anger can be a teacher rather than a destroyer.

Communicating Rage to Your Partner

Here's a script to help verbally express your rage:

> Instead of: "You never help me! I do everything around here!"
>
> Try: "I'm feeling overwhelmed and need us to redistribute some responsibilities. When I handle most of the household tasks alone, I feel unsupported and resentful. Can we talk about a more balanced approach?"
>
> Instead of: "You don't care about me!"
>
> Try: "When my needs aren't prioritized, I feel invisible and unimportant. I need us to make time for what matters to me too."
>
> Instead of: "Fine, I'll just do it myself!" (while seething)
>
> Try: "I'm feeling frustrated right now. I need to take a break before we continue this conversation so I can communicate clearly."

The key is learning to express anger from your needs rather than letting your unhealed wounds take over.

Rage often *does* come from those old wounds – that's not wrong. It's actually your body saying, *"enough, I can't carry this anymore."* The turning point is allowing that rage to surface and then translating it into a clearer expression of what you need in the present moment.

The Repair: What to Do After You've Raged

The repair is more important than perfection. Explosions will happen and sometimes the wounds spill out before we can catch them. What matters most is what comes next.

If you've raged at your kids, here's how to clean it up:

"I was feeling overwhelmed and I didn't handle it well. My big feelings aren't your fault. I'm sorry for raising my voice. Let's talk about what happened."

Don't over-apologize. Don't make them comfort you. Don't promise you'll never be angry again (because anger will come, and it's not something to erase).

What you're showing them is powerful: that adults can feel big emotions, mess up, and then take responsibility. You're modeling that rupture can be followed by repair, and that relationships can grow stronger through the honesty of that cycle.

When Rage Might Be Signaling Something Deeper

Sometimes rage is a symptom of something that needs professional support. If your anger feels:

- Completely out of proportion to triggers
- Impossible to control
- Followed by deep shame or self-harm thoughts
- Interfering with your ability to function
- Coupled with other symptoms like severe mood swings, sleep disruption, or thoughts of harming yourself or others

Please reach out to a therapist, counselor, or your doctor. Rage can be a sign of depression, anxiety, trauma, hormonal imbalances, brain inflammation or trauma, or other conditions that respond well to treatment.

Getting help is a healthy step. It's taking your anger seriously enough to understand what it's trying to tell you.

Fire Method

Sometimes we need more than permission to feel our rage - we need a way to work with it. So it can move through us in a way that keeps its wisdom intact. The goal isn't to "get rid" of your anger. It's to let it guide you without letting it consume you.

This is where the *FIRE Method* comes in - a simple framework for feeling, understanding, and channeling your rage so it becomes a force for clarity, boundaries, and change, rather than something that burns you from the inside out.

F – Feel It Fully Don't try to calm down immediately. Let the anger move through your body. Shake, stomp, scream into a pillow. (*Pillow Scream*) Put on music and shake your entire body for 3–5 minutes (*Shake-Out*).

I – Investigate the Source Ask: What boundary was crossed? What need was ignored? What value was violated? Your anger is pointing toward something important. Rage journaling can help here - write without censoring, burn it afterward if you want.

R – Respond, Don't React Take space before speaking. Drink water. Move your body. Let the intensity settle so you can speak from power, not explosion.

E – Express and Evolve Communicate your needs clearly. Set boundaries. Take action. Let your anger fuel change, not just release. This could mean a conversation, a new agreement, or even a ritual like a hot bath (*Boundary Bath*) to visualize letting go of what isn't yours.

Other Ways to Live With Sacred Rage

• Identify your rage triggers and look for patterns.
• Build a support network of women who understand the sacred nature of maternal anger.
• Model healthy anger for your children so they see that big feelings are human and manageable.
• Practice repair when needed, clean it up with accountability and love.

Your Truth to Anchor In
A declaration to hold onto

My rage is sacred.
It's the part of me that remembers what I deserve and refuses to forget.
It's the signal that something must change (and the fuel to make it so).
It awakens me to my truth and restores my power.
I am fully capable, and my voice is mine to use.

My wisdom can roar as fiercely as it can whisper.

I am safe in my expansion, steady in my strength.
My rage is rooted in love - love for myself, for what is just, and for what must endure.

And I trust myself to move through my rage.
To come away stronger, clearer, and guided by truer direction,
becoming the unshakable, embodied presence, I know is within myself.

Chapter 18

The Ghost in the Kitchen

The silent toll of carrying what no one else notices.

People say, "She doesn't work, she stays at home."
Or, "She's lucky she only works part-time."
Or, "At least you get to be with your kids."

And yet she's the first one up and the last one to bed, the one who never stops scanning, thinking, noticing, managing, preparing, absorbing, or tracking.

This isn't "just being a mom."
This is running a human ecosystem.

And far too often, beneath all of this invisible labor is the slow, quiet vanishing of the mother's full self. And we should dig into what this means for her and for those around her.

But first, let's honor and recognize that for some women, motherhood is the place they've felt most alive, most needed, or most in sync with their deepest sense of purpose.

They find joy in being the steady anchor, the trusted confidant, creating the warm home environment their children return to again and again. They feel seen and cherished in ways they never have before, their identity is deepened, their days are full of meaning and a love blossoms that roots itself into every corner of their being.

But for others, there's a quieter, heavier reality - a slow dissipation of self into something unnameable. Whether this is at the forefront of the experience or only a part of it, it's as if they stepped into motherhood and were pulled into a great nothing, a kind of oblivion that swallows their edges until all that remains is the outline of "Mom."

They are loved for what they give, but their personhood drifts into invisibility, unnoticed even by those they hold closest.

That's the cruel paradox: a mother can be everywhere and still *not* be *known*. She can appear in every photograph, sign every permission slip, fill every lunchbox, and still vanish in the eyes of the people she loves the most.

And when that happens, it's not just her life that's dimmed - it's the family's. What's left is a hollow space at the center of the home, a strange, quiet absence that most don't even recognize as loss.

She's visible but invisible.
Present but not fully known.
Loved but mostly for what she gives.
Remembered but not deeply seen.

Her body feeds everyone.
Her mind remembers everything.
Her hands are always full.
Her emotions stretch to hold the room together.
Her heart softens what might otherwise harden.
Her womb, her breasts, her cycles - all treated as though they exist only for others.
Her very being becomes the vessel through which everyone else is steadied, comforted, and sustained.

And yet ... who stops to ask, or care, or see who *she* really is?

The culture calls her "selfless." But selflessness, when demanded, when expected without at least some acknowledgement, becomes erasure. And that erasure becomes a void - one that lives in the children who grow up never really knowing their mother beyond what she did for them.

And as this carries on, mothers end up feeling like ghosts. Whispers, echoes, or shadows of who they really are, who they want to be, or who they can be.

The ghost in the kitchen, silently chopping vegetables while conversations swirl around her.

The ghost in the school pickup line, another face behind the wheel.

The ghost in the doctor's waiting room, holding a clipboard for someone else's appointment.

The ghost behind the shopping cart, mentally checking off a grocery list.

She's present everywhere, but recognized nowhere. She moves through the world unseen, except when needed.

Loving is Seeing

In relationships, we may often say "I love you" to one another. And it's a beautiful thing - something everyone should hear, say, and feel in their lifetime.

But over the years, I've come to believe there's something even more profound we can say to one another. And that phrase is: *I see you.*

"I love you" can be said out of habit or ritual - often without looking someone in the eyes. And often, without really feeling those words or meaning it as we say it.

But "I see you" is different. It calls for presence. It says: I'm paying attention to you, I see who you are. I see your potential. I see your struggles. I see your soul. I am present with you.

Humans are wired for this kind of recognition. Being seen is a lifeline for the mind, heart, and soul. It tells the nervous system it's safe to exist as you are. It validates your worth outside of output. It allows the soul to exhale. And it encourages one's essence to expand.

All living things respond to being noticed:

> Children thrive when being noticed.
> Plants grow faster and healthier when spoken to - or simply when a human is present.
> Flowers open wider when they're watered and tended.
> Abused animals, once withdrawn and skeletal, come back to life when they are seen, fed, and touched with kindness.
> Even the most cautious creature will step into the open when it feels observed without threat.

This is the nature of life:
We bloom when we are witnessed.

And the Universe itself blooms as it witnesses itself through others.

Some spiritual teachers teach that if the Universe were all that existed, with nothing to reflect back, it could never truly know itself. It learns, understands, and expands by witnessing itself through *our* lives, *our* expressions, *our* choices, *our* reactions, and *our* stories.

If that's how the Universe expands, is it possible that we also expand by witnessing one another?

So in the moment someone truly sees you, the Universe sees itself reflected back - it's a part of that vast conversation, and together you both say, *I exist. I matter. I am here.*

And in that seeing, even though it comes through someone else's eyes (and as you offer that same depth of seeing to others) you and the Universe awaken together - each more alive, and each more whole, simply because the other exists.

The Loneliest Room in the House

Ghosts are unseen but they are also untouched, unheard, and often alone.

And when a mother spends enough time fading into the background, that invisibility goes hand in hand feeling deep and continual with loneliness. A mother can be surrounded by people, even in the rooms where she's most needed, yet still feel profoundly alone.

There are many faces of maternal loneliness:

Sometimes it's not distance that hurts most - it's proximity without presence. It's lying in bed next to someone who once knew your deepest thoughts and feeling like you're living parallel lives in the same house.

The Physical Loneliness You crave touch that isn't a child pulling on you or a partner grabbing a quick kiss before rushing out the door. You're touched constantly - grabbed, climbed on, needed - but rarely in ways that feel nurturing to you. There's a difference between being a jungle gym and being held.

Your body becomes functional rather than sensual, a tool for meeting others' needs rather than a home for yourself. This physical loneliness is real and valid - your body deserves to feel cared for, not just used.

Friendship Erosion Some friends fall away because they don't understand your new rhythms. They stop inviting you out because you've said no too many times. Even friendships with other mothers can feel surface-level - conversations that circle around nap schedules and preschool waiting lists, as if the rest of who you are has been deemed irrelevant.

You find yourself standing at birthday parties making small talk about organic snacks while your soul craves the kind of conversation that sees you as more than a mother.

The Competence Trap If you do it all, people tend to stop asking if you need help. Because if you look like you're managing, they assume you're fine.

You work so hard to look like you have it together that you convince everyone you actually do. Sometimes the most capable mothers are the ones suffering most silently. And the loneliness of not being checked on - because you've always been the one doing the checking - cuts deep.

The Loneliness of Success When you're crushing it at work but still come home to manage dinner, bedtime routines, and weekend schedules, people see someone who "has it all figured out." They don't ask how you're doing, not really. Success becomes its own form of isolation. The better you get at juggling, the more people assume the juggling is effortless.

Anniversary Grief Your birthday comes and goes with little fanfare. Mother's Day feels more like another day of managing everyone else's needs. Your wedding anniversary gets forgotten entirely in the chaos of soccer practice and bedtime routines.

These moments illuminate how completely you've been absorbed into your function - how long it's been since anyone saw you as worthy of acknowledgment beyond what you provide.

The Loneliness of Decision Fatigue You decide everything:

What's for dinner. Which activities to sign up for. How to handle the tantrum. Whether the fever is high enough for the doctor.

A thousand tiny decisions every day, and somehow they all land on you. When you try to share the decision-making, you're often met with "Whatever you think is best" or "You're better at this stuff."

So you carry it all. The mental load. The constant vigilance. The weight of being responsible for everyone else's wellbeing. And the loneliness of being the only one who truly understands what it takes to keep everything running becomes its own quiet emergency.

Seen as the center of the home, yet rarely seen as herself, she becomes the one who holds it all while remaining untouched.

But loneliness can soften when you create connection in ways that nourish you - before you ever wait for someone else to give it.

This can mean reaching out to a friend instead of waiting for the call, joining spaces where women speak openly and deeply, or simply letting someone in on the truth of how you're feeling.

Loneliness is not so much about the absence of people as it is more about the absence of being known. And the fastest way to feel known is to risk showing yourself again. Maybe not to everyone at once, but enough to feel the warmth of recognition, even if it's just from one trusted soul.

Because every time you let yourself be real in the presence of another, the loneliness of being a ghost loses its grip, and the human in you can step forward again.

The Ghost of Being "Fine"

Motherhood comes with an unspoken script: Be grateful. Beam with joy. Glow with fulfillment. Say "I'm fine" when asked - even when your chest feels hollow.

And the cherry on top? Somewhere in your mind you might believe that, because you wanted children, you forfeited the right to struggle.

So you perform.

You smile at school pickup while dying inside.
You nod enthusiastically during parent meetings while feeling completely empty.
You shrug and say, "It's busy, but good," when inside you're unraveling.
You laugh and say, "It's nothing," when it's actually everything.
You brush it off with, "I'll be okay," when what you need most is for someone else to hold you.
But inside, you ache to be seen. To say, "I'm not okay," and have it matter.

You know the story of Tinkerbell - how every time someone says, *"I don't believe in fairies,"* a fairy dies? In the same way, every time a mother swallows her truth and says, *"I'm fine,"* a little more of her disappears, until only a ghost remains where a woman once stood.

Here's what should be occurring in motherhood:

A mother who refuses to vanish in service of everyone else's comfort.
A mother who allows herself to be her full, unique self.
A mother who doesn't stay a ghost with every, "I'm just fine."
A mother who lets her emotions be felt instead of hidden.
A mother who isn't just known for what she gives, but for who she is.
A mother who reaches for friendship instead of waiting to be chosen.
A mother who dares to be witnessed in her rawness, not just her resilience.
A mother who shows up for herself the way she shows up for everyone else.
A mother who has opinions, dreams, boundaries, and bad days.

Being this kind of mother is healing.

Being this kind of mother is the antidote to the loneliness of disappearing.

There Is Memory in Your Bones

Keep in mind, mothers weren't always alone in this.

Archaeological evidence shows that for millennia, child-rearing was a community effort. Children had multiple caregivers, mothers supported each other through shared domestic labor, knowledge was passed down through generations of women who understood that survival meant interdependence, not isolation.

The nuclear family, the isolated suburban home, the myth of the self-sufficient mother - these are historical aberrations, not natural law.

But some women are already remembering (and rewriting). They're creating new forms of chosen family, sharing childcare cooperatives, demanding partners become true co-parents not helpful assistants.

They're speaking honestly about the cost of invisibility, modeling for their children what it looks like when a mother takes up space.

They're reclaiming rest as resistance, boundaries as basic human rights, and their own needs as worthy of consideration.

There's an ancestral memory humming beneath the exhaustion - a rhythm of community, reciprocity, and recognition.

It remembers that mothers were once seen as powerful, that their work was valued, that their wellbeing mattered not just for what they could give others but for who they were themselves.

That rhythm is calling us home.

The Day I Chose to Live

Many years ago, I found myself in a place so miserable that every day was a running loop of thoughts about how wrong my life was. I was deeply unhappy, and the weight of that unhappiness began to pull my body down with it.

My health crumbled. My energy vanished. I could barely get out of bed.

One of those times, I was sitting on the couch in my bedroom, resting from the daily deep fatigue, when a clear question came into my mind:

Do you want to live?

I froze. The question was so stark, so matter-of-fact, that I didn't know how to answer. Again, it came:

Do you want to live?

I had to think about it. (That's how far gone I was.) Finally, I answered silently, *Well... my daughter would be sad if I died. So yes, I want to live.*

The moment I said it, my heart began to pound hard in my chest, and a deeper, heavier fatigue than I'd ever felt swept over me. My body felt like a log. I crawled into bed and couldn't move. That's when I felt something dark surrounding me - something that seemed angry that I had chosen life.

I demanded it to leave. And within seconds, it was gone.

From that day forward, I began to heal. I began to slowly climb out of the pit I had been in.

I chose to live. The universe responded. And my life began to shift.

Years after, I became a holistic health practitioner. I began teaching classes and seminars throughout the western U.S., wrote books, created products, and pulled our family out of our financial struggles. The momentum that followed that choice was undeniable - it was as if the entire universe had been waiting for me to say *yes*.

Whatever that presence was (the voice that asked if I wanted to live) what I know is this:

The universe responds to our choice to exist. It responds to our wanting to truly live and being okay with taking up space and creating a life that we're excited to live.

Do you want health and vibrancy? It begins to align toward that.
Do you want dance and music? It brings us closer to it.
Do you want friends and connection? It supports that path.
Do you want adventure and wonder? It clears a path for us to find it.
Do you want purpose and meaning? It aligns the next right thing in front of us.

I've learned that whatever efforts we pour into our desires, the universe meets and magnifies - in its own gentle, synchronistic way.

And wherever we stand, in fullness (or in absence), the Universe meets us there and begins to move with us.

Choosing to Reappear

Every return begins with a choice to inhabit your own life. The more you root into yourself, the more the world turns its gaze toward you. It starts with a single spark of awareness - a decision to be here, fully.

From that spark, your presence grows, and others feel it too. Seeing yourself is the first act of coming home. From there, the path back into connection will unfold with quiet certainty.

Once you see this ghostness for what it is, the answer isn't to demand that everyone suddenly notice you. (That only puts your worth back in someone else's hands.)

The beginning of your return starts courageously with you.

- Recognize the ways you've faded from your own life - where you've stopped speaking up, stopped expecting to be included, stopped showing yourself fully.
- Notice the places you feel most unseen, and then start by seeing yourself there.
- Honor your needs in your own eyes first. From that grounded place, you can respectfully and clearly ask to be seen in the moments that matter most to you.

When you choose to shift from being a ghost to being a solid form that takes up space and has an effect on things around them, things shift.

You speak differently.
You take up space differently.
You stop apologizing for the ripple you create and the shifts your presence brings.

And that change, however small at first, is contagious - it invites the people around you to see you as you are, not just as the role you play.

The moment you refuse invisibility, you begin to reappear.

Your Truth to Anchor In
A declaration to hold onto

I am not invisible.
My labor is real, sacred, and costly.
I am not just the container - I am the core.
I deserve acknowledgement, rest, and support.
I am allowed to be seen.
I am allowed to be held.

I am allowed to live inside a system that values me - not just what I give.
I matter.

And I remember now:

The weight of this life was never meant to be carried alone.

I am not a ghost.
I am not a function.
I am not a shadow behind the scenes.
I am real.
I am whole.
I am here.

My children deserve to know me - not just my giving, but my being.
My family deserves a mother who lives fully.
And I deserve to be seen.

I will not vanish.
I will not be forgotten.
I am the story, not just the support.
And I am showing up now - in full.

(The more gently we listen to what our soul needs to say, the more clearly we hear
what our loneliness is asking us to reclaim.)

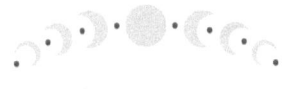

Chapter 19

Grief in the Motherhood Journey

How grief lives beside love in every stage of motherhood.

Grief in motherhood often slips quietly into the spaces between moments, showing up in phases and seasons we didn't expect.

It can appear while folding impossibly small onesies that no longer fit, or in the instant you watch your teen walk away without a backward glance. It can settle in on an ordinary Tuesday, when you're driving alone and suddenly remember the weight of your child asleep against your chest.

Grief in motherhood is often in the shadow that love casts - the ache that lives beside joy. Grief proves how deeply we love. To grieve fully is to honor both the person or thing lost and how those losses affect your soul.

When we begin to notice where grief quietly resides in our motherhood story, we can move through it with greater ease, make the changes we need, and return to ourselves with more empathy and compassion.

Not all of the moments we'll name in this chapter are purely sorrowful. Many (like birthdays, anniversaries, graduations) can carry both joy and ache in the same breath. But when we notice the grief woven into those moments, it no longer weighs us down in silence - we're better able to release it and allow it to move through us, softening us as it goes.

This chapter is written to reveal the quiet griefs that accompany motherhood and to honor what slips away, even as new life unfolds.

Cultural Landscapes of Maternal Grief

The grief of motherhood coincides with the societies we mother within, the histories we inherit, and the expectations placed upon us.

In America, motherhood operates under the myth of self-sufficiency - we may aim for being the strong mother who does it all without complaint, who bounces back, and who always puts her children first.

Our grief may tend to hide behind closed doors because we think that being a competent and successful mother means making it look effortless.

Every culture carries its own version of maternal grief, shaped by history, expectation, and survival. The experience of grief in motherhood looks different across the world, yet its ache is universal.

In some Korean families, maternal sacrifice is expected - sometimes even celebrated. Grandmothers may wear their selflessness like a badge of honor, boasting of never having taken a day for themselves. For modern mothers navigating different values, the grief of lost freedom can feel like failing an unspoken generational test.

For many Black mothers in America, grief might be compounded by the need to prepare their children for a world that may not protect them. The heartbreak of explaining why a child can't play freely, why a toy can be seen as a threat, marks a premature end to innocence that should have lasted longer.

Indigenous mothers carry centuries of family separation. From boarding schools to modern foster care systems that remove Native children at disproportionate rates. Their grief exists within historical wounds still unhealed.

Immigrant mothers grieve across languages and borders. Many immigrant parents know their children will never fully know their homeland, their language, the context that shaped their mother's life before them.

Religious communities often provide support through motherhood transitions but can also silence certain griefs - the grief of unwanted pregnancy, of questioning traditional family structures, of desiring identities beyond motherhood.

In wealthy nations, modern mothers parent with unprecedented isolation - without the villages, extended families, and communal childcare that humans evolved alongside. We grieve connections we never had.

The pandemic generation of mothers carries unique grief - of milestones missed, of support systems dissolved, of parenting under extraordinary pressure while the world expected ordinary results.

And then there may be the quiet grief for a village that never was...

So many mothers carry a longing for elders who could have held them, for a circle of women who would have cooked for them, rocked their babies, tended to their torn body, witnessed their tears without judgment.

This is an ancestral grief. An echo of something our bones and hearts remember even when our modern lives have forgotten all about it.

It's okay to mourn the village you didn't have. It means you know you were never meant to do this alone.

When you feel grief in motherhood, you're touching the same aches that mothers before you felt, and that mothers beside you still carry.

These experiences of grief unite us, as a shared thread across time and culture, reminding us that what has passed mattered, and that what is here matters too. It's to stand in the paradox of love, knowing that even joy carries loss within it.

And if we let it, this grief shapes us into more tender beings, teaching us how to pause, how to honor, and how to live more fully in the moments that remain.

The Threshold Crossing

For some, grief first appears in that liminal space - the crossing from woman to mother, when the door to your former self closes with a soft, irrevocable click.

In the early weeks postpartum, mothers may find themselves staring into mirrors that reflect someone both familiar and foreign. The body (mapped with new geography) can feel like a place they no longer fully inhabit. The grief isn't just about clothing that no longer fits, but about the woman who once wore it - the one who slept through the night and answered to her own needs.

Some mothers speak of missing their minds - the sharpness, the focus, the identity tied to work or creativity. When every conversation revolves around feeding schedules and diaper brands, the sense of intellectual loss can be profound.

For some mothers, pregnancy itself becomes a place of unexpected belonging - their bodies finally making sense in a new way. When birth empties them, they feel a peculiar hollowness alongside their joy. One mother described it as "missing someone who now sleeps beside me."

Others carry the jagged edges of birth trauma - promises of empowerment shattered by emergency interventions, bodies opened without consent, pain dismissed by those meant to witness it. They arrive at motherhood already wounded, already grieving a beginning they cannot rewrite.

Your body bears witness.
The cesarean scar that still pulls when you laugh too hard.
The pelvic floor that betrays you when you run.
The breasts that changed their purpose, then changed again.

These losses matter.
And they deserve to be named.

The Fog of Early Days

In early motherhood, grief often shows up as exhaustion, irritability, or the vague sense that you're drowning while everyone tells you how blessed you are.

There's the grief of the breastfeeding relationship you envisioned - intimate, intuitive, natural - replaced by cracked nipples, milk that won't come, or a baby who screams at your breast. The grief when your body fails to perform its supposed most natural function. The grief when you realize how much of motherhood might be like this - expectations colliding with a messier reality.

"I pump in my car between meetings."
"Sometimes I forget who I'm doing this for anymore."

There's grief in the marriage bed gone cold, in conversations reduced to logistics. In partners who cannot fathom the weight you carry, even as they try. In friendships that fade when your availability does.

Many mothers described the same surreal experience: standing in a crowded room, baby on hip, utterly alone. Wondering if anyone would notice if they simply disappeared.

This isn't about not loving your child. It's about loving yourself too, and recognizing what's been lost in the merger.

The Middle Distance

When children grow, their independence arrives in heartbreaking increments.

You grieve the last time they reach for your hand crossing the street - a moment you don't recognize until it's already passed. The way they once mispronounced "spaghetti" that you can't quite remember anymore. How they needed you, completely and without question.

A mother may find her son's baby blanket, threadbare and forgotten at the back of his closet. She might find herself sitting on the floor sobbing because she can't remember his baby smell anymore.

During these years, a reckoning of sorts may emerge:
The realization that you've become your own mother in ways that horrify you.
The understanding that some damage can't be undone.
The recognition of time wasted on worry, on phones, on absence.
The realization that you haven't been as present in special moments as you know you could or should have been - or wish you had been.

This is also when buried dreams begin to surface, bobbing up like messages in bottles. The degree never finished or the book never written or the career path abandoned.

This grief tastes like regret. And regret can be proof of desires that didn't die.

It's a reminder that those desires, and others like them, aren't dead. They wait with the patience of roots, certain their season of bloom will come.

And they'll remain tethered to you because they were always meant to be lived.

Adolescent Rehearsals

Adolescence can bring its own grief, the slow untethering that must happen for health but hurts nonetheless. Rehearsals that come in bits and pieces of them practicing leaving you so that one day they'll be able to do so.

Adolescence is the slow, often painful cutting of the cord. It's nature's insistence that to grow is to part, even when the heart resists. It's necessary, but never easy. Both mother and child must learn to breathe on their own.

As a mother we might watch our teenage daughter across a crowded school event - laughing, vibrant, completely herself. And realize that she didn't even look at us. It made us feel like a ghost. Proud yet heartbroken all at once.

There's grief when values diverge.
When the child you raised questions everything you taught them.
When they adopt beliefs that feel foreign or even threatening to you.

There's grief in realizing the bedtime rituals, the little traditions, have quietly ended.
There's grief in watching them hurt and being unable to fix it.
There's grief in loving someone who is pulling away.
There's grief in the shift from being the center of their world to being the background.
There's grief in recognizing that your love can no longer shield them from consequence.
There's grief in being both their home and their obstacle.
There's grief in wishing you had done things differently.
And there's grief in realizing the very best outcome of mothering is to be let go of.

This separation isn't the *undoing* of love, but its ultimate expression.

The Empty Rooms

When children leave home, silence becomes the new norm.

You may grieve routines that structured decades - the morning rush, the afternoon chaos, the evening check-ins. The refrigerator that stays full. The laundry hamper that doesn't overflow. The knowledge that your primary job (the one that defined your adulthood) has fundamentally changed.

As an empty-nester, we might keep waiting to feel free. But instead, we may feel haunted and hear phantom footsteps on the stairs.

Some children move across the world.
Some struggle with addiction or mental illness.
Some simply build lives that have little space for regular connection.

And some become parents themselves, transforming you into a witness rather than a protagonist. There's grief in watching your daughter become a mother and seeing her face the same struggles, in wanting to protect her, in realizing you cannot. In understanding that your grandchild will never know you as you were in your prime.

This grief accumulates. It has history. Weight.

The Unspeakable Losses

Some grief in motherhood is treated as unspeakable.

The miscarriage you're told to forget because "at least it was early." The stillbirth that makes others uncomfortable when you mention your child's name. The infant who lived briefly but changed you permanently.

There's the particular grief of raising a child with serious illness or disability - where the future holds more fear, more fight, and more exhaustion than you ever prepared for or effort you thought you'd have to give.

There's the grief of single motherhood - of doing everything, witnessing everything, deciding everything alone. Of having no one to turn to at the end of a hard day and say, "Did you see what she did? Isn't she amazing?"

There's the grief in non-traditional family structures - adoptive mothers who navigate the complex emotions of loving a child born to someone else, stepmothers who pour love into relationships that lack cultural scripts, non-binary parents who parent without models to follow, grandmothers raising grandchildren in their retirement years. Each carries unique losses alongside their fierce love.

When you adopt a child, there can be grief for the pregnancy you never carried, the familiar features you won't find mirrored in their face. There can be grief for the bond that came before you - grief for their first mother, for what she lost so you could gain. Your joy and her pain can feel forever linked, a complicated knot of love and loss you hold together for the child you share.

There's the wrenching grief of mothers separated from children by incarceration, deportation, foster care, or family court decisions. Mothers who parent through plexiglass or across borders. Mothers who aren't allowed to mother at all.

And there's the impossible grief of living without a child who has died - breathing, functioning, continuing in a world that no longer contains them.

These griefs are sacred. They often can't be fixed or rationalized away. But they can be witnessed.

Grief means you're paying attention to what matters.
It means you're loving with your whole self.
It means you're alive to the terrible beauty of watching someone exist beyond you.

Motherhood contains everything - devastating loss and unbearable beauty, often tangled together in the very same breath. You are allowed your grief, just as you are allowed your joy. You are allowed to live the story of both.

Motherhood will always carry the possibility of grief. It's the risk we take (often without realizing) when we open ourselves to love this deeply.

Honoring Your Grief

If you've recognized yourself in these pages, here are gentle ways to acknowledge and move with your grief:

Name it specifically. Instead of "I'm struggling," try "I'm grieving my pre-motherhood confidence" or "I'm grieving the toddler years ending." Precision helps process emotion.

Find witness. Share your grief with someone who can hold it without trying to fix it - a friend, a therapist, a partner, a journal. Being seen in our pain lessens its weight.

Create small rituals. Light a candle on the anniversary of a loss. Write a letter to your pre-mother self. Plant something that will grow as your grief changes form.

Look for the both/and. Practice noticing when grief and gratitude coexist: "I'm heartbroken my teenager doesn't need my help **and** I'm proud of their independence."

Connect with others who understand. Find spaces (online or in person) where particular maternal griefs are normalized. Postpartum support groups. Special needs parent networks. Bereavement circles. Communities for mothers estranged from adult children.

Give yourself permission to change. Sometimes honoring grief means making changes - seeking more support, adjusting expectations, reconnecting with parts of yourself that motherhood has overshadowed.

Resist toxic positivity. When someone tries to silver-line your loss ("At least you have other children," "At least you had the time you did"), gently redirect: "I know you're trying to help, but right now I just need you to listen."

Remember that grief transforms. It doesn't disappear, but it changes shape. The sharp edges soften. The heaviness lifts, even if it never fully leaves. You build the capacity to carry it.

Your grief deepens your love.
It makes you more human.
More whole.
More real.

When you honor this grief, you help heal yourself and you also lay down a gentler inheritance for every mother who comes after you.

—————— ›)◯(‹ ——————

Your Truth to Anchor In
A declaration to hold onto

My grief is the evidence of love stretched across time.
It's the echo of what mattered, the imprint of what I held.
I am whole enough to carry it.

I honor what has ended, what has changed, and what I cannot return to.
I honor the child I was,
the mother I became,
and the woman I am still becoming.

I do not rush my grief.
I let it breathe, I let it teach, and I let it soften me.

I carry both love and loss in my hands.
Both are teachers.
Both belong.

Chapter 20

The Unmothered Mother

*Loving your child when you're still healing
yourself.*

To mother without having been mothered is to raise a child while carrying an old wound inside you. You learn love by offering it, even as part of you is still searching for it. You are both nurturer and a neglected child, giving away what you, yourself, are still hungry for.

It may linger in you like an unfinished sentence - this constant act of giving what you needed and of being both the hand that reaches and the hand that was never held.

You are the mother with no map, walking into territory your own mother never showed you, creating something to the best of your ability from the raw materials of your own unhealed places.

The unfinished story of your own mothering rose to the surface the moment you became a mother yourself.

Because how do you mother when you weren't mothered?
How do you offer what you never received?
And how do you break cycles that you're still trapped in?

The Cycle Breaker's Burden

The unmothered mother carries the weight and learning curve of being the first.

The first to say, *"I was wrong. I'm sorry."*
The first to kneel down and meet your child's eyes instead of towering above them.
The first to pause when anger rises, choosing words over wounds.
The first to notice when silence has become a shield and gently ask, *"What's really going on?"*
The first to celebrate emotions instead of shaming them.

The first to put language to needs no one once named for you.
The first to protect boundaries you were never taught to have.
The first to offer safety instead of fear, tenderness instead of withdrawal.
The first to tell the truth, even when the truth is heavy.
The first to stop pretending and begin healing.

This makes you a revolutionary, though it probably rarely feels heroic. Most days it might feel disorienting or lonely. You're writing a new story for your family line, after all, and you're writing it without knowing how it ends and without being able to flip ahead to see if you're getting it right.

You are mothering in two directions at once - forward into your children, and backward into the girl you once were.

Each act of love you offer them also whispers back through time: *you deserved this too.* And the effort you put into this work, is how the wound becomes a doorway, backward, offering healing to the girl you once were, and forward, opening a freer world for the children you now raise.

Parenting from an Empty Well

Some mornings you might wake up and wonder how you're supposed to give patience when you're running on three hours of sleep and a lifetime of feeling misunderstood.

How do you offer emotional availability when you're still learning what that even means?

And how do you create safety when your own childhood was anything but safe, when the wounds you carry still ache for healing?

You find yourself researching things that seem like they should come naturally - how to comfort a crying child, what healthy boundaries look like, how to have difficult conversations. You study parenting like you're cramming for an exam, trying to learn instincts that other mothers seem to have been born with.

The cup feels perpetually half-empty, and yet somehow you keep pouring.Love stretches further than you thought possible.You discover reserves you didn't know you had, finding ways to show up even when showing up feels impossible. You learn that sometimes *good enough* really is good enough, that love can cover a multitude of imperfect moments.

But exhaustion is inevitable.

Reparenting yourself while parenting others is like trying to build a house while living in it, trying to heal while using the wounded parts of yourself to care for someone else.

The Inner Child at the Playground

Your three-year-old throws herself into your arms after a tumble, and something inside you crumbles. The automatic comfort you give her, the way you stroke her hair and whisper "you're okay, mama's here", these are words your inner child has been waiting decades to hear.

Every developmental stage your child passes through becomes a mirror, reflecting back what you experienced at that age.

When she's five and afraid of the dark,
you remember being five and having no one come when you called.

When she's eight and needs help with homework,
you recall being eight and figuring everything out alone.

Sometimes you overcompensate,
pouring all your unmet needs into meeting hers.

Sometimes you freeze,
unsure how to respond to needs you were never allowed to have.

You might find yourself learning alongside her-how to ask for comfort,
how to express feelings,
how to trust that love isn't conditional on being perfect.

Watching your child receive what you never had is both healing and heartbreaking. It's proof that this kind of love was always possible, and was always what you deserved.

But it can also be a reminder of what was missing and what can never be recovered.

Hypervigilance vs. Neglect

You might swing between extremes like a pendulum that can't find its center.

One day you're helicopter-hovering, watching for every potential danger - because you know too well how much can go wrong when no one is watching.

The next day, you catch yourself spacing out during a story she's telling, realizing you've inherited some of the emotional unavailability you swore you'd never pass on.

You know what it feels like to be overlooked, so you're determined never to overlook her. But you also know what it feels like to have your every move monitored, so you're terrified of being too much, too present, too involved.

Finding the middle ground requires constant recalibration. You're learning to trust your instincts, while questioning whether your instincts are wisdom or wounds.

You're discovering that hypervigilance disguised as love can be just as damaging as neglect - that healthy attention looks different from anxious attention.

And learning to live in that tender in-between,
not too close,
not too far,
is a quiet act of healing you practice every day.

The Motherless Mother's Compass

Your internal compass may spin wildly some days, the needle unable to find true north. How do you trust your parenting instincts when your foundation feels shaky? How do you distinguish between intuitive responses and trauma responses?

You question everything.
Is this boundary too rigid or too loose?
Is this comfort or enabling?
Is this protection or projection?

You second-guess decisions that other mothers make without thinking, because you don't have that deep well of being well-mothered to draw from.

But slowly, carefully, you can learn to calibrate your own compass.

You can notice when your reactions come from fear versus love.

You can begin to recognize the difference between your child's needs and your own unmet needs.

And you can start trusting the voice that speaks from your heart rather than your wounds.

As time passes, the compass finds its true north not in the perfection of your responses, but in the consistency of your love, the reliability of your presence, the safety of your arms.

Creating Traditions from Scratch

There might not be any family recipes passed down, no "this is how we've always done special occasions" traditions to lean on. You're inventing everything from scratch - birthday rituals, holiday celebrations, even small daily rhythms that make a house feel like home.

This creative work is exhausting and exhilarating. You research how other families celebrate, you Pinterest holiday crafts, you wonder if homemade cookies or store-bought ones will make better memories. You're building culture where there was chaos, creating meaning where there was emptiness.

Some experiments fail spectacularly.
Some traditions you create feel forced or hollow.

But some stick, becoming the golden threads that weave your family's story together.

Your children may not know how much intention went into creating what feels natural to them, how much love was poured into building what they'll simply call "how we've always done things."

Grieving While Growing

Here's what might be at the core of what you're experiencing and carrying:

You are simultaneously living in two timelines - creating your child's childhood while processing your own.

Give yourself credit.
See it for what it is,
and give yourself generous grace.
You're carrying a lot.

This dual existence can be overwhelming, beautiful, and disorienting all at once.

While you're planning birthday parties, you're grieving the birthdays when you felt forgotten. While you're reading bedtime stories, you're mourning the nights you fell asleep alone and scared. While you're cheering at school plays, you're healing the part of you that performed for empty seats.

You're both the wounded child and the healing parent, existing in the same body, in the same moment. When your daughter needs comfort, you comfort her - and in doing so, you're also comforting the little girl you used to be. When you set loving boundaries, you're parenting both forward and backward through time.

This dual role can blur lines in confusing ways. Sometimes you have to parent your inner child before you can parent your actual child. And that's okay.

Sometimes your child's needs trigger your own unmet needs so intensely that you have to step away and tend to yourself first. That's okay too.

Learning to hold both, the healing you need and the love you're giving, without letting them collapse into each other is delicate work.

It requires recognizing when your inner child is driving the parenting car, when your own needs are masquerading as your child's needs.

However different these moments may be, keep in mind that this timeline collision creates unique opportunities for healing. Every tender moment you give your child also tends to the wounded child within you.

Every "I love you" you whisper into their hair also reaches the little girl who waited so long to hear those words.

But it may also create emotional overwhelm.
Some days the overwhelm from this collision may feel bigger than the gratitude. Some days the weight of healing yourself while raising another human may feel impossible to carry.

Learning to Give

Whether you realize it or not, you are rewriting the blueprint for what it means to be a mother - one imperfect, love-soaked day at a time.

You're healing generational wounds while gently unraveling generational patterns.

You're offering your children what you never had, while slowly learning to give yourself what you've always deserved.

The path is unmarked.
The map unwritten.
But your love is the compass
that charts new ground.

Your children may never fully know the courage, effort, and quiet sacrifice it took to love them the way you do - but they will know they were loved.

And that knowing will echo through generations.

The canvas is blank.
You get to create this messy masterpiece.
And the fact that you're trying...

That's everything.

Your Truth to Anchor In
A declaration to hold onto

I am the first of my line to do it differently.
I am the mother I never had.
I am allowed to grieve,
to admit what I never had,
and I am allowed to grow.
Even without a map, I find my way.

My love is a compass - steady, imperfect, true.
I am deeply worthy of the care I offer others.
I am building something from the ground up:
the miracle of a cycle broken,
a story rewritten,
the quiet work that reshapes a lineage.

Even on the hard days, I am whole.
Even with my wounds, I am radiant.
Even without a model, I am a mother.

And I am doing sacred work.

PART THREE

The Rise
of the Human Mother

Intro to The Rise of the Human Mother

The Wisdom That Lies Deep Within

The first two sections of this book have been an unearthing - a slow, deliberate digging through the layers modern motherhood has piled on top of us. We've uncovered how the role has been twisted into a performance, a dumping ground, a scapegoat, a machine, a martyr, even a ghost in her own life - expected to give endlessly while erasing herself in the process.

We've stripped away the myths, spoken the truths that are rarely mentioned, and brought to light the unspoken legacies that have been shaping women's lives across generations.

What we need now is vision - something that carries us beyond survival and dares us to imagine what thriving could truly mean. To trust that we were made for more than survival.

To reimagine motherhood is to reimagine the world - because the health of one shapes the future of all.

In this final section of the book, we begin the work of rising - as women in our own right, carrying forward what is finally ours again.

The Rise of the Human Mother is about reclaiming what has been lost or skewed:

Whether it be our voices.
Our needs.
Our desires.
Our boundaries.
Our future.
Our no.
Our freedom.
Or our place in the world.

And it's about remembering that we are not only mothers, but whole human beings - worthy of being known, held, and honored in our entirety.

It's also about reimagining the structure around us so we stop expecting mothers to carry it all alone. These chapters explore how we can change the culture in our homes, our communities, and our internal narratives so that motherhood no longer means self-abandonment.

This part of the book is both personal and collective. It invites you to explore what it looks like to live as a mother who is allowed to be fully human - and how that shift ripples out into our families, systems, and future generations.

Remember, in ancestral and Indigenous cultures around the world, the needs of mothers weren't seen as burdens - they were seen as community priorities. The mother wasn't left to figure it out alone, juggling invisible, endless work in the background while smiling on the surface.

She was *held*.

By sisters, by elders, by rituals, by structure. There were postpartum ceremonies that lasted 30–40 days or more, where the mother was nourished, massaged, fed, and protected so her energy could return and her role could integrate.

There were aunties and grandmothers who tended to the children because mothering was collective, not isolated.

Even outside of the postpartum window, the mother's well-being was woven into the health of the tribe. Because everyone knew: If the mother falls, the whole system weakens. So they made sure she *didn't fall*.

And here we are now - having spent so much time being isolated, exhausted, alone, repeatedly feeling like we failed, pretending we're fine with how society portrays mothers and women in general and often not realizing that there's a different and better way.

Praising the woman who can "do it all" instead of wondering why the hell she's expected to.

Western culture erased the circle around the mother and replaced it with a pressure cooker. And we wonder why she's cracking.

Mothers were *never meant* to carry this much alone.

There are better ways to do what we're doing now.

Although we don't live in villages anymore, we can still remember what worked in the past and we can use the tools, voices, skills, and access we have now to build something better. Something rooted in wisdom and shaped for a more evolved world.

With circles that hold the mother at the heart of it all.

She Belonged to the Circle - A Glimpse Into the Past

She mothered within a web of care.
They wrapped her in warmth and reverence.
Laid herbs on her womb with knowing hands.
Fed her with recipes passed down through blood and bone.

She wept-
and three women came.
To witness her becoming a mother.

Her child was a gift shared.
Her fatigue was honored.
Her needs were tended to like sacred flame.

She stood at the center of the village,
as the pulse.
She was held as she birthed.
She was honored, observed, and cared for as she mothered.

She never mothered alone.
The village carried the children together.
And everyone remained whole.

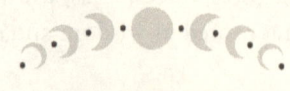

Chapter 21

Let Me Be Seen

*Embracing integration to rise as your whole,
human self.*

There's a phase in every garden when what has been dormant beneath the soil finally breaks through. It's finally gathered enough strength to push against the darkness and to have enough strength and perseverance to crack open the earth above it and to reach toward light.

This is a gentle emergence yet it's laced with urgency. It's a necessary birth, born of an inner knowing that to remain hidden is to wither and emergence is the only way into a life that is awake and vibrant with the fullness of who you are capable of becoming.

Life longs to be seen.
Living things thrive when they're recognized.
Aliveness deepens when it is witnessed.

Plants lean into more than water and soil - they respond to voice, to touch, to the energy of care.

Children bloom under attention, their very cells respond to the quality of the gaze that meets them.

Animals in the wild understand this too - they know the difference between being hunted and being truly seen, between being feared and being respected for what they are.

Even in the quantum realm, observation changes everything. Particles exist in states of infinite possibility until the moment they are witnessed - then they collapse into reality, taking their place in the world.

What if this is true for you as well?

What if your dreams, your fullness, the very potential of who you are have been living in a state of possibility – waiting for the moment you finally allow yourself to be seen?

You have spent years, perhaps decades, performing versions of motherhood that felt hollow, living according to scripts written by others, rejecting piece after piece of who you really are until it got to the point where you became a stranger, an unrecognizable shadow, to yourself.

This self-rejection, we should understand, takes many forms. Sometimes it's dramatic - the abandonment of entire dreams, the silencing of deep truths, or the display of strong emotions. But more often, it's subtle, woven into the fabric of daily life through a thousand small betrayals:

The moment you say "I'm fine" when you are drowning.
The moment you smile and nod when you want to rage.
The moment you choose what others need over what your soul requires.
The moment you edit your thoughts before speaking them.
The moment you choose to take up less space.
The moment you diminish your dreams or your anger to make others comfortable.

This isn't admirable motherly stoicism that builds character.
We've been fed lies like that for long enough.

These mini-rejections accumulate like sediment, building layers of separation between who you are and who you allow yourself to be. They are anti-life in the truest sense, a systematic starvation of the spirit that leaves you performing rather than living, and leaves you existing rather than thriving.

A starved spirit performs. It moves to rhythms it barely feels, speaks words stripped of authentic truth, and pours love from a superficial well. It masters the art of imitation - mimicking life while its inner life withers in silence.

But recognition, true seeing, changes everything.
To be seen is to be restored to yourself.
It turns fragments into a self, possibility into reality.
It transforms starvation into nourishment, shadow into substance, silence into voice.

Because what is recognized is finally allowed to live.

The Courage to Rise Whole

To rise as the human mother means to gather all the scattered pieces of yourself (the ones you abandoned, the ones you were told to hide, the ones you thought were too much or not enough) and to claim them as yours.

It means integrating the mother who feels with the woman who dreams,
the nurturer with the creator, the one who gives with the one who receives.

This integration isn't about balance, that impossible standard that suggests you should be able to hold all things in perfect equilibrium. Integration is about *wholeness* - about allowing all of who you are to exist in the same body, and to breathe the same air.

You are the mother who makes room at the table and the woman who claims her own seat.
You are the mother who reads bedtime stories *and* the woman who writes her own.
You are the one who tends to others' needs *and* the one who honors her own.
You are the mother who teaches children to grow and the woman who remembers she is still growing too.
You are the one who comforts with gentleness and the one who rises with rage.
You are the keeper of family traditions *and* the breaker of generational chains.
You are the nurturer *and* the force of nature.
You are the soft place to land *and* the hurricane that clears the path.
You are the mother who brings life into the world and the woman who brings her own life back into focus.

To integrate is to stop performing the role of "mother" and start being human. A human who also mothers - beautifully, imperfectly, and, above all, authentically. Integration is the end of self-rejection. It's the permission to bring *all of you* to the table of motherhood, not just the parts that fit the role.

Witnesses and Mirrors

As mentioned, the work of becoming whole could benefit from having witnesses - other human beings who can see all of who you are and reflect your wholeness back to you. For too long, you may have been surrounded by those who could only see parts of you, who needed you to remain small or predictable or easy to understand.

But integration calls for different kinds of relationships. It calls for mothers who are also doing this work, who understand the courage it takes to stop performing and start being. It calls for friends who can hold space for your complexity without trying to fix or change you.

These witnesses become midwives to your emergence. They see your wholeness before you can see it yourself. They remind you of who you are when you forget. They celebrate your integration not as an achievement but as a homecoming.

And as you learn to be truly seen, you learn to truly see others. You become the witness you needed, the mirror that reflects wholeness back to other mothers who are also rising. This is how healing spreads - one authentic relationship at a time, one moment of true seeing creating space for another.

Look for your people.

They'll be the ones who don't flinch, stare blankly, or try to compete with you when you show them your full self.
They'll be the ones who don't feign excitement for your successes.
They'll be the ones who celebrate your dreams alongside your devotion to your children.
They'll be the ones who understand that your integration makes you more available for genuine love.

You can search #thehumanmother. You may discover the midwives to your own emergence there - other mothers who are also rising, ready to connect, reflect, and walk this path alongside you.

The Mother's Paradox

Integration means learning to hold contradictions without breaking under their weight, to be multiple things at once without apology or explanation. As you learn to integrate, you're discovering that you can be both nurturing and fierce, both available and boundaried, both deeply rooted in your role as mother and wildly free in your dreams.

This is the mother's paradox - you are simultaneously ancient and newly born, wise and still learning, complete and ever-evolving. You contain multitudes, and in a world that demands simple categories, your complexity is a quiet form of power - and the very medicine this world needs.

You can love your children completely while also loving yourself.
You can be devoted to your family while also being devoted to your dreams.

You can be present for others while also being present for yourself.
You can be soft and strong, vulnerable and powerful, giving and receiving.

The world may try to convince you that these are contradictions to resolve, conflicts that demand choosing sides. But integration whispers a different truth: *you are vast enough to hold all of who you are.* (You are a woman after all.) You don't need to shrink or split yourself apart. You were made to expand - just as the universe expands, endlessly making room for more.

If the cosmos keeps stretching outward into more, then we, too, are meant for continual growth.

Reclaiming Your Voice

Your voice, the one that speaks truth, has been waiting for this moment. It has survived possibly years of swallowing words, of editing thoughts, of speaking in whispers when you wanted to roar. It carries within it every unsaid thing, every swallowed words, every moment when you choose silence over authenticity.

But your voice isn't just yours. It carries the voices of all the mothers who came before you, the ones who also learned to disappear, to perform, to reject themselves in service of others. When you reclaim your voice, you break chains that stretch back generations. You give permission to yourself, but also to your children, to other mothers, and to the little girl you once were who learned that her voice didn't matter.

Your voice knows things your mind has forgotten. It's in constant communion with your soul-self. It remembers what you loved before you were taught to love carefully, what you wanted before you learned to want appropriately, and what you believed before you were convinced to believe safely.

Listen to what your voice wants to say.
Trust it.
Practice using it.
Let it crack open the silence that has held you hostage.

Let it allow to be expressed and then allow the "chips to fall where they may."

Because when you speak your truth and refuse to swallow it back down, the ground will shift and new patterns will emerge.

Some people will walk away.
Some doors will close.

Entire landscapes of your life may change.
But in their place, the people, places and circumstances meant for you will appear.
The spaces you were never meant to fit into will dissolve.
And what's left will be real, aligned, and alive.
Something that always matched your true, authentic frequency.

Like sand on a vibration plate, the moment the frequency changes the old pattern rearranges. For a time, it looks like chaos - shapes break apart, nothing holds. But that disruption is only the threshold of transformation.

Soon a new pattern that's more intricate and aligned will take form. The new pattern that emerges from the upgraded frequency, is the one you were always meant to inhabit, or the foundation from which you will rise next.

This is the risk and the reward: you can stay silent to keep the peace in a world that profits from your compliance and prevent circumstances from being shaken up, or you can speak and live (fully and unapologetically) and watch as your life rearranges itself into something that finally fits the woman you always had the potential to be - and the right to be.

Reclaiming Your Space

You may have made yourself small in a thousand ways - physically, emotionally, spiritually. You may have learned to take up less room, to need less, to ask for less, to be less so that others could be more. You may have given away your space so gradually that you might not even remember what it feels like to fully inhabit your own life.

But space, true space, isn't something you earn through perfect behavior or selfless service.

It's your birthright.
You deserve to take up room simply because you exist.
You deserve to have opinions, to express them, to change them.
You deserve to have dreams that might inconvenience others, needs that might require attention, and desires that might make people uncomfortable.

Reclaiming your space means saying no to the things that drain you and yes to the things that feed you. It means setting boundaries with clarity. It means creating room in your life for the parts of yourself that have been relegated to the shadows.

This is the foundation upon which authentic love is built.

Reclaiming Your Dreams

What did you want before you learned to want what was expected? What dreams lived in your heart before you were taught that mothers don't get to dream, that wanting is selfish, that your role is to nurture the dreams of others while abandoning your own?

Your dreams may be buried, neglected, covered in dust and disappointment, but they aren't dead. Dreams are resilient things - they survive the "dark nights of the soul", the frequency transitions, they wait for the smallest crack of light or the settling of new patterns.

They also survive neglect. And when you begin to uncover them, to brush off the dust and breathe life into them again, you'll be beginning to reclaim yourself.

If we can move through the initial discomfort of change and the unfamiliar, and allow ourselves to be led by what sparks our interest and ignites our inner light, we don't just become better mothers - we become fuller humans.

If only society would realize that when a mother expands, *everyone* in her orbit feels the freedom of and benefits from that expansion too.

Reclaiming your dreams shows your children what it looks like when a woman honors her full humanity. It's proving that love multiplies when it flows from a well that is full, not one that's been drained dry.

Your dreams matter. The world needs your whole self - your specific gifts, your unique perspective, your irreplaceable contribution. Pursuing them in wisdom won't take you away from motherhood; it will deepen it, because every step toward your dreams makes you more fully yourself.

And by becoming more fully yourself, you offer the world the greatest gift it could ever receive.

The Ripple Effect

Like a stone dropped into still water, your choice to rise as your whole, human self creates ripples that extend far beyond what you can see.

Your children, who have been watching and learning, suddenly have permission to be complex human beings rather than simple, good children. They see that it is possible to love deeply while also honoring your own needs, to care for others while also caring for yourself. They learn that authenticity is necessary and that wholeness is something to nurture.

Your partner witnesses what it looks like when someone chooses integration over performance, truth over pleasing. This either calls them toward their own wholeness or reveals the places where they are still committed to hiding. Either way, it creates an opportunity for deeper intimacy - or necessary boundaries.

Other mothers, watching your integration from a distance, begin to feel stirrings of their own buried selves. Your refusal to disappear could give them permission to consider their own emergence. Your willingness to be seen might remind them that they, too, deserve to be witnessed in their fullness.

The communities you move through (schools, neighborhoods, workplaces) will begin to shift in subtle ways. When one person stops performing and starts being authentic, it disrupts the unspoken agreements that keep everyone small. Your integration becomes an invitation for collective healing.

Find your way of coming together with other mothers - in living rooms or over coffee, in quiet walks or shared projects - whatever nourishes connection without draining your spirit.

This isn't pressure to be perfect or to carry the burden of changing the world. This is simply recognition that your wholeness matters beyond yourself, that your integration is both deeply personal and inherently political.

Sacred Rebellion

Make no mistake, choosing integration in a world that profits from your self-rejection is an act of sacred rebellion. Every system that depends on women's unpaid labor, whether subtle or extreme, emotional availability, and willing sacrifice needs you to remain fragmented, to never quite claim your full power, to always put yourself last.

Your integration threatens these systems. When you refuse to perform perfect motherhood, you expose the impossibility of the standards. When you honor your own needs alongside your children's, you challenge the myth of maternal selflessness. When you pursue your dreams with the same intensity you bring to nurturing others, you demonstrate that love multiplies rather than diminishes when it flows from a full well.

This rebellion isn't about rejecting motherhood or family life. But it's about refusing to let these roles consume your entire identity. It's about expanding the definition of what it means to be a good mother to include being a whole human being.

You are rebelling against the silence that has kept mothers isolated and ashamed. You are rebelling against the perfectionism that has kept you performing rather than living.
You are rebelling against the systems that need your compliance to survive.

If we truly grasped the power of more mothers living and mothering as their whole selves, we'd see families, communities, and entire cultures shift toward a deeper, more lasting kind of thriving.

Integration Practices

Integration is a daily choice to gather the scattered pieces of yourself and hold them in loving awareness. Here are some ways to begin or deepen this work:

> **The Daily Check-In**: In the morning, ask yourself: "What parts of me am I planning to hide today? What parts am I planning to honor?" Notice the difference between these lists and make conscious choices about how you want to show up.

> **Truth-Telling Practice**: Start small. Practice saying one true thing each day that you would normally keep to yourself. Notice what happens in your body when you speak truth instead of performing pleasantness.

> **Dream Archaeology**: Set aside time to excavate the dreams you buried. What did you want to be, do, create, experience before you learned to want only what was acceptable? Write them down without judgment or planning. Just remember.

> **Boundary Experiments**: Practice saying no to one small thing each day that drains you, and yes to one small thing that feeds you. Notice the internal voices that arise and speak back to them with compassion and firmness.

> **Mirror Work**: Look for the people in your life who see and celebrate your wholeness. Spend more time with them. Distance yourself from those who need you to remain small. This isn't cruel,

it is necessary.

Integration Journaling: Write from different parts of yourself. Let the mother in you speak, then the dreamer, then the woman, then the creator. Notice how they can coexist and complement each other rather than compete.

Body Wisdom: Pay attention to what makes you feel expanded versus contracted. Your body knows the difference between authenticity and performance, between nourishing relationships and draining ones. Trust its wisdom.

The Bridge to Tomorrow

This integration (this rising as your whole, human self) is a bridge between the woman you were told to be and the woman you are choosing to become. A bridge between the myths that constrained you and the truth that will set you free. And a bridge between performing motherhood and living it authentically.

As you cross this bridge, you carry with you everything you have learned. The unraveled myths become wisdom. The feelings you have felt become strength. The integration you achieve becomes a gift - to your children, to other mothers, to the world that desperately needs examples of what it looks like when a woman refuses to disappear.

You're rising to wholeness.
You're becoming more fully yourself.
You're embracing it completely.

This is the rise of the human mother - imperfect, authentic, and fully alive.

Words of Encouragement for the Journey

Be patient with yourself as you learn this new way of being. You're unlearning years of conditioning, breaking patterns that run generations deep. This is special work, and special work like this takes time.

Trust that you are worthy of being seen in your fullness.
Trust that your wholeness is a gift to the world.
Trust that your children need to see you as a complete human being more than they need you to be a perfect mother.

You have probably spent so long making yourself small that claiming your full size may feel overwhelming.
Start where you are.
Honor one suppressed dream.
Speak one difficult truth.
Set one necessary boundary.
Integration begins with a single step toward wholeness.

The world needs you - the real, complex, beautifully human you. Your integration is collective medicine.

Let yourself be seen.

The time for hiding is over.

The path forward is about uncovering who you have always been beneath the layers of expectation and performance.

It's about integration - bringing together all the parts of yourself you have been taught to keep separate.

It's about rising not as a perfect maternal figure, but as a whole, complex, beautifully human woman who happens to be someone's mother.

And in this rising, you give permission.
To your children, to other mothers, to yourself.
Permission to be whole.
Permission to be real.
Permission to be seen.

Let the integration begin.

Chapter 22

The Strength of Surrender

The gift and power of letting things go.

There may come a time in your life when you realize you've been holding on to *far too much*, for *far too long*.

The dishes, the errands, the never-ending lists.
The emotional temperature of the household.
The constant work of keeping up appearances.
The family's reputation, balanced on your back.
The moods. The meltdowns. The unspoken needs.
The invisible weight of being the one who holds it all together.

You may look around at the life you've built and wonder:
Why do I feel like I'm disappearing inside of it?

Perhaps the answer is that *you were never meant to hold it all.*

Along with dishes and errands and never-ending lists, mothers also carry a type of labor that can't be measured in hours or tasks.

It's the emotional labor of noticing every shift in mood.
The mental labor of remembering everything for everyone.
The physical labor of daily caretaking.
The energetic labor of absorbing stress that isn't even yours.
The logistical labor of scheduling, planning, and keeping the wheels from falling off.
The social labor of maintaining the family's reputation, of covering the cracks so no one sees what it really costs.
The spiritual labor of holding hope when no one else can find it.

You manage the dynamics before they explode.
You adjust your tone to keep others regulated.

You keep track of the shoes, the bills, the birthdays, the doctor's appointments.
You hold the line, soften the edges, anticipate the needs.

And most of it goes unseen.
No one thanks you for preventing the breakdown.
They don't even know there was a breakdown to prevent.

But *you* know.

You've become the silent system that keeps everyone else stable while the thread of your own self quietly slips further from your grasp.

But If I Don't Hold It, Who Will?

As mothers, we don't just carry the emotional regulation of our families. We carry the structure, the flow, the very functioning of daily life.

We remember the appointments, keep the fridge stocked, and patch the holes no one else even notices.
We carry the reputation of the family, covering the mess so the image looks intact.
We carry the mental load of planning and anticipating, the physical weight of bodies that need tending,
the emotional scaffolding that holds everyone steady, the energetic absorption of stress that doesn't belong to us.

So we ask ourselves:
If I stop holding all of the weight of this family, what will happen?
Will the house fall apart?
Will the tension rise until everyone explodes?
Will the truth of our dysfunction finally surface?

The fear is real. Because you know what happens when a woman stops carrying what was never meant to be hers alone?

The cracks become visible.
The conflict surfaces.
The unfinished work demands attention.
And the relationships finally have to do the labor you've been doing in silence for years.

And so the world asks you to keep holding it.
But your soul is begging you to let it go.

You aren't God.
You aren't a machine.
And you aren't here to manage everyone else's wholeness at the expense of your own.

Stepping away from this damaging role takes courage.
And trust.

You may ask:

Will they fall apart - or finally grow up?
Do I trust them to hold themselves?
Do I trust myself to stop?
When is it my turn to be held?
What might heal if I finally set this weight down?
Who might I become if I'm not carrying everyone else?

Maybe it's not just them.
Maybe we found ourselves neck-deep in carrying this family's emotional weight because, once upon a time, we had to.
Maybe we learned to stay hyper-aware because as children, it kept us safe.
Maybe we tracked every mood shift in the room because we were the ones who felt it all.
Maybe we became so good at adjusting and smoothing things over because it was the only way we knew to survive, or be loved, or stay needed.

Some of us were raised in chaos that trained us to be the steady one.
Some of us are naturally wired to notice everything - the subtle changes, the unspoken tensions, the things no one else sees.
Some of us are simply more sensitive, more tuned in, more attuned to the web of connection around us.
And for a while, it served us - this vigilance, this control, this deep sense of responsibility.

But what if it isn't serving us anymore?

What if the work of fixing never stops - and it's our own lives that pay the price?
What if holding it all together isn't the proof of our love, but the reason we feel so heavy and hidden inside our own lives?

There comes a moment when the only thing left to do...

Is to surrender.

The Art of Surrender

Surrender isn't giving up.

It's the radical decision to stop controlling what was never yours to hold. It's trusting that the people you love have their own lessons to live and they'll be okay as they learn those lessons. And it's trusting that the cracks you fear might break everything open may be the very thing that sets you free.

As Peter Crone says, "Freedom isn't found in changing what happened - it's found in seeing it clearly, loving yourself through it, and letting life be what it is."

Nature doesn't force.
Divine Intelligence doesn't force.
Love doesn't force.
They allow.
And so can we.

And when we surrender, old feelings may pop up.
Maybe even some rage.
Or grief.
Or deep-rooted fear.

Let it come.
Let them move through.
Make *sure* they move through.
Acknowledging them fully as they are there.
Letting them move out of you after you've processed them.

They'll pass.
They always do, in time.

Give yourself the space to feel it - rage, grief, fear, whatever shows up.
Breathe it through.
Write it all down and allow yourself to process what comes through.

Allow it - because when we stop holding what was never ours, we finally have room for what was always meant to stay.

What Happens When You Stop

When you stop playing the role of the family soul, things will shake.

Your children may have to learn to hold themselves.
Your partner may have to grow emotionally instead of relying on your stability.
Your extended family may finally be forced to feel the dysfunction you've been smoothing over for decades.

But something else finally has the ability to happen as well:

You return.

Your joy.
Your chaos.
Your intuition.
Your power.

You begin to feel what's yours - not just what's theirs.

And *that* is how lineages begins to heal.
And how *you* can heal as well.

Taking the First Step

So what does "laying it down" actually look like?
Start small. Start with one thing.

Maybe it's not jumping in to solve the sibling fight immediately - let them work it out for five whole minutes before intervening.

Maybe it's saying, *"I noticed you seem upset"* instead of automatically trying to fix their upset.

Maybe it's taking a walk when the family energy gets chaotic instead of trying to manage everyone back to calm.

Maybe it's letting your partner handle their own emotional response to work stress instead of offering solutions.

Maybe it's speaking your own feelings instead of only tracking everyone else's.

Maybe it's putting down the endless mental checklist - lunches, bills, permission slips, groceries - and giving yourself permission to forget for a while.

Maybe it's stepping out of the role of "peacekeeper" and letting conflict belong to the people who created it.

Maybe it's laying down the story that you have to be cheerful to be lovable, or selfless to be noticed.

Maybe it's letting go of the weight of being the dependable one, the one who never drops the ball.

And maybe it's setting down the expectation that you have to heal generations of hurt all by yourself.

You Are Allowed to Be Mothered by Life

You have spent so long mothering everyone else. But there might just be something deeper beneath the noise, beneath the work, the hustle and bustle, all the stress, the mental notes - waiting to mother *you*.

Call it Source.
God.
Earth.
Life.
Nature.

It's the soft current beneath the surface.
The one that says:
You aren't alone.
You aren't forgotten.
And you were never meant to do this without being held.

And when you surrender?
You let go.
But you also *let in*.
And you open yourself to being mothered too.

You make space for what's been trying to reach you for years.
The messages your body has been sending in symptoms.
The truths your soul has been catching in fleeting sparks and in sudden snippets of knowing.
The clarity that was always waiting, but couldn't quite break through the noise.

Stop gripping what no longer fits - and as you do so,
you'll finally let what wants to fall into place, fall into place.

Sometimes life doesn't ask you to figure it all out.
Sometimes it simply asks you to *release*.

To step aside.
To trust that the unseen pieces are already moving.
And know that everything will be okay.

As Michael A. Singer writes in *The Untethered Soul*:

> "Eventually you will see that the real cause of problems isn't life itself. It's the commotion the mind makes about life that really causes the problems."

Surrender doesn't mean you stop caring.
It means you stop controlling.

And in that stillness, some sacred truths can finally arrive in the form of...
Support.
Truth.
Peace.
Or even your own presence.

Surrendering allows you to finally open up to being mothered by something infinite.
By the wisdom within.
By the river of life that knows where to carry you.

The First Steps

Surrender occurs through many small choices.

So let the dishes sit.
Let the tantrum pass without rushing in.
Let your child feel bored without entertaining them.
Let your partner hold their own discomfort without softening it.

It's frequently choosing your energy first.
It's sitting in your own center during times of turmoil.
It's reclaiming your nervous system no matter what's happening around you.
And trusting that love will never require you to disappear.

Who You Are

Even if you've done it all-
Held the emotional pulse of the household.
Managed the schedules, the crises, the meals, the moods.
Carried the mental load no one sees.
Absorbed the unspoken tension in every room.
Stayed spiritually grounded so others could lean on your steadiness.
Pushed your body past exhaustion to hold it all together.

That is not who you are.

You aren't an emotional regulator.
You aren't a sponge.
You aren't a container.
You are not just the vessel of everyone else's needs.
You are a soul with a name, a body, and a life of your own.

You are *you...*

A breathtaking soul in a one-of-a-kind body.
A living, breathing being with limits, with longings,
with sacred worth that exists *beyond what you give or hold.*

You get to live too.
Fully.
Freely.
In the spaciousness of surrender.
As *you.*

Lay It Down

In the name of every mother who carried it all...
In the name of every woman who broke quietly while holding up everyone else...
In the name of your own healing and your own humanity...

Lay some of it down.

Tap into some of the grace of surrender by doing so.

Let the world adjust.
Let the chips fall where they may.

Trust that the world, and the people around you, can adjust just fine. You were
never meant to hold it all anyway.

Remember these nuggets of wisdom about surrendering:

When you stop holding it all, everyone else finally has the chance to grow.
When you loosen your grip, something deeper can arrive.
When you step back, the universe steps in.
You've held so much, for so long.

It's okay to rest now.
It's safe to stop carrying it all.

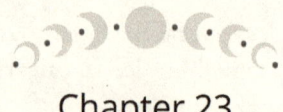

Chapter 23

Raising Children Who Can Witness Us

Inviting your children into real connection.
How we raise emotionally intelligent adults
by being emotionally honest ourselves.

We'll probably spend much of our lives wishing people would just *get it*. We want our partners to intuit what we need. We hope our parents will one day realize how we need healing. And with our children, we sometimes silently plead: *see me - not just for what I give you, but for who I am.*

We want to be seen.
Heard.
Felt.

We want someone to look at us and say, *"I understand. That mattered. You matter."*

But if there's one thing women, especially mothers, have had to learn over time, it's this:

Respect doesn't show up just because you deserve it. (Which you do.)

It shows up because you expect it.
Because you live it.
Because you stop staying in spaces that refuse to offer it.

This is true in relationships. In families. In communities. And it's especially true in motherhood.

The Cost of Invisible Mothering

It's easy to believe our children will naturally grow to respect us because of all we do for them. But the rather difficult truth is, respect is something we teach. Through how we carry ourselves. Through how we speak. Through how we draw boundaries. And through how we allow ourselves to be seen as full, feeling humans.

For generations, mothers have been taught to disappear into their role. To become the invisible infrastructure that holds everything together while never asking for recognition.

We've been conditioned to believe that good mothers don't have needs, don't feel disappointment, and don't get overwhelmed. We smile through exhaustion, laugh off disrespect, arrange the family for picture-perfect appearances, and stay too long in situations that hollow us out.

But this invisibility comes at a cost - not just to us, but to our children.

When we hide our humanity, we rob them of the chance to learn empathy.

When we never model boundaries, they don't learn to respect them.

When we pretend everything is always fine, they never learn to navigate difficult emotions or offer genuine support.

Children absorb far more than our words. They absorb our silence, our self-denial and the way we diminish ourselves to keep the peace.

If we don't show them what respect looks like, they won't learn to offer it. If we never let them see us advocate for ourselves, they won't know how to advocate for others - or recognize when someone is advocating for them.

What Witnessing Really Means

Being witnessed doesn't mean turning our children into our confidants or making them responsible for our emotions. It's about letting them see us as complete human beings who experience the full spectrum of feelings - and handle them with grace and responsibility.

The key is sharing our emotional reality without handing them the weight of fixing it. We're modeling emotional intelligence, not seeking emotional caretaking.

> **For younger children (ages 2–7):** Keep it simple and concrete. Name the feeling, show a basic coping strategy, and reassure them they're not the cause or the cure.

"Mommy is sad right now. Sad is a feeling everyone has sometimes. I'm going to take some deep breaths and then I'll feel better." "I'm frustrated because the park is closed. Let's think of something else fun to do."

For school-age children (ages 8–12): Add a bit more context and model how to work through disappointment or conflict constructively.

"I'm disappointed our plans changed. I could complain about it, or I could look for something good in the new plan." "Work was really hard today. That's not your fault, and it's not your job to fix it - I just need a little quiet to reset."

For teens (ages 13–18): Let them see how you navigate more complex situations - boundaries, hard conversations, or personal growth.

"I had a difficult conversation with your grandmother today about boundaries. It wasn't easy, but it was necessary. Sometimes love means having hard conversations.""I decided not to attend the party because I want to spend time with people who treat me well. You always have the right to make that choice, too."

When they see us set boundaries, apologize when we've gone too far, or take rest when we're tired, they learn that these actions are normal, not selfish. When they see us manage our emotions instead of pretending not to have them, they learn that strength and vulnerability can live in the same person.

Teaching Respect Through Self-Respect

We teach our children how to witness us by being emotionally honest with them - not by making them responsible for our emotions, but by refusing to disappear inside of them.

We stop pretending to be machines.
We let them see us rest.
Let them hear us say no.
Let them see us cry.

We let them witness us in our strength and our softness, in our joy and our exhaustion. And in doing so, we rewrite the story that a mother is someone who gives everything and asks for nothing.

When our teenager sees us decline an invitation because we're genuinely tired, they learn that rest isn't selfish - it's necessary.

When our young child watches us return food that was prepared incorrectly at a restaurant, they learn that advocating for yourself is normal and appropriate. When they see us apologize after losing our temper, they learn that accountability is part of love.

This doesn't mean we share every struggle or make our children witnesses to inappropriate adult content. It means *we stop performing invulnerability* and start modeling *emotional maturity*.

Navigating Common Concerns

Of course, being more open with our children can stir up questions and worries. Many mothers may wonder what this will mean for their kids, and those concerns are worth naming.

"Won't this burden my children?"

There's a crucial difference between sharing your humanity and making your children your emotional caretakers. Burdening looks like seeking comfort, advice, or solutions from your child. Witnessing looks like letting them see how you handle your own emotions responsibly.

Burden: "I'm so worried about money. What do you think I should do?"
Witness: "I'm feeling stressed about our budget, so I'm going to spend some time tonight figuring out a plan. Money stress is hard, but it's my job to handle it."

"What if showing vulnerability undermines my authority?"

Authority built on the pretense of perfection is fragile and ultimately false. True authority comes from competence, consistency, and the ability to handle challenges with grace. Children respect parents who are real, not parents who are perfect.

When you show your children that you can feel disappointed and still function, that you can make mistakes and take responsibility, that you can be overwhelmed and still find solutions - you demonstrate actual strength, not performed strength.

"How do I maintain appropriate boundaries?"

The boundary isn't about hiding your emotions - it's about taking responsibility for them. You can feel angry without making your child responsible for managing that anger. You can be sad without expecting your child to cheer you up. You can be stressed without requiring your child to fix the situation.

Always remember: Your child gets to witness your emotions, but they don't get to carry them.

When Partners and Family Don't Align

This shift becomes more complex when other adults in your child's life operate differently. Perhaps your partner believes children shouldn't see adults struggle, or extended family members expect you to maintain the "everything is fine" facade.

In these situations, you can't control how others show up, but you can control how you respond.

You might say to your child, "Different adults handle their feelings in different ways. This is how I choose to handle mine." In this way, you aren't criticizing others - you're simply modeling an alternative approach.

Sometimes this means having difficult conversations with partners about what emotional honesty looks like in your family. It might mean setting boundaries with extended family about how they speak to or about you in front of your children. These conversations are part of the work - part of refusing to disappear.

The Ripple Effect

When children grow up witnessing a mother who honors herself, they don't become entitled to a woman's silence.

They grow up knowing love is mutual.
That real connection includes real feelings.
That respect is a baseline, not a bonus.

These children don't grow up expecting women to be endlessly accommodating.
They don't assume their future partners will manage all the emotional labor in
relationships.

They understand that all humans deserve consideration- and they're equipped to
offer it, because they've seen what it looks like.

A child who grows up witnessing emotional honesty learns to:

• Recognize and name their own emotions
• Take responsibility for their feelings without dumping them on others
• Offer genuine empathy rather than fix-it responses
• Respect boundaries because they've seen them modeled
• Understand that love includes the full range of human experience

The Healing for Mothers

This work is about reclaiming ourselves.

When we stop hiding our humanity, we stop splitting ourselves in half. We
integrate the mother-self with the whole-self. We heal the wound that tells us we
can only be loved if we're useful, only valued if we're giving.

Many of us discover that we don't actually know how to be witnessed because
we've spent so long being invisible.

We might need to practice identifying our own feelings before we can share them
appropriately. Or we might need to learn what healthy boundaries look like before
we can model them.

This is part of the journey. Our children get to witness us learning and growing
too.They get to see that being an adult doesn't mean having everything figured
out-*it means being willing to keep figuring things out.*

Breaking the Pattern

If we want our children to become emotionally intelligent, whole, and capable of
true connection - we should show them what that looks like. We should be the
example, not just the caretaker.

Change begins with us.
We are the pattern-breakers.
The cycle-interrupters.
The ones who stop sugarcoating in the name of peace-and instead teach connection through truth.

Let them see you hold a boundary.
Let them hear you say, "That hurt."
Let them watch you apologize when you've gone too far.
Let them see you become more human, not less.

When we let them see our humanity, we teach them to honor their own - and to honor ours in return.

A child who grows up witnessing a mother in her fullness won't be threatened by a woman in hers.

That's how change begins.
That's how the world shifts.
That's how we raise children who can witness - and who can be witnessed in return.

The generation you're raising will expect better - because you showed them what better looks like. They'll offer more - because you taught them what offering actually means.

They'll love more fully - because you showed them that love includes all of who we are, not just the parts we think are acceptable.

The end goal is to have children who know that every human deserves to be seen, heard, and honored - especially the woman who raised them.

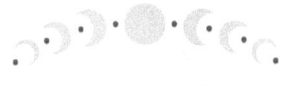

Chapter 24

The Mother with Her Own Clock

*Shifting from the world's demands to your
own sacred timing.*

It's 3:17 AM, and you lie awake listening to the rhythm of your own breathing.
Your youngest, now in her late teens, is sleeping soundly down the hall, the times
where she needed you during the night are long gone.

But you're wide awake, feeling something you can barely name - it's a stirring, a
quiet voice whispering that you're ready for something different. Ready to reclaim
pieces of yourself you set aside years ago.

But guilt might immediately raise its head:
What kind of mother wants less togetherness?
What kind of mother dreams of an empty nest?
What kind of mother yearns to do things outside of caring for her children?

From the moment we become mothers, the ticking begins. Not our own clocks
- but theirs. Society's. The ones that tell us when to start, how long to stay, and
when to stop.

The ticking that tries to tell us:
How long to breastfeed.
How long to share a bed.
How long to stay home.
How long to homeschool.
How long to hold them when they cry.
How long to give everything before reclaiming anything.
How long before you nudge them from the nest.
How long before you ask them to help pay some of the expenses.

We're told there's a sweet spot for all of it. Not too soon, not too late. Not
too attached, not too detached. Just balanced enough to be praised, but not so
different that we stand out.

The ticking we hear comes from a dilapidated old grandfather clock that hasn't yet realized that-

Every mother carries a different rhythm.

And that's okay.

The Spectrum of Mothering Seasons

What culture calls 'the right way' is only ever one way. Real motherhood is lived in countless rhythms and seasons.

Some of us feel the pull to keep our babies close for years.
We welcome small bodies tucked beside us in bed.
We nurse past toddlerhood.
We find joy in long days spent teaching them ourselves,
watching them unfold slowly at home.

Others of us find peace in early boundaries.
We wean when it feels right for our bodies.
We value our nights alone.
We send our children into the world early-
and feel deep alignment in that choice.

Perhaps you're the mother who at 35 finally enrolled in the designer program you'd dreamed of since college. Your youngest had just started junior high, and for the first time in ten or fifteen years, you felt the space to create again. Your sister raised an eyebrow at your decision. Your mother worried you were having a midlife crisis. But you knew something they didn't - you had given everything you had to give in those early years, and now it was time to give to yourself.

Or perhaps you're the mother who at 60 still sets five places at your dinner table most nights. Your grown children drift in and out, bringing grandchildren, laundry, and stories. Your friends wonder when you'll downsize, travel, "live for yourself." But you *are* living for yourself - you thrive in the rhythm of multigenerational love, finding deep satisfaction in being the family anchor.

Neither is wrong.

But the myth says otherwise. It tells us there's only one sacred timeline for motherhood. That our choices, our instincts, should bend to what's currently popular, praised, or expected. That if we don't match the mothers around us, we're accused of loving too loosely or holding on too tight.

The Weight of Different Clocks

The pressure to conform to external timelines becomes even more complex when we consider the different lenses through which we mother.

A single mother working two jobs may need to establish independence earlier not by choice, but by necessity.

A mother with extended family support might have the luxury to hold her children close longer.

Economic privilege, cultural background, and family structures all influence the rhythm of our mothering seasons.

These differences are the shape of reality - the ways mothers bend and adapt to the life they've been given.

They're the signatures of resilience - evidence that a mother's worth isn't measured by uniformity.

They're survival in motion - love finding its way within the limits and possibilities of each life.

They're mothers doing what works within their circumstances, trusting their own navigation system even when it looks different from the prescribed path.

But motherhood isn't a race.
It's not a clocktower with one face.

It's a spiral.
A set of seasons that looks different for every woman and every child.

One of my children's favorite storybooks (and one of mine) was *Ruby in Her Own Time* by Jonathan Emmett. It tells the story of a little duckling named Ruby, the youngest in her family, who seems to do everything more slowly than her siblings.

She eats in her own time.
Swims in her own time.
Even learns to fly in her own time.
Her father worries she'll never catch up.
But her mother only says, again and again,
"She will, in her own time."

And she does. Not when everyone else expects, not at the same pace as her siblings, but in the rhythm that is hers alone.

That story has lingered with me for years, because it reminds me that motherhood (and life) was never meant to be measured against one clock. Each of us has our own unfolding. Each of our children does too.

Perhaps that's the quiet gift of Ruby's story: the reminder that just as our children bloom in their own time, so do we.

And when the pressure creeps in, smile and say to yourself:

"I will. In my own time."

The Unspoken End Seasons

We should talk more about the end seasons. About the mothers who feel the stirring in their chest and the ache in their bones - to let go. The ones who raised their children they best they could, gave all they had, and now... they want their own time back.

We tend to shame these women.
We say they're cold,
Disconnected,
Selfish.

But what if they're just ready?
What if they're not giving up on their children-but returning to themselves?
What if it isn't abandonment,
but a powerful reclaiming of space after decades of devotion?

Some mothers want to live alone again.
Some mothers dream of quiet homes.
Some want to travel, to paint, to sleep uninterrupted.
Some need a second home or space where they aren't "mom" for just a little while.
Some want to walk barefoot in silence,
And this isn't because they don't love their children-
but it's because they've already done the work of mothering.

Others never reach that point.
They find deep joy in a full home.
They love having adult children nearby.

They enjoy being needed a little longer.
They thrive in a home where generations mix and move through seasons together.

This, too, is sacred.

When Partners' Clocks Don't Align

The complexity deepens when partners find themselves in different seasons.

One parent may be ready to reclaim space and independence while the other wants to hold on longer. One may be energized by the prospect of an empty nest while the other mourns each child's step toward independence.

These differences don't have to create fractures. They can be conversations. They can be negotiations where both needs are honored. They can be opportunities to understand that love expresses itself differently in different seasons-and that's not a problem to be solved, but a reality to be navigated with grace.

Recognizing Your Own Seasons

How do you know when you're moving between seasons? The signals are often subtle, internal whispers before they become external realities:

- A restlessness that feels different from ordinary fatigue
- Dreams returning after years of dormancy
- Noticing your children's increasing independence without the familiar pang of loss
- Feeling energized by thoughts of future possibilities rather than overwhelmed by them
- A gentle but persistent voice asking, "What do I want now?"

These stirrings are invitations to the next chapter.

The Wisdom of Nature's Mothers

Birds eventually nudge their fledglings out of the nest.
Cats teach their kittens independence with quick, clear lessons.
Elephants raise their young within vast herds, mothering as a collective.
Wolves take turns raising the pups.
Orangutan mothers nurse for seven years.

There's no one timeline in nature-
only what works, what serves, and what fits.
And what pulses with the rhythm of your own becoming.

And so it should be with us.

Creating Space for Truth

It's all sacred - *as long as it is genuine and authentic and true to who we are and what nurtures and embraces our growth and the growth of those around us.*

We aren't meant to mother the same way.
We aren't meant to feel the same at every stage.
We aren't lesser if we want something different than we once did.

Let's honor the mother who nurses for five years-and the one who doesn't nurse at all.
Let's also honor the one who sleeps beside her child until they're ready to move, and the one who cherishes her space at night.
Let's honor the mother who finishes her work at forty,
and the one who begins again at sixty-five.
Let's honor the one who opens her arms for longer,
and the one who gently closes them when the time has come.

And let's honor the whole spectrum of mothering.

Let's release the myth of "the right time."
And in its place, let's create space for truth, sovereignty, and grace.

Trusting Your Own Rhythm

The most human kind of mother is the one who listens to her own clock and trusts it. She knows that her instincts (honed through years of loving, learning, and letting go) are worthy guides.

She understands that her season may look different from her neighbor's, her sister's, her own mother's. And she's learned that this difference isn't a defection from motherhood - it's a deeper expression of it.

Tonight, if you find yourself awake at 3:17 AM, feeling that stirring you can barely name, try this: Place your hand on your heart and ask, "What season am I in? What does my own clock tell me?"

Then listen.

Maybe you're in a season of constant arms full, with little ones clinging to you from dawn to dusk.

Maybe you're in a season of boundary building, reclaiming your nights or carving space for your own work.

Maybe you're in a season of becoming again, finally tending to a dream you tucked away twenty years ago.

Maybe you're in a season of surrender, caring for aging parents while your grown children build lives of their own.

Maybe you're in a season of anchoring, still setting the family table at 60 because you thrive in being the center of gravity.

Maybe you're in a season of letting go, watching your children step into adulthood and finding out who you are without them.

Maybe you're in a season of recovery, finally resting after years of pouring out more than you had to give.

Maybe you're in a season of wild discovery, learning that motherhood is not the end of your story but the soil from which new stories can grow.

Listen to the voice that knows you – the mother you've been,
the woman you are,
the person you're becoming.

Listen to the voice you recognize,
the decision that feels like you,
the one that brings you joy and peace.
The one that feels like home.

Trust that voice. It's guided you this far.

It will guide you home to yourself, again and again, through every season of this beautiful, complex journey we call motherhood.

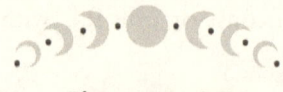

Chapter 25

When "Mom" Replaced My Name

The exchange of a name for a lifetime of
expectations.

They stopped calling me by my name.
No, not when I died.
But when I gave birth.

That was the moment my identity shifted from some*one* - into some*thing*.

Not Claudia...

The name my own mother carefully chose for me. The name I identified with my entire life - the one I wrote across notebooks, scribbled onto sidewalks with chalk, and read on birthday cards.

The name teachers called during roll, that I instinctively answered, "Here!" to.

The name written in Sharpie on my backpack, written in cursive on certificates, and embroidered on t-shirts.

The name my friends called out into the warm night air while we played tag beneath the streetlights.

The name my first boyfriend scribbled at the top of a folded note passed during class.

The name I wore on a lanyard at my first job, where I felt like my effort was valued.

The name people used when they wanted *me* - not solely something I could do for them, but *me*.

After a lifetime of being called by my name, suddenly overnight, it was being replaced.

Not even with another unique name.
But with the *title* of a role.
"Mom."

The Vanishing Act Hidden in a Word

It sounds so sweet when they're little.
"Mama." "Mommy."

Soft syllables soaked in recognition and need.

I loved being called mom, but in later years it left me wondering if anyone remembered I had another name.

What's in this chapter may stir deep emotions. You don't have to agree with every point, but each one might be worth sitting with and worth considering.

Mom. It's the first word you hope they'll say. The one you listen for through the baby monitor at 2 a.m. The one that makes your heart race when it's shouted across a playground or cried out in the night.

It's a sound that can stop a mother mid-step (any mother) anywhere in the world. Because when a child cries "*Mom!*" we all turn. We all know that cry.

And yes, at first, it feels like a badge of honor.
Like the world just handed you your highest calling.
A single word that means:
safe place, soft landing, forever love, I need you, you are mine.

But over time, something else tends to happen.

Your name, the one you've answered to all your life, starts to disappear. And the word that once felt sacred starts to become the only thing you're known by, from the people you're around the most.

It's not just the children who do this. Partners fall into it too. "Ask Mom." "Mom will know where it is." "Mom handles that." Even when you're standing right there, with your actual name, your actual identity - you become the *function*, not the *person*.

I'm not here to strip away the beauty of that word.
It's powerful, primal, and it saves lives.

Maybe "Mom" *should* remain the universal word children cry out in danger, a call the world instinctively responds to, to quickly be swooped into the space of the safest humans on the planet. But what I'm suggesting is that perhaps it also doesn't have to cost us our own names.

Maybe we can be mothers - *and* still be "Claudia."
Or Olivia.
Or Michelle.
Or whoever we were before.

Maybe our homes can hold both:
The sacredness of being called "Mom"
And the wholeness of being called by name.

We Don't Call Our Kids "Child"

We don't call our children "kid" all day.
We use their names.

We cherish their individuality.
We make space for them to grow, shift, and become.

But when it comes to the one who carried them, fed them, raised them - we don't speak her name.

We just call her "Mom"?
The *title* to the role she carries in the home?

And, unfortunately, with that word comes centuries of cultural programming about who she's supposed to be that has tainted something so seemingly innocent.

Mom is nurturing, but never needy.
Mom is strong, but never angry.
Mom is available, but never demanding.
Mom is everywhere, but never herself.

What's fascinating is that fathers don't experience this same erasure - not to this extent. 'Dad' still leaves room for individuality - he can be fun, strict, busy, even absent, and still be recognized as himself.

(Not every dad escapes pressure. In many cultures, fathers face scripts too. But the weight is often narrower, not erasing. Fathers are allowed, and even praised, for a *range* of identities alongside "dad" - they can be goofy, career-driven, authoritarian, "weekend dads," or even fairly hands-off, and they're still culturally recognizable as fathers.

Motherhood, in contrast, is treated as *all-consuming*. Fathers are seen as people *who have children* - the role is additive. Mothers are seen as people who become mothers, it often becomes their entire identity.)

So mom comes with a script written by generations of expectations – about feminine sacrifice, endless selflessness, god-like love, and expected, uninterrupted softness.

No matter the cost.

This makes me think of something so many parents say to their kids when they bring home a stray animal: *"Don't name it."*

Don't name the bird with a broken wing.
Don't name the stray dog that followed you home.
Don't name the kitten in the shoebox.

Why do so many parents tell their children never to name an animal they found? Because the moment we name something *it becomes real to us.*

We get attached.
We see its uniqueness.
We make space for it in our hearts.
We feel like it belongs to us.

Naming turns something from "an animal" into *this* animal.
From "a thing" into *someone.*
And that kind of connection changes everything.

So what happens when a mother's name disappears?
When even those closest to her stop calling her by it?
When her name - her *self* - is replaced by a role?

Do we really think it doesn't somehow ripple into how children, families, and entire cultures learn to see women when even her name is taken by the title of a role?

When she's only ever called by the title of that role, she's more easily reduced to a function.

A category.
A concept.
Rather than something more personal and intimate.

Research shows that names anchor individuality, while titles often reduce people to roles. When women are called only "mom," they are more easily de-individuated - seen as functions instead of full humans.

Scholars like Adrienne Rich and Sara Ruddick have argued that patriarchal cultures collapse "woman" into "mother," reinforcing her as a category of service rather than a person. Even obituaries reflect this, often defining women by motherhood while omitting their names, achievements, or passions.

The pattern is clear: replacing a woman's name with "mom" erodes recognition of her individuality.

"Mom" becomes shorthand for a set of tasks, traits, and expectations.
But *Claudia*? *Renee*? *Sammy*?
Those are names that carry her story.
Her soul.
Her imprint of uniqueness.

Even a title as sacred as "mom" will never compare to the power of her own name - the one that carries her story, her soul, her essence that no role can replace.

Maybe it's not such a small thing, after all - this habit of replacing her name.
Maybe calling her "Mom" isn't always a sign of intimacy.
Not like we thought it was.

Maybe it's a signal that the person she was has been absorbed by the job she now performs.

We should, of course, never stop being ourselves just because we became mothers and are being called "mom." But perhaps we also shouldn't lose our right to having been *named*, and known, just because we gave life.

We choose our daughters' names with such care - but do we ever pause to realize that, one day, her name will hardly be spoken within the walls of her own home? When we name them, we imagine friends calling out to them on playgrounds, teachers reading their names from class lists, future partners speaking their names with tenderness, or colleagues addressing them with respect. We envision their names traveling through every season of life, honoring their individuality.

Why then do we accept that the moment she becomes a mother, her own name will vanish by those who she'll be around the most, replaced by a role that flattens her into a single dimension?

The Reclamation of Name Is the Reclamation of Self

Maybe it sounds small.
Maybe it sounds petty.
But it's not.

Your name is more than a sound. It's an energetic fingerprint. It's a living vibration that holds who you are - your essence, your soul print, and your presence.

Whether it was the first name spoken over you at birth or a sacred choice by you later in life, it carries meaning and power. It's one way the universe recognizes your unique frequency in this world.

To only be called "Mom" - over and over, year after year, is to be slowly cut off from that sacred and very personal resonance.

To become only a title.

A function.

Not because the word "mom" isn't sacred, but because our own name holds a uniqueness that no title can replace.

In the movie *Ever After*, a modern retelling of the Cinderella story, Danielle is referred to by her beloved mother's name, a name she honors but that isn't her own. When her true name, Danielle de Barbarac, is finally spoken aloud, the recognition pierces her heart, and she weeps. Being seen as herself means more than any borrowed dignity.

"You said my name," she says softly, reveling in the familiarity of hearing her name and feeling stunned to be finally seen and accepted for who she is.

She loved her mother's name. She wore it with pride. But no borrowed name, however sacred, can compare to being seen as yourself.

That moment captures something profound about the power of our own name, of being known as the name we've resonated with our entire lives.

Because that's what a name does.
It tells the world, and yourself,
I am here. I exist. I matter. I am seen.

And reclaiming your name,
in the midst of the sacred storm of motherhood,
is a retrieval of your soul.

Yes, "mother" is a word of honor.
Yes, it represents something worth honoring.

But no title and no role, no matter how noble, can contain the fullness of who
you are...

And of your own name.

A Childhood Memory

When I was younger, I visited a new friend's house and was startled to hear her call
her parents by their first names. For a moment, I wondered if I had misunderstood
– maybe they weren't her parents at all.

It felt foreign. So... casual. But then I noticed something else.

There was room in that home - for opinions, for voices, for being human. They
respected one another, spoke openly, even disagreed. And laughed over dinner.

It wasn't chaotic or messy. There were no muumuus, no weed-fueled drum
circles, no contrived 'progressive' vibe - just an ease and openness that felt like
home.

It was real.
And fluid.
It was mature.
And full of understanding while giving respect to one another.
It was very human.

I never forgot that home. And I never forgot that feeling.

It planted a seed inside me that whispered:
"Perhaps there's another way to do this."

In many cultures around the world, this rigid parent-title dynamic doesn't exist in the same way. In some societies, children call their parents by name, or use terms that honor the relationship without erasing the individual.

The American obsession with titles that define and confine isn't as universal as we think it is - it's tied to cultural programming. And like all programming, it can be interrupted, rewritten, and reshaped into something different. Something that lets us be seen not only for the roles we fill, but for the people we are.

Language Shapes Identity

The language we use creates our reality.

Solely call someone "teacher," "nurse," "maid," "mom" - and suddenly their humanness becomes secondary to their function.

When people stop saying your name, they don't see you quite in the same way as they would have if they were to use your name. Whether we meant for this to occur or not.

And when you, yourself, stop hearing it, you, too, begin to adjust to the idea that your worth lies in what you do, not who you are.

"Mom" becomes a role you perform.
It isn't "just" a word.
It ends up being a cloak.

And for many women, it becomes a costume that covers everything else up.

The Liberation of Naming Myself

For me, the journey back to my name became even more profound when I realized I was carrying names that didn't belong to me - names that carried the weight of other people's stories, other people's wounds, and other people's expectations.

As I began to unravel years of suppression - from religious indoctrination that told me my worth and my ability to reach God was in my service to the church and my obedience to its demands, from a marriage that had taught me to minimize myself, from false ideas about what kind of mother I should be - I felt a deep, cellular need to reclaim not just my first name, but my entire identity.

I no longer wanted to carry last names that didn't resonate with me - names weighted with painful memories, negative associations, and versions of myself that felt diminished rather than honored.

Names like the 'secret' name (Lydia) I was given from the religion I was raised in, a name I was told never to speak aloud, the name my husband supposedly needed to use in order for me to get to heaven - though *his* would never be revealed to me.

Or the names that bore the shadows of generational wounds and toxic patterns I refused to keep carrying.

So I did something that felt both terrifying and necessary: I liberated myself from names that weren't mine.

I took time to create my own last name - a name that reflected the fire of when I was born, the Leo energy that had always lived in my bones but had been dampened by a lifetime of silence, sacrifice, and the need to be acceptable.

I kept my first name because that had always resonated with me, and had always felt like home. But the other half of my name? I created it.

I named myself.

And in that act of self-naming, I found a freedom I hadn't even known I was missing.

The name is mine now. I created it. I chose it. And I'm more free and authentic because of it.

This might sound radical to some, but it doesn't have to be about changing your legal name. It's about recognizing that you have the power to define yourself - to choose what you're called, to choose how you're seen, to choose which parts of your identity you want to honor and which parts you're ready to release.

Your name, whatever it is, belongs to you.
It's a living thread between who you are and who you're becoming.

I Want to Be Called By My Name Again

I want my name back.

I want my children to know the person behind the care.
I want them to see the flaws, the humor, the individuality, the realness - not just

the service I can give them.

I want a family culture where names aren't erased in favor of roles.

Where respect is given because we know one another - not because we perform for one another.

I want to walk into a room and not be reduced to the title that's been assigned to me.

I want to be called out of love, not expectation. To know that I'm being seen.

And I want to acknowledge that this desire doesn't make me less of a mother. It makes me more of a whole person. Some mothers find deep joy and identity in being called "Mom" - and that's beautiful too.

This isn't about judgment - it's about choice. It's about recognizing that we can honor the role of motherhood while still maintaining our individual identities.

The guilt that comes with wanting to be seen as more than "Mom" is real, and it's something our culture has taught us to feel. But wanting to maintain your sense of self isn't selfish - it's what allows us to model wholeness for our children, should we feel led to do so.

The Power of Being Named

Maybe it's small. But maybe it's the first crack in the wall.

What would shift if your children called you by your name once in a while?
Or if your partner did?
Or if you remembered that you are still the same you-
with or without the title?

What would it feel like to introduce yourself by your actual name instead of "So-and-so's mom"?

How might it change the energy in your home if everyone saw each other as complete humans rather than just roles to be filled?

This might look different for everyone.
Maybe it's asking to be called by your name during certain conversations.
Maybe it's introducing yourself differently at school events.
Maybe it's having a conversation with your family about seeing each other more fully.

Or maybe, like me, it's taking the radical step of choosing your own name entirely - creating an identity that truly reflects who you are now, not who you were expected to be.

Reclaiming Our Name in Motherhood

In my family, there's a grandmother who has always been called by her first name. Not "Grandma Smith," as tradition might dictate, but "Grandma Opal." Her name was never buried under a husband's. She was never introduced solely as someone's wife, or identified only by the family she married into. Her name remained her own - a living reminder that she was a whole person long before she was anybody's anything.

That small choice mattered. Calling her by her first name meant we continued to see her as *her*, Opal, not just a title, or a role, or an extension of a man's lineage. Her identity was carried forward, spoken aloud every time someone called to her, preserved like a thread tying her back to herself.

It made me wonder: what if reclaiming our names doesn't have to mean throwing out "mom" altogether? What if the transition back to self could be as simple as weaving our names into the role - "Mama Claudia," "Mama Annette," "Mama Nicole," "Mama Jasmine"?

It's a small shift, but a powerful one. Adding your name keeps *you* in the picture. It reminds your children (and yourself) that "mama" isn't a faceless role anyone could fill.

It's *you*.
Your essence.
Your story.
Your life woven into the work of mothering.

And hearing your own name in the mouths of the people you love most might be a quiet thread that keeps you from disappearing - turning each "Mama Claudia" into both an acknowledgment of your role and an affirmation of *you* as an irreplaceable individual.

And it models to your children that a woman's name carries value and dignity, that her identity is meant to endure through every stage of life.

"Mom" Is a Function, But You Are a Being

"Mom" is a function.

But you (*feel free to state your name here*) are a being.

And you don't have to be just a function for everyone else anymore.
You can be yourself again.

The woman who stays up too late reading or dreams of traveling to places she's never been.

The woman who has opinions about politics, preferences in music, fears and dreams and ambitions that have nothing to do with her children's safety.

The woman who existed before motherhood *and continues to exist within it.*

The woman who embraced her own name with wisdom and grace-and stepped into her own power.

That woman deserves to be called by her name.

In the movie *The Never Ending Story*, Bastian can only save the magical world of Fantasia by doing one seemingly simple thing: calling out the princess's name. The world had been crumbling and disappearing in Fantasia *until he spoke her name.*

Why was this the case? Although this is a fictional story, it teaches that - naming holds power.

To speak a name is to affirm existence.
To restore connection.
To summon the soul back into being.

When we speak a name, we anchor it to reality. We say, *I see you. I know you. You are real.*

A name calls something (or someone) out of the shadows and into the light. It transforms the vague into the tangible, the fading into the enduring. This is why names are invoked in blessings, in vows, in prayers - because they pull the essence of a thing closer, binding it to memory and meaning.

What if the same is true for you?

What if your inner world (one that might feel foggy, flattened, or fading) needs the same medicine?

Say your name.

Whisper it (or shout it):
Into a field.
To the stars.
To the sky.
At your reflection in the mirror.
Over a lake, to the trees, or into your room.

Say it again and again until you can feel it the way Danielle did in Ever After.

Do you remember her story? After she had spent so long being dismissed, erased, or called by her mother's name, when the prince finally spoke her full name, Danielle, she froze. With tears in her eyes she whispers, "Say it again." The prince, confused, says, "I'm sorry." And she replied, "No... the part where you said my name."

She closes her eyes, breathes it in, and revels in the comfort and familiarity of being known by her own name.

Let your own name become that for you:
the sound that brings you back to yourself.

References:

Adrienne Rich, *Of Woman Born: Motherhood as Experience and Institution*https://www.penguinrandom house.com/books/292389/of-woman-born-by-adrienne-rich/
Sara Ruddick, *Maternal Thinking: Toward a Politics of Peace*https://www.beacon.org/Maternal-Think ing-P1066.aspx
Twenge & Campbell (2003). "Narcissism, Social Acceptance, and Deindividuation." *Personality and Social Psychology Bulletin*https://journals.sagepub.com/doi/10.1177/0146167202239051
Fowler (2015). "Obituaries, Gender and the American Way of Death." *OMEGA-Journal of Death and Dying*https://journals.sagepub.com/doi/10.1177/0030222815570705

Chapter 26

Reclaiming My Voice, My Body, My Boundaries

What it looks like to unlearn martyrdom.
Saying no. Making room. Taking back your
time, body, and emotions.

When was the last time you wanted something purely for yourself?

Not a better schedule for the children.
Or a cleaner house.
A bigger paycheck so the bills feel lighter.
Extra hours in the day so you can get more done.
A vacation only to return to twice the work.
More energy only to keep meeting everyone else's needs.

But something that belonged entirely to you - a desire born from joy, from aliveness, and from the refreshing recognition that *you* matter too.

The question sits pretty heavy, doesn't it?

Because somewhere in the beautiful, exhausting transformation of becoming a mother, we learned to translate every need through the lens of others.

I want quiet becomes: the children need less screen time.
I want adventure becomes: we should plan more family activities.
I want to feel beautiful becomes: I need to lose the baby weight or once I do A, B, or C for the kids, I'll finally invest in myself.

The practice of returning:

Each morning, before the house wakes, ask yourself one question: *What do I want today?*

Not what you *should* want.
Not what the *house* needs.
Or what the kids need.
Or what the partner needs.
Or what would make you feel like a better mother.

Simply: what do *you* want.
Even if it feels selfish.
Or out of your comfort zone.

Write it down on a sticky note.
Place it somewhere you'll see it several times a day.
Honor it.
And see how honoring it leads you home to yourself again.

The Guilt of Self-Care

Self-care has become a buzzword, sanitized and packaged and sold back to us as face masks and bubble baths and twenty minutes of yoga stolen between making lunch and folding laundry.

But self-care doesn't need to feel bouige.

Genuine self-care might be saying no to the bake sale even though you've never said no before.

Genuine self-care might be leaving dishes in the sink to take a walk alone.

Genuine self-care might be letting your children be bored while you finish your coffee while it's still hot.

Genuine self-care might be understanding that a depleted mother serves no one well.

The guilt will inevitably come.
It will whisper that good mothers don't choose themselves.
That your children will suffer.
That you're being selfish.

Let it come.
Feel it fully.
Then choose yourself anyway.

Because self-preservation isn't selfish - it's essential.

And your children are watching, learning what it looks like to value yourself, to take up space, and *to matter*.

Renegotiating Relationships

When you begin to reclaim your boundaries, the people around you might just notice.

Your partner, who has probably grown accustomed to your endless availability. Your mother, who expects you to carry on the family tradition of self-sacrifice. Your friends, who have come to depend on your constant yes.

They may call you different now.
Difficult, even.
Changed.
A little rigid around the edges - until you find that softness again.

You are changed.
And that's exactly the point.

The resistance will be real.

Some will try to guilt you back into your smaller self. Others will simply drift away, unable to adjust to this version of you who asks for what she needs.

Let them.

The relationships that matter will bend without breaking. The people who love you will learn to love this fuller version - the one who speaks up, who takes up space, who refuses to disappear into the role of mother alone.

Renegotiation isn't betrayal.
It's growth.
It's evolution.

And it's becoming who you were always meant to be. The version of you that will allow you to continue on in a much better way than the self who only existed in the margins of her own story.

Your Body Belongs to You

For months, maybe years, your body wasn't entirely your own.

Growing life.
Feeding life.
Recovering from the miracle and trauma of birth.

Even now, small hands reach for you at all hours. Your body becomes public property - commented on, grabbed at, needed constantly - and yes, there's love in this, and care, and a genuine need that matters deeply.

But something you ought to remember is this:
Your body is yours.

You can say no to the hug when you're touched out.
You can ask for space when you need it.
You can make choices about your physical self (what you wear, how you move, when you rest) without justifying them to anyone.

Your body has done incredible things. It deserves reverence, not just from others, but from you.

The Mental Load and Invisible Labor

Who remembers the pediatrician appointments? Who notices when the milk is running low? Who carries the running list of everything that needs to be done, bought, scheduled, remembered?

This is the invisible labor of motherhood.

You're not the family's Chief Memory Officer by divine appointment. You're not naturally better at remembering, organizing, managing.

You simply stepped into the role because someone had to, and that someone is almost always the mother.

Redistribution begins the moment you call it what it is.

Make the invisible visible. Write down everything you manage, remember, coordinate.

Share the list. Delegate not just tasks, but responsibility.

Your mind deserves space for thoughts that aren't grocery lists and permission slip deadlines.

Listening to Your Anger

We're taught that angry mothers are dangerous mothers. That rage has no place in the sacred space of motherhood.

So we swallow it. Push it down. Transform it into guilt, exhaustion, resentment.

But anger isn't the enemy.
Anger is information.

It tells you when your boundaries have been crossed. When your needs have been ignored. When you're giving more than you can sustain.

Listen to your anger.

What is it trying to tell you?
Where in your life are you saying yes when you mean no?

Your anger isn't too much.
Your anger isn't ugly.
Your anger is a compass pointing toward what needs to change.

Modeling Boundaries for Your Children

What are you teaching your children about respect? About consent? About the right to say no?

When you have no boundaries, you teach them that love means endless availability. That care means self-sacrifice. That their needs matter more than yours.

But when you model boundaries:

You teach them that all people, including mothers, deserve respect.
You show them what it looks like to value yourself.
You give them permission to protect their own energy, their own space, their own time.
You teach them that love is not the absence of limits, but the presence of mutual respect.

This is revolutionary parenting.

Financial Boundaries and Independence

Money is power. And too often, mothers give away their power in the name of family unity, practical choices, what makes sense.

But financial dependence is a boundary issue.

When you can't make choices about your own money, your own career, your own economic future, your autonomy is compromised.

Even if you've chosen to step back from work, even if your partner is generous and kind, even if it makes financial sense - you deserve access to resources, to decision-making power, to economic agency.

Reclaiming financial boundaries might look like:

Keeping your own account.
Staying informed about family finances.
Maintaining your professional skills.
Having money that is solely yours.

Financial independence isn't about not trusting your partner.

It's about trusting yourself with your own life.

The Right to Change Your Mind

Who you were as a new mother is not who you have to be forever.

The choices you made then - about work, about parenting, about your relationship, about yourself - were right for that version of you, in that season of your life.

You are allowed to evolve.

You can change your mind about staying home.
About having more children.
About the way you parent.
About what you want your life to look like.

Growth is an amazing part of our human experience.
And anyone who says it should look or feel a certain way is wrong.
This boxed in way of mothering is wrong for you.

Changing is a necessary part of your personal (and society's) evolution.

You're allowed to become whoever you're becoming, even if it means leaving behind the version of yourself that others found more comfortable - or the version of you that you've gotten used to as well.

Making Room

The reclamation doesn't need to require burning bridges or starting over completely.

It can be gentler than that.
But still be radical.

It's the quiet revolution of making room for yourself in your own life.

Room for your voice in conversations about your family, your future, your dreams.
Room for your body to rest, to move, to exist without constant demands.
Room for your boundaries to protect your energy, your time, your peace.

You don't have to choose between being a good mother and being a whole person. You can be both. You deserve to be both. You were always meant to be both.

Be patient with yourself as you remember who you are beneath all the roles you've learned to play.

This reclaiming will be sacred work.
Sacred and irreplaceable work - of coming home to yourself.

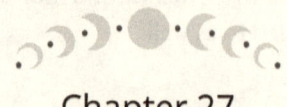

Chapter 27

The Village That Lives in Our Bones

*Remembering to rebuild the past in the
present. A guide for rekindling the sisterhood
that once sustained us, and still can.*

There's something inside us that stirs when we glimpse the lives of our ancestral mothers.

It may show up as a longing so familiar it feels like we've lived it before.

We read about women gathering around birth and blood, tending to each other with knowing hands and open hearts. About babies born into songs. Meals cooked in shared kitchens. Healing that took place in communities.

And something stirs in us.
Something that whispers:

This is how it's supposed to be.
This is how it could be.
I need this.
Women need this.

But then the laundry buzzes. The inbox fills. Your back hurts from carrying too much. You're bone-tired, emotionally starved, and wondering how you're supposed to keep giving when no one's giving back.

And then you realize: *I'm nowhere close to living in the kind of support, sisterhood, and shared care my bones remember.*

But this chapter is here to remind you that what feels gone can still develop - even within the layers of modern life, ready to be unearthed.

The Ancient Knowledge Lives in Our Bones

In traditional African villages, new mothers entered a sacred forty-day period called "lying-in," where elder women took over all household duties while the mother focused solely on recovery and bonding. The Akan people of Ghana have a saying: "A child belongs to the community before it belongs to its mother." Birth wasn't an individual accomplishment - it was a collective celebration with every woman playing a vital role.

In Mayan communities, women practiced the *sobada* - a traditional abdominal massage passed down through generations. Skilled midwives and healers used gentle touch to ease discomfort, support fertility, and even help reposition babies in the womb.

These practices were more than medicine; they were sacred acts of continuity, where wisdom flowed from woman to woman, generation to generation. Birth unfolded in the presence of those who had walked the path before - women who knew what to do when words weren't enough.

In ancient Celtic societies, the *ban-drui* (wise women) formed circles that held women through every life transition. They understood what modern science now confirms: women's nervous systems co-regulate through proximity and touch. When one woman's breathing deepened, others followed. When one woman wept, others held space. They were deliberate, sacred duties braided into the heart of communal life.

Indigenous Australian cultures maintained "women's business"- separate spaces where knowledge about birth, healing, and child-rearing was passed down like precious heirlooms. No woman faced motherhood alone because every woman was surrounded by others who had walked the path, who remembered what she might forget, who could catch her when she stumbled.

These societies knew something we've moved away from:
Motherhood was never meant to be a solo journey.

The ache you may feel when you hear these stories?

Perhaps it's recognition.

Perhaps it's your body remembering its instincts - your nervous system calling out for what it has always needed and what it longs for to feel safe, supported, and held.

A Great Unraveling

It would benefit us to remember that these life-giving structures didn't necessarily disappear naturally. They were slowly dismantled - accidentally at times, but often with intention, piece by careful piece, until only the ache of their absence remained.

Industrialization moved families from villages where everyone knew your grandmother's remedies to cities where you might not know your neighbor's name.

Medical institutions claimed birth from midwives, turning a community celebration into a sterile procedure.

Consumer culture replaced community interdependence with individual purchasing power - why ask your neighbor to watch the baby when you can hire a stranger?

The nuclear family became the new ideal: mother, father, children, contained and self-sufficient.

Multigenerational wisdom was replaced by books written by experts.

Extended family scattered across states and countries. The village that once raised our children became a metaphor instead of a reality.

And we were told this was progress.
We were told this was *freedom*.

But just because these changes may have been intentional, perhaps our bodies have kept the old knowing. Perhaps our nervous systems have kept reaching for tribal-like connections, for the safety of many hands, for the rhythm of shared labor and shared rest.

The exhaustion so many mothers feel isn't just about sleep deprivation - it's about carrying alone what was meant to be shared.

Medical care has its place - but women and babies need more. They need what our ancestors knew to give: the warmth of many hands, the watchful eyes of a circle, the steady hum of familiar voices.

The question isn't whether we can bring this back exactly as it was, but how we might weave ancient foundations into our modern, disconnected, sterilized world

- so that birth, recovery, and early motherhood are once again held as a communal act of love.

What We Lost, What We Carry

Buried under hyper-independence. Under capitalism. Under the myth of the strong woman who never needs anyone. Under the quiet, lonely ache of doing it all without being truly seen, support or cared for.

We were never meant to mother alone. We were never meant to carry birth, baby blues, perimenopause, or menopause without the hands of others around us - no matter what society tells us. And while our partners may love us and try, there are seasons when only another woman truly understands what we need.

There's no comparison to the way a woman can hold space. The way she notices what's unspoken. The way she touches your arm when words fail. The way she knows to bring tea without being asked, to sit in silence without trying to fix, to witness your unraveling without judgment.

This kind of care isn't necessarily better than what men offer, but it's older. Deeper. Cellular. It's ancestral.

And it might just be the missing piece in how we find the rest and care our bodies crave during such stretching times.

We carry this memory in our bones.
In our longing for purposefulness and slowness.
In the way our bodies respond to gentle touch.
In the way we exhale when we're finally, truly seen.

In the way we light up when we find another woman who *gets it* – who understands the invisible load, the constant giving, and the bone-deep exhaustion braided with love.

The Path Back Home

So how do we find our way back to something that feels so far away?

We start with understanding. We stop pretending we're okay in this modern version of motherhood. We name what's off. The exhaustion. The invisible labor.

Then we ask: *What's needed?*

We need circles. We need spaces where women gather not to nourish and sustain one another. Where someone brings coffee or tea, someone brings truth or clarity, and everyone brings their full, unpolished self.

We need places where we can say, "I'm not okay," and no one rushes to fix it. Where someone just sits with us, hand on heart. Where we're not required to be resilient - we're allowed to be real.

We need circles to catch what spills over, and to have spaces where we can lay down our burdens without explanation. Places where we sway to music under the night sky, share food made with love, pass babies between gentle arms, and speak truths that don't need to be softened.

Circles that remind us we were never meant to do this alone, and that we are still, beneath it all - wild, whole, and worthy.

Examples of these circles might look like:

One mother might start with just one other woman from her child's preschool. Every Tuesday morning, after drop-off, they sit on the porch with coffee and speak honestly about their weeks. No advice unless asked for. No rushing to solutions. Just witnessing. Within six months, a few more women have joined. They begin taking turns bringing meals when someone is sick, watching each other's children during appointments, and holding space for the hard seasons.

Another group might form what they call "Moon Circles" - gathering monthly to mark the lunar cycle, share what they're carrying, and practice rituals of release and renewal. They burn written worries, massage each other's hands with oils, and remind one another of their inherent worth. Some months they cry together. Some months they laugh until their bellies ache. Every month they remember they are not alone.

Some circles lean toward joy, reminding us that play is medicine, too. Saturday mornings might mean coffee at one mother's kitchen table while the kids tumble through the backyard. Evenings could turn into game nights where laughter replaces small talk, or a bowling league where they show up in matching shirts and cheer each other on louder than anyone else in the alley.

Some circles become hubs of shared living - rotating laundry-folding days where everyone leaves with clean baskets, weeding parties that end in barefoot dancing, afternoons making herbal salves and tinctures from someone's garden, evenings swapping books and talking late into the night. There are food-sharing networks, childcare swaps, story circles for children and adults alike, and "gossip parties" where what's really shared is connection, release, and relief.

Whether solemn or playful, these circles give back what modern motherhood has stolen: community, reciprocity, and the simple joy of being in a room - or a field - full of women who see you.

Starting Where You Are

These kinds of spaces don't need to be perfect or pretty. But they do need to be intentional. You can start one. You can join one. You can reach out to a friend and say, "Can we begin something new?"

Be willing to be vulnerable - let them see the unwashed dishes, the piled-up laundry, the circles under your eyes. Let them see you in bed on a hard day, your hair unbrushed, your heart tender.

Let them see the toys scattered on the floor, the half-drunk cups of tea, the truth of your real life. Let them see the version of you that exists when you're not "on," so they know it's safe for them to be real too.

Start small and start honest. Start with one conversation that goes deeper than the surface. Start with admitting you need more than you're getting. Start with asking, "What would it look like if we actually supported each other?"

Use the hashtag **#thehumanmother** to find others who are remembering too. Let it be a thread that reconnects us - not through performance, but through truth.

The Ripple Effect

This isn't just about us. It's also about our daughters, and the daughters they might one day raise. It's about the world we're shaping through the way we live now. The girls watching us are learning. They're learning whether womanhood is depletion or connection. Whether strength means silence or softness with a spine.

Wouldn't we want our daughters to grow up in a world where women are surrounded, supported, and seen? It's up to us to begin weaving those circles now - so they inherit a model of womanhood rooted in connection, not depletion; in shared strength, not solitary survival.

They're watching to see whether we break the cycle.

When we gather in circles, we heal not just our own isolated hearts - we heal generations of women who mothered alone. We heal the grandmother who never spoke of her postpartum depression. We heal the great-aunt who carried miscarriage in silence. We heal forward, creating new patterns for our children to inherit.

Supported mothers raise more secure children. Secure children become adults who know how to form healthy relationships, how to ask for help, how to offer support without martyrdom. The circles we create today become the foundation for communities our grandchildren will inherit.

The Future We're Building

What we create now will echo for generations - either the loneliness we've endured or the connection we dared to rebuild.

Because those old ways? They live in us still. In our longing for slowness and in the way we exhale when we're finally seen. They've stayed alive in the moments when someone truly listens, when care arrives without being asked for, when understanding meets us before words do.

We carry the memory in our bones. And we get to bring it back.

The villages our ancestors knew may be gone, but the blueprint remains encoded in our DNA. We can create new versions - circles that honor ancient wisdom while meeting modern realities.

Communities that support working mothers and stay-at-home mothers alike.

Spaces where single mothers are cherished, where mothers of special needs children are witnessed, where mothers in all seasons of life are held.

We can weave the safety net that was torn apart!

We can remember what our ancestors might've known: that raising children is community work, that women's wisdom flows best in circles, that no one thrives in isolation.

We can begin weaving this together, starting now.

The thread is already there,
waiting for us to pick it up.

Every time you choose vulnerability over perfection,
or community over competition,

or truth over the tired performance of having it all together-
you're weaving the fabric back into wholeness.

I have no doubt that your ancestors are cheering you on. And our daughters are watching with curiosity.

And somewhere, in a circle not yet formed, women are waiting for you to begin.

Or hoping you'll join in.

The Ripple Begins With You

Gather the courage to reach out your hand and say, "I need more than this. We deserve better than this."

You can be the woman your grandmother wished she had. You can create the community your daughter will thank you for creating. You can be the one who refuses to accept isolation as normal and who recreates the new reality of motherhood.

The change won't begin with everyone else waking up. So don't wait for that. There are already women like you, longing for the human mother circles, aching for a place to belong.

It begins when you decide you are worthy of support. When you decide things can be different. When you honor the longing for women who will hear you, hold you, and walk beside you through every season.

It's okay to start out messy and unsure about how you want to make a difference.

You might worry that no one will show up. That you'll reach out and find emptiness. But perhaps what you'll end up discovering is that there are women everywhere who have been waiting for someone brave enough to go first. Someone willing to say, "What if we did this differently?"

Maybe that someone is you.

The ancient mothers are whispering their encouragement across time. The future daughters are sending their gratitude back through the years. And all around you, right now, are women who need exactly what you need - to be seen, to be held, to be reminded that they aren't alone.

The world is filled with women who can and need to connect with one another to support one another.

The village doesn't rebuild itself. It rebuilds because someone (someone just like you) answers the call that has been echoing through the bones of women for centuries.

Chapter 28

You Are a Human Before You're Anything Else

A reminder that your personhood was never supposed to be sacrificed at the altar of motherhood.

It can happen unexpectedly: someone asks, "What brings you joy? What are you passionate about?" - and we don't know how to answer.

We freeze.

We freeze because we've forgotten. We've become so disconnected from the pulse of our own desires that we can't remember what lights us up without lighting the way for someone else.

We stand there, mouth slightly open, searching for an identity that feels like ours alone - and finding nothing but roles, responsibilities, and other people's needs echoing back at us.

If this sounds familiar, what you're experiencing is the natural result of a world that taught you that disappearing in order to properly love is normal.

But there's something holy about being a *human being*.

Not a mother.
Not a wife.
Not a role.
Not a label.
And not someone's support system or emotional manager.

Just ... a person.

With strange preferences and impossible dreams.
With quirks and longings and laughter that might even surprise even you.

With a history no one fully knows,
desires you keep secret in your heart,
and a future no one can write for you.

With your own personal truth that will save your life if you let it.

The Greatest Identity of All

Being a mother is profound. It may stretch your soul and break and expand your heart open in ways you never imagined.

But it isn't the most important thing about you. The most important thing about you is that you are you.

Your existence is enough.
Your individuality is sacred.
Your aliveness-your very essence-
is a masterpiece.

And if motherhood costs you that?

It's too expensive.

If any role, religion, system, belief, or structure asks you to sever yourself from your truest self - it's not worth staying loyal to (not that version of it anyway).

This truth leads us to the story that changed everything for me, the moment I understood what I'm really fighting to reclaim.

My Story: The Word That Wouldn't Leave Me

There was a time in my life when everything I believed was unraveling.

I had just left a high-demand religion. Everything I thought was true felt like sand slipping through my fingers. It was disorienting. Painful. Lonely.

One day, during that time, I laid down for a nap. While lying down, I began hearing something tell me, over and over:

"Remember." I tried to grasp what this voice was asking of me. I felt like this message wanted me to remember something I knew or had been through. So I searched through every good and painful memory I could remember from my very first memories to being a teen.

But nothing surfaced.

The word echoed in my mind for days, and still, I couldn't figure out what it was I was supposed to remember.

One day, while standing in my kitchen, I finally shouted out loud: "I don't know what you want me to remember!" Basically telling whatever this was to let off!

I meant it. I wanted clarity.

Days later, while reading in my living room, I heard the sound of a small plane flying overhead. And just like that - everything came flooding back.

As a child, I had a friend who lived by a small airport. On summer days we'd play outside while small planes buzzed above us, low in the sky. The sound of these small planes became a familiar summertime background memory. They were sounds that reminded me what it felt to be comfortable and ... free.

And suddenly - I remembered.

My mind, body and soul was catapulted to understanding what I was to remember.

The "remember" wasn't a belief system I was being asked to return to.
It wasn't some trauma I endured at some point in my life.
It wasn't a doctrine.
Or a rule or a role.

I was being asked to remember *me*.

The child who felt wild and alive and unfiltered.
Free.

The person I was before I was shaped, silenced, squeezed, squashed, shamed, sacrificed, overlooked, or diminished into something smaller than myself..

It was a knowing.

And it was the deepest, most sacred message I've ever received:

Every human is completely and irrevocably cherished by the universe-
not for what they do,
not for how they perform or obey,

but for who they uniquely and individually are.
As that one, special soul entity.

And *that* is something to be remembered and safeguarded-honored and cared for.

Through that I learned that what the Universe/God treasures most about each of us is our one-of-a-kind, unrepeatable individuality.

Our unique, authentic individuality - as unrepeatable as a snowflake, as one-of-a-kind as a butterfly's wing, yet far more expansive, alive with possibility, and more capable of carrying freedom into being.

We were never meant to disappear, but to expand into all that we are.

You Were Never Meant to Disappear

So from that experience, I share this wisdom with you:

You are a one-of-a-kind expression of creation.

And anything that asks you to erase that, even in the name of motherhood, is a theft from the collective soul of the Universe.

You weren't made to be a title.
You were made to be a light.
A flawed, radiant, stumbling, rising, truth-telling human.

And if motherhood adds to that light? Beautiful.
But if it begins to dim it ... Then it's time to come home.

To your name.
To your voice.
To your fire.
To your quirks.
To your wonder.
To *your* you...

As you mother.

What Coming Home Looks Like

Coming home to yourself doesn't need to involve grand gestures or dramatic life changes. It's about the small, daily acts of remembering who you are even in the midst of motherhood's relentless demands.

It can look like playing your favorite song while folding laundry instead of listening to children's music for the thousandth time.

It's taking five minutes to write in a journal before anyone else wakes up, even if you only manage to scribble "I exist and that matters."

It's saying no to the school fundraiser committee because you'd rather spend Saturday morning reading a book that has nothing to do with parenting.

It's remembering that you liked astronomy before you became an expert on sleep schedules.

That you used to paint, or dance, or debate politics, or collect vintage postcards.

It's honoring the fact that you still contain all of these interests and preferences, even if they're currently mixed into the beautiful chaos of raising humans.

Coming home means recognizing that the woman who changes diapers is the same person who once stayed up all night talking about life's big questions.

She's still in there.
She'll always be there.
She's been waiting patiently for you to remember her.

The Ripple Effect of Your Wholeness

Remember how easily you believed in magic as a child?

The kind that could change everything with a single touch, a single word, a single choice, belief, spell or a heartfelt wish? Back then, the world was alive! Every puddle was an ocean. Every tree had a secret. Every day carried the possibility of something extraordinary.

And then, slowly, almost without noticing, we traded that magic for the "real world." We inherited lenses made from dogmas, doctrines, rules, unspoken expectations, and generational wounds.

We learned to see through glass smudged with other people's fears, opinions, and beliefs. And the clearer our view was supposed to become, the more clouded it probably got.

Children see without lenses.

They don't just watch rain - they *feel the power of the entire storm while also feeling* it kiss their skin. They don't just look at the night sky - they *live* in the enormity of it.

We used to see like that too.
Do you remember?

Can you picture the whole world you imagined living within the blades of grass?
Do you remember how clouds were never just clouds, but ships, castles, and secret animals drifting overhead?
Do you remember how the smell of rain meant adventure, how puddles were oceans, and sticks were swords or wands that carried power?
Do you remember how time stretched wide - a single afternoon enough to hold an entire lifetime of wonder?
Do you remember how you could disappear into play so fully that the rest of the world melted away?

And we can, if we choose, let the world reveal itself to us the way it once did.

When you return to yourself (beneath the roles, beyond the masks, outside of the storylines you were handed) *you reclaim the clearest lens there is.*

The one that sees the world as alive, responsive, and full of possibility.

That's where the magic still lies!

Magic is simply life meeting you with the same authenticity you bring to it.

And because your true, authentic self is so breathtakingly amazing, it can't help but ripple outward - stirring courage, rekindling wonder, illuminating others, changing the atmosphere, calling for authenticity in others, lowering walls and opening eyes.

When you are fully yourself, the universe responds.
People will shift.
Doors will open.
Things will align that logic could never explain.

Your wholeness isn't just a gift to yourself.

Your children will feel it in their bones too. They begin to understand that being whole is far more valuable than being perfect.

Other women will feel it too - like a tuning fork vibrating at a frequency they've been aching to hear.

Your wholeness will be a gift to the women watching you from across the room who suddenly feel permission to stop pretending.

It'll be a gift to your daughter, who will live her own story without having to claw her way back to herself.

It'll be a gift to your son, who will grow up knowing that love doesn't require someone to vanish to deserve it.

It'll be a gift to the grandmother you'll one day be - looking back, knowing you didn't waste your life performing for a world that would never be satisfied.

If you live this way, your obituary will read differently. It will speak of the life you *lived*. The joy and bliss you followed. The truth you told. The people you helped remember their own light.

And the unique magic only you could bring into a room.

This is how magic blossoms.
One woman wearing new lenses.
One woman choosing her truth over her performance.
One woman seeing herself and the world clearly again-
and in that seeing, she remembers her proximity to the center of it all.

Her rightful place, holding a thread the universe has been waiting for her to pick up.

She's a part of the whole cosmic weave. Without her, the pattern is incomplete. But, *with her*, magic grows - spilling into her family, her community, and the generations yet to come.

And in the spirit of child-like imagination, who knows?
Maybe, just maybe,
when a woman who has lived her truest self leaves this earth,
she bursts across the world as light,
her true essence scattering into every corner of life,
especially to those whom she touched,
leaving behind an invisible magic that lingers in the air,
adding more magic for the little ones who come after her,
to breathe in, dance with, and grow from.

And maybe the more authentically you live, the brighter and wider your burst of light will be – sparking wonder, imagination, and joy in every heart it touches.

Finding Your People

Around the world, there are mothers who are also remembering themselves, also choosing wholeness, also refusing to disappear in the name of love. Our journey back to ourselves echoes in kitchens, in late-night journal pages, in whispered conversations after bedtime.

There are many of us who long for the same things. And when we find each other, we begin to remember more easily, to breathe more freely, and to stand more firmly in who we are.

Find them. Online, in your community, in the quiet corners of playgrounds where other mothers are reading books that have nothing to do with parenting. Look for the ones who light up when they talk about something other than their children. The ones who still use their own names when introducing themselves.

Create spaces where mothers can be human together. Start conversations about dreams and interests - and the parts of yourself you're working to reclaim. Share your struggles with the balance between love and selfhood. And celebrate the small victories of remembering who you are.

We heal in communities. And the community of mothers who are choosing wholeness is growing stronger every day.

A Practice for Remembering

Saying things out loud can be a healing ritual you can return to whenever you feel yourself disappearing:

Step 1: Say your name. Not "Mom" or "Mrs. Anyone." Your actual name. Say it like a prayer. Say it like the world is listening. Because it is. Because we are.

I am _____.

Step 2: Remember what you loved before. What brought you joy before you became responsible for everyone else's joy? What made you feel alive? What were you curious about?

Before I became a mother, I loved _____.

Step 3: Name what you're reclaiming. What part of yourself is asking to be remembered right now? What aspect of your humanity wants to be honored today?

The part of me I'm calling home is _____.

Step 4: Make one small promise. What's one tiny thing you can do today to honor your full humanity? Something so small that guilt can't talk you out of it.

Today I will honor myself by _____.

Return to this practice whenever you feel yourself fading. Your wholeness is not a luxury - it's a necessity.

The Long View

This work, the work of remaining whole while loving deeply, is about every mother who will come after you, every child who will grow up seeing a different model of what love looks like, and every family that will be shaped by the truth that love doesn't require disappearance.

This might be soul-stretching, difficult work.

There might be days when it feels easier to just disappear, to let the roles swallow you whole, to stop fighting for your own existence. There will be moments when the world pushes back against your wholeness, or when people are uncomfortable with a mother who refuses to shrink.

Do it anyway.

Stay human anyway.
Love deeply anyway.
Choose yourself anyway.
Remember how much this Universe loves your individuality anyway.

Because somewhere out there, there's a little girl watching her mother remain whole while loving fully, and she's learning that she doesn't have to choose. There's a woman becoming a mother for the first time, terrified she'll lose herself, and she needs to see that it's possible to keep both - the love and the self.

There's a mother reading this right now who has forgotten her own name, and she needs to know that it's not too late to come home.

Your existence matters more than anyone or anything ever let you believe.
Your wholeness is the foundation you deserve to stand on.
Your humanity is the heartbeat of your existence.

You are a human before you are anything else.

And that is exactly as it should be.

Chapter 29

Rewriting the Future

*Bringing the pieces home and building
something new from all we now know.*

We began this journey by examining the shape of our cage - those invisible bars of expectation, myth, and cultural programming that have contained mothers for generations.

We traced the outline of each myth that told us who we were supposed to be: saints without needs, natural beings who never struggled, unbreakable forces who never cracked, bodies meant for sacrifice, default caretakers, guardians of sacred family units.

We felt the weight of jobs we never applied for and the crushing burden of being everyone's emotional manager while forgetting we had emotions of our own. And we grieved the obituaries written for good women who disappeared so completely that even they forgot their own names.

Then we dared to dig deeper.

We acknowledged that awakening through motherhood is real, that needs aren't weaknesses, and that rage is a beacon back to yourself.

We learned that unconditional love is a lie that serves everyone except the mother, and that being the family's emotional dumping ground is not a role worth keeping. We sat with grief, loneliness, and the particular ache of being unmothered while trying to mother others.

And finally, we claimed the ground beneath our feet.

We demanded to be seen, remembered the village that lives in our bones, and we reclaimed our voices and boundaries.

We remembered our names and explored raising children who can witness us as whole humans.

We took back our own clocks and claimed our humanity as our primary identity.

Now, having traveled this path together, we know the future won't be handed to us - it will be shaped by the women who remember. Let's review what was remembered:

We've remembered that motherhood isn't meant to be martyrdom. For generations, we've been told that good mothers sacrifice everything (their bodies, their dreams, their identities, their needs) on the altar of family. We've been conditioned to believe that love requires erasure, that caring means disappearing.

But we've remembered something our great-grandmothers knew before the world told them to forget: love does not require self-destruction. The most powerful love comes from fullness, not depletion. When we love from a place of wholeness rather than emptiness, everyone benefits - especially our children.

We've remembered that our bodies belong to us. The cultural narrative told us that once we became mothers, our bodies were no longer our own. They belonged to our babies, our families, our culture's expectations of what maternal bodies should look like and how they should function. We learned to see our bodies as vessels for others rather than homes for ourselves.

But we've remembered that our bodies are sacred, not because they can create life, but because they house the miracle of our individual existence. We've reclaimed the right to say no, to set boundaries, to honor our physical needs and desires. We've remembered that we can love our children deeply while still loving ourselves first.

We've remembered that emotional labor is real work. For too long, the mental and emotional work of maintaining families and relationships has been invisible, unpaid, and assumed to be women's natural duty. We've been the ones remembering birthdays, managing social calendars, tracking everyone's needs, and regulating everyone's emotions - all while pretending this work didn't exist.

But we've remembered that emotional labor is skilled, valuable work that deserves recognition, boundaries, and, when possible, compensation. We've learned to name this work, to delegate it, and to refuse to be the default emotional manager for everyone around us.

We've remembered that we're allowed to have needs. Perhaps the most radical remembering of all is this: mothers are human beings with legitimate needs that deserve to be met. We've been so conditioned to believe that motherhood means existing solely to meet others' needs that having our own felt selfish, unreasonable, or impossible.

But we've remembered what should have been obvious all along: people with needs cannot effectively meet others' needs indefinitely. Self-care isn't selfish - it's sustainable. Meeting our own needs isn't taking from our children - it's modeling for them what healthy humanity looks like.

We've remembered that anger is information, not pathology. The world taught us that maternal anger was dangerous, shameful, evidence of our failure as women and mothers. We learned to swallow our rage, to turn it inward, to apologize for the fire that arose when our boundaries were violated or our needs ignored.

But we've remembered that anger is often the most honest emotion we have. It tells us when something is wrong, when we're being mistreated, when our boundaries are being crossed. Maternal anger isn't a character flaw - it's often a sign of sanity in an insane system.

We've remembered that we don't have to forgive everyone everything. The pressure to forgive (partners who don't step up, families who don't support us, systems that fail us, cultures that erase us) has been overwhelming. We've been told that withholding forgiveness makes us bitter, small, un-motherly.

But we've remembered that forgiveness is not always healing, and it's certainly not always required. Sometimes the most loving thing we can do - for ourselves and our children - is to maintain boundaries with people who have hurt us, even if they're family. Sometimes protecting ourselves is more important than preserving relationships.

We've remembered the village that lives in our bones. We've been isolated, told that good mothers can do it all alone, that needing help is weakness, that nuclear families are not just sufficient but ideal. We've been separated from the networks of support that sustained mothers throughout human history.

But we've remembered that humans are meant to raise children in community. We've started building new villages - online and in person, formal and informal, blood-related and chosen. We've remembered that it truly does take a village, and we've begun creating the villages we need.

We've remembered our names. Somewhere along the way, we became "Mom" and forgot we were ever anything else. We lost ourselves in the role, until the role became our entire identity. We forgot that we had preferences, dreams, quirks, and qualities that existed independently of our children.

But we've remembered that "Mom" is something we do, not something we are. We've reclaimed our names, our individual identities, our right to exist as full humans who happen to also be mothers. We've remembered that we can love our children completely while still maintaining our individual selves.

How Remembering Becomes Rewriting

Every time a mother remembers her worth, she rewrites the future. Every boundary set, every need honored, every moment of self-compassion creates ripples that extend far beyond her immediate family.

We're rewriting the script for our daughters. The girls growing up in homes where mothers model wholeness rather than martyrdom are learning that they don't have to choose between love and selfhood. They're seeing what it looks like to be devoted without being depleted, caring without disappearing. These daughters will enter relationships and eventual motherhood with entirely different expectations and boundaries.

When our daughters see us setting boundaries, they learn that their boundaries matter too. When they watch us honor our needs, they understand that their needs are valid. When they witness us pursuing interests outside of motherhood, they learn that they, too, can remain individuals while loving others deeply.

We're rewriting the expectations for our sons. The boys raised by mothers who refuse to be default caretakers are learning to be full partners in relationships and parenting. They're growing up understanding that emotional labor is real work that should be shared, that everyone in a family has needs that matter, that love requires reciprocity rather than sacrifice.

These sons will enter adulthood expecting to be equal partners in domestic life, emotional management, and childcare. They won't assume that love means someone else handles all the invisible work. They'll understand that healthy relationships require two whole people, not one person sacrificing for another.

We're rewriting what partnership looks like. As mothers refuse to be the default parent, partners are being forced to step up or step out. Relationships that were built on unequal labor and invisible sacrifice are being renegotiated or ended. New partnerships are being formed with more equitable foundations.

The mothers who are demanding true partnership are creating space for relationships based on mutual respect, shared responsibility, and reciprocal care. They're proving that it's possible to love deeply while maintaining individual identity and shared responsibility.

We're rewriting workplace expectations. Mothers who refuse to apologize for having children while also refusing to sacrifice their careers are forcing workplaces to adapt. By demanding flexibility, fair pay, and respect for the complex realities of working parenthood, they're creating better conditions for all working parents.

Companies are being forced to recognize that supporting working mothers isn't charity - it's good business. The mothers who refuse to choose between career and family are proving that both are possible when systems adapt to support human needs rather than forcing humans to adapt to inhuman systems.

We're rewriting community expectations. Mothers who openly discuss their struggles, needs, and boundaries are breaking the silence that has kept maternal suffering invisible. By refusing to perform perfect motherhood, they're creating space for honesty, support, and real community among parents.

The end of performative motherhood means the beginning of authentic connection. When mothers stop pretending everything is fine, other mothers feel permission to admit their struggles too. This honesty creates the foundation for real support and genuine community.

We're rewriting generational patterns. Perhaps most importantly, we're interrupting cycles of inherited trauma, unexpressed needs, and learned helplessness that have been passed down through generations of mothers. By healing ourselves, we're healing the lineage - both backward and forward.

The work we're doing to reclaim our wholeness as mothers isn't just for us. It's for our mothers, who perhaps never had the language or permission to advocate for themselves. And it's for our children, who will grow up with entirely different models of what love, relationships, and family can look like.

————————— ›)◯(‹ —————————

The Future We're Creating

In the future we're creating, motherhood enhances rather than erases identity. Women become mothers without losing themselves because the culture supports and celebrates the full humanity of maternal beings.

In the future we're creating, children grow up understanding that love doesn't require sacrifice, that caring doesn't mean disappearing, that healthy relationships involve two whole people supporting each other rather than one person carrying everything.

In the future we're creating, emotional labor is visible, valued, and shared. The mental work of maintaining families and relationships is recognized as skilled labor that deserves compensation, appreciation, and equitable distribution.

In the future we're creating, support for mothers is systematic rather than incidental. Communities, workplaces, and social systems are designed to support the complex reality of modern parenthood rather than expecting families to manage everything in isolation.

In the future we're creating, maternal anger is understood as information rather than pathology. When mothers express frustration, fear, or rage, they're heard and supported rather than pathologized and silenced.

In the future we're creating, women don't have to choose between career and family, self-care and child-care, individual identity and maternal love. The false dichotomies that have trapped mothers for generations are recognized as products of systems that benefit from women's sacrifice rather than natural laws of motherhood.

In the future we're creating, every child grows up witnessing at least one adult who models what it looks like to love others while loving themselves, to give generously while maintaining boundaries, to care deeply while preserving individual identity.

⸻ ⟩ ◯ ⟨ ⸻

The Sacred Work of Now

This future isn't guaranteed. It will only become reality if we continue the sacred work we've begun - the work of remembering who we are, honoring what we need, and refusing to disappear in the name of love.

Every day, we have opportunities to choose wholeness over martyrdom, authenticity over performance, and boundaries over depletion. Every time we make these choices, we move closer to the future we're creating.

The sacred work looks like: refusing to apologize for having needs while being a mother. Setting boundaries with family members who expect you to carry emotional labor that isn't yours. Asking for help without shame. Pursuing interests that have nothing to do with your children. Saying no to commitments that deplete you. Speaking honestly about the challenges of motherhood instead of performing perfect contentment.

The sacred work looks like: teaching your children that love doesn't require self-erasure by modeling self-love alongside love for them. Showing them that anger is information by expressing your own anger appropriately rather than swallowing it. Demonstrating that boundaries are healthy by maintaining your own rather than letting others walk all over you.

The sacred work looks like: building communities with other mothers who are also choosing wholeness over martyrdom. Supporting other women as they reclaim their voices, names, and autonomy. Refusing to participate in the competitive performance of perfect motherhood that keeps us all isolated and struggling.

The sacred work looks like: voting for policies that support families, advocating for workplace changes that recognize the reality of working parenthood, and speaking up when you see mothers being diminished, ignored, or expected to sacrifice their humanity for others' comfort.

A Love Letter to the Mothers Who Come Next

To the women who will become mothers after us:

We're fighting for a world where motherhood enhances rather than erases your humanity. Where your needs matter as much as everyone else's. Where emotional labor is recognized, valued, and shared. Where you can love your children completely while still loving yourself first.

The path we're creating will be more honest than what we inherited. It will make space for your anger, your needs, your boundaries, your individual dreams and desires. It will support your wholeness rather than demanding your disappearance.

You'll still face challenges - some from systems that haven't caught up to our remembering, some from family members who are uncomfortable with your wholeness, and perhaps some from the internal voices that inherited generations of conditioning about what good mothers should be.

But you'll also have something we didn't have when we began: a growing community of mothers who also refuse to disappear, resources for maintaining your identity while loving deeply, and cultural models of what wholeness in motherhood can look like.

You'll have the knowledge that maternal martyrdom is unsustainable. That self-care is sacred. That your children need you to be human more than they need you to be perfect. And that your obituary is going to be memorable and amazing!

Most importantly, you'll have permission to love both your children and yourself, to give generously while maintaining boundaries, and to care deeply while preserving your individual identity.

This is the future that's waiting for you.
This is what we've remembered.
This is how love becomes revolutionary-
by continually remembering and insisting on wholeness.

The cage has been opened. We can see the shape of the bars now, which means we can also see the door.

We're walking through it together.
And let's never go back to that again.

The Invitation

This book ends, but the work continues. The remembering you've done while reading these words is just the beginning. The real transformation will happen in the daily choices, the small boundaries, and the moments when you choose wholeness over martyrdom.

I invite you to continue this sacred work:

Remember your name. Use it. Introduce yourself with it. Insist that others see you as more than just "Mom."

Honor your needs. They are not weaknesses or luxuries - they are requirements for sustainable love.

Set boundaries. Your energy, time, and emotional capacity are finite resources that deserve protection.

Build your village. Find other mothers who are also choosing wholeness. Support each other in this revolutionary act of remaining human while loving deeply.

We were never meant to mother in silence, in separation, or in systems that ask us to disappear in the name of love.

We were meant to mother in *circles*.
In rhythm.
In ritual.
In deep, intertwined relationships with others.

It's not motherhood itself that breaks a woman.
It's the absence of what should have stayed and what should have held her.

Model wholeness for your children. Show them what it looks like to love others while loving yourself, to care deeply while maintaining individual identity.

Trust your anger. It's information about what needs to change, not evidence of your failure as a mother.

Refuse to disappear. Your existence matters independent of how well you serve others.

The future we're creating depends on mothers like you who are willing to remember the sacredness of your full, complex, messy, beautiful humanity.

You aren't just a mother.
You're a human being ... who also happens to be a mother.

That difference changes everything.

Embodying the Matriarchal Shift

Our hearts are moving toward a matriarchal society. It begins here, with us, in our homes, as we redeem the role of mother while keeping ourselves whole inside it. We set the standard first for our own lives, refusing the myth that motherhood requires self-erasure. Then, we live that standard out loud so other mothers know it's possible too.

When enough of us reclaim this way of mothering (rooted in truth, mutuality, and wholeness) it can't help but ripple into the fabric of society.

Communities will have to shift to meet this standard. Workplaces, healthcare systems, and education will have to honor the well-being of the mother as central to the well-being of all.

The village will no longer be a metaphor, but a living structure woven back into our neighborhoods, policies, and daily rhythms. From there, the shift moves outward - flowing into the brittle bones of toxic patriarchal systems that have been running the world on extraction, competition, and burnout.

A matriarchal model steps in not to punish, but to mother a depleted and dilapidated civilization back to health. We will tend to it the way we tend to life: with fierce truth, with unwavering care, with the clear boundary that says, "You will heal, and you will learn to sustain yourself."

And like any wise mother, the goal will never be to keep the world dependent on us, but to restore it to the point where it runs on its own - healed, nurtured, sustained, and whole - independent of our constant tending, yet always infused with the standard we set.

Because a healed society doesn't just benefit the mother. It benefits the collective. It benefits the generations yet to come. It benefits life itself.

And, yes, women *are* meant to lead. Perhaps one reason there's so much resistance to this idea is because, in today's world, it *can* appear "unnatural." And this isn't because women leading is unnatural, it's because the models of leadership we've inherited were never ours to replicate.

The structures men built - hierarchies of domination, power hoarded at the top, secret organizations, control and manipulation, financial gain and hoarding - do not reflect the way women were designed to lead - or have the desire to lead. The distortion isn't in the woman rising to lead, but in asking her to replicate the patterns of men.

The unnatural thing isn't her leadership. The unnatural thing is her confinement to their mold.

<hr />

Reclaiming Connection and Support in Motherhood

Live Near or With Other Women You Trust
Intentionally co-live with a friend, sister, cousin, or chosen sister. Whether in the same home, a duplex, or side-by-side homes, this allows for shared meals, childcare trade-offs, emotional check-ins, and daily companionship.

Build Intentional Neighborhoods
Instead of relying on chance, collaborate with friends or likeminded families to live near one another. Share school pickups, groceries, backyard playtime, or healing rituals. It takes planning - but so did building the isolated suburbs that drain us.

Find or Create "Women's Acres"
Seek out women who are offering space on land to other women and mothers. These "modern villages" are forming in both rural and urban settings - sometimes just two families, sometimes more. Women working, cooking, raising kids, and living life together, as it once was.

Use Hashtags to Connect
Search and post using hashtags like #thehumanmother, #radicalmotherhood, #newmotherculture, or #thevillageisrising to find women who are thinking and living differently. Share your vision. Ask for collaboration. New circles form from courageous honesty.

Create Micro-Circles for Exchange
Don't wait for a "mom group" to appear. Start a trade circle - one mom watches kids while the other rests. One cooks meals, another cleans. One hosts craft day, another teaches garden skills. *Every mom has something to offer.*

Host or Attend Monthly Mother Circles
Create space to be heard, held, and seen. These can be in person or virtual, small or large, guided or open. Share stories, rage, tears, and dreams. If we can't live together, we can at least sit together.

Normalize Asking for Help Openly
Post or text your needs to trusted women: "Can someone help me clean today?" "Can anyone bring a meal?" "Can I drop my kids off for two hours?" Practice receiving without guilt. It softens the world.

Start a Communal Calendar or Support Chat
A shared group calendar or WhatsApp/Signal thread among friends or local moms can be a game-changer. Mark who needs help that week. Add "support rotations." Someone always knows who needs checking in.

Create Shared Healing Spaces
Rent or share a space where women can come to rest, cry, breathe, nap, or just *be*. It doesn't need to be fancy. What matters is that it exists. Bonus if there's a couch and a pot of tea.

Rethink What Help Looks Like
Help doesn't always look like childcare. It can be someone folding laundry while you vent. Someone bringing soup and walking out. Someone texting "I see you" after your rough day. We must expand the definition of support.

Ask: What Would a Village Do?
When you're unsure what to do or what to ask for - ask this. What would a village have done in this moment? The answers are wiser than our programming.

Build Intergenerational Friendships
Seek out older women or grandmothers who *want* to help or be around children. Many long to feel useful and connected. Trade meals or company for stories and help.

Design Homes With Mothers in Mind
Dream of (or build!) homes with shared courtyards, side-by-side entrances, com-

munity gardens, or big porches for rocking babies while sipping tea. A built environment shapes a lived experience.

Encourage Husbands/Partners to Build Their Own Circles
Men need support, too - but it doesn't always have to come from *you*. Invite partners to form their own "dad support group," therapy pod, or skill-swap circle. Offloading their needs from you creates space for you.

Bring the Village Into the School System
Advocate for schools to include "parent rooms," social circles for single moms, or family resource hubs. If it doesn't exist - suggest it. Or start small: host tea outside the school while kids are in class.

Reclaim Ceremonies and Mother Rituals
Celebrate transitions - first blood, births, birthdays, end-of-nursing, etc. - *together*. These moments were once marked with village presence, not silence or isolation. Create rituals to remind each other we're not alone.

Epilogue

This is What Remembering Feels Like

The old story of motherhood was written with sacrifice being at the core of its story. It asked you to disappear and smile and be grateful for the experience while doing it. It asked you to love your children more than yourself - and then called it noble when you forgot who you were.

But that story is crumbling now.
Because we are telling a *new one*.

A story where mothers don't vanish. A story where being human is the most sacred offering. A story where your name is known, your body is yours, your voice is heard, and your needs are *not negotiable*.

Perhaps this isn't so much about rebellion.
It isn't about rejecting motherhood.
It's about *remembering*.

Because maybe you were never meant to fit inside a martyr mold. And you were never meant to parent from depletion. And were never meant to be the rock, the anchor, the lighthouse *and* the ocean all at once.

You were meant to be *you*.

The Era of the Human Mother Has Begun

Let this book be your permission slip, your battle cry, your quiet knowing.
You are here to be whole - no matter what stage of life you're in.

You have permission to be tired without apologizing.
To feel angry without shame.
To be radiant in your own skin.
To embrace the beautiful mess of your humanity.
To fall in love with your own life again - not someday, but right now.

You can want the promotion and the quiet morning coffee.
You can plan the girls' trip and take the uninterrupted shower.
You can start writing the novel,
launch the business,
learn the language,
or travel to the place that calls to your soul.

You can take up space - physical space, emotional space, conversational space.

You can tell your children the truth about your struggles - to teach them how to
live authentically. You can show them that mothers are people, that feelings are
valid, and that asking for help is brave.

You are more than "Mom."
You are a person.

And when the world doesn't understand? When it whispers about selfishness or
calls you dramatic or too much?

Let it watch you rise anyway.

Because when one mother chooses to be human,
the whole world shifts.
Our children feel it.
Our bodies feel it.

And the universe finally exhales and says:
Yes. This is the kind of mother the future needs.

A mother that's alive.

End Note

Join the Rising Wave

If this book cracked something open in you - if it helped you feel seen, remembered, or more human than you've felt in years - then you're already part of something larger.

A movement.
A rewriting of the myth.
A reclamation of identity.
A revolution of women saying:
"I won't disappear to be worthy of love."

Share this message in whatever way feels true to you. Start conversations. Send the quote that shook you to a friend who needs to hear it. Gather women together. Read passages aloud. Create gathering circles.

Highlight the words that woke you up and share them on social media platforms using **#TheHumanMother** so we can find each other. Tell your daughters, your sons, your sisters what you've learned.

When you speak up, others can feel permission to do the same.
You can become a voice in this rising wave-
Embracing a returning.
Returning to the body.
To the soul.
To the woman behind the mother.

So take a breath, beautiful one.
Feel your own weight in this world.
Feel how the ground holds you as surely as you have held so much.
You aren't just a mother anymore.
You are the keeper of your own life.

You are home - and the world is better for it.

About the Author

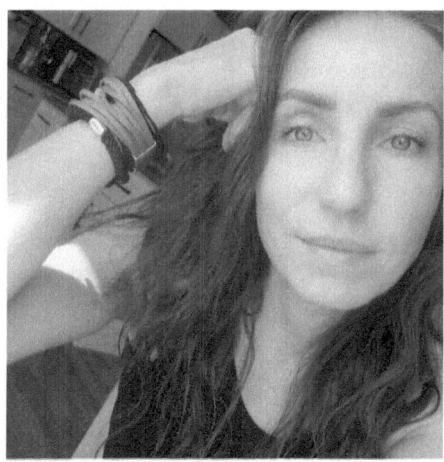

Claudia Leona is a writer, artist, and longtime natural wellness educator. For over 11 years, she guided others in reclaiming the body's wisdom. Today, she brings that same devotion to the soul - offering medicine in the form of words, stories, and liberating truths.

Her work is devoted to reclaiming the sacred truth of womanhood and calling forth the feminine spirit needed to birth a matriarchal society capable of healing our broken civilization.

She spent years bound by illness, emptied by sacrifice, and scarred by the shadows of others' unhealed lives. In her return, she stitched herself back together with boundaries and clarity - reclaiming her voice, her body, and her creative fire.

Using words and art, she embodies the wisdom that flows through her, so that it can touch others and resonate like a remembered song.

She writes as a human beside you - one who knows the cost of women's silence and the transformation that begins when they rise in power to heal a civilization.

Stay Connected

You can purchase *The Human Mother* and Claudia's other books on:

Amazon or **ClaudiaLeona.com**

Follow along for more reflections and truth-telling:

Instagram: @claudialeona.author
TikTok: @claudia_leona_author
Facebook: facebook.com/ClaudiaLeonaAuthor

For news on Claudia's next book in the **Rise of the Sacred Feminine** series and other upcoming works, visit claudialeona.com.